Nestorius and his Teaching

a fresh examination of the evidence

Nestorius and his Teaching

a fresh examination of the evidence

by

J. F. BETHUNE-BAKER, B.D.

With special reference to the newly recovered
Apology of Nestorius
(*The Bazaar of Heraclides*)

Wipf and Stock Publishers
150 West Broadway • Eugene OR 97401
1998

Nestorius and His Teachings

A Fresh Examination of the Evidence

By J.F. Bethune-Baker

ISBN: 1-57910-194-1

Printed by *Wipf and Stock Publishers* *150 West Broadway • Eugene OR 97401* *1998*

NESTORIO

ILLI VERITATIS DIVINAE INDAGATORI

SIVE VICTORI SEV PARVM FELICI

VIRO PROPOSITI PRAE CETEROS TENACI

MONACHO EPISCOPO EXVLI

NEC NON ECCLESIAE NESTORIANAE

RERVM SACRARVM OLIM FAVTRICI INSIGNI

SERAS IN VLTIMOS NOMINIS CHRISTI PRAECONI

ANTIQVA PRO FIDE QVAM DIV INFANDA PERPESSAE

NON SINE DEO SVPERSTITI

OMNIVM CHRISTIANORVM PRECIBVS OPIBVS RESTITVENDAE

STVDIA HAEC QVALIACVMQVE

VTINAM SANAE DOCTRINAE ET IPSA ADFVTVRA

NOTIS IGNOTVS

DEDICO

Donec spiro, sano dogmati adsum. (Nestorius *apud* Marium Mercatorem.)

ὁ θεὸς δὲ οὐδεμίαν ἔχει πρὸς ἡμᾶς φυσικὴν σχέσιν, ὡς οἱ τῶν αἱρέσεων κτισταὶ θέλουσιν...εἰ μή τις μέρος αὐτοῦ καὶ ὁμοουσίους ἡμᾶς τῷ θεῷ τολμήσει λέγειν· καὶ οὐκ οἶδ ὅπως ἀνέξεταί τις ἐπαΐων τούτου θεὸν ἐγνωκώς, ἀπιδὼν εἰς τὸν βίον τὸν ἡμέτερον, ἐν ὅσοις φυρόμεθα κακοῖς.

(Clem. Al. *Strom.* II xvi)

O God, Who didst put it into the heart of Ezra the priest to bring again Thy people from their captivity, teaching them Thy Holy Scripture and renewing among them Thy godly discipline; mercifully grant that we who desire to restore this church and repair the desolations thereof, may be blessed in our endeavour, and strengthened for the work Thou wouldest have done; through Jesus Christ our Lord.

(Memorial of the English Mission to the Assyrian Christians, composed by Archbishop Benson.)

PREFACE

THE following pages are an attempt to reexamine the teaching of Nestorius, and the conclusion to which they lead is that Nestorius was not "Nestorian".

I am aware that to some, for whose point of view I have a deep respect, a question which has been the subject of consideration and decision by a General Council of the Church is a *chose jugée*, and any attempt to reopen it is idle and on the part of a Churchman even disloyal. I have given further on some of the reasons why I think that this general demurrer does not apply to the case of Nestorius. But I desire at once to express my conviction, apart from any ecclesiastical theories, that the doctrinal decisions of a General Council of the Church, properly conducted, are infinitely more likely to embody, as nearly as it can be embodied in words, a true interpretation of the facts of human life—to give us a true theory of the relation between God and man—than are the reflexions of any individual thinker or school of theologians. That the General Council which condemned the teaching of Nestorius erred in matters of faith might be a conclusion to which we should be very unwilling to come. But we are not called upon to enter on this question. Councils come into existence to express the *communis sensus fidelium*, which sums up a vast range of religious experience; and their decisions need to be confirmed by subsequent acceptance by the Church as a whole. This "consensus of the faithful" has ratified the doctrinal decisions of the Council of Ephesus, and the question immediately before us is only, Did Nestorius mean what the Council thought he meant?

To others such a question as is considered here is one of merely antiquarian interest and may be left to "scholars" who are condemned by unfortunate circumstances, or their own misguided choice of a vocation, to trivial details which cannot claim attention from any one who is in touch with the realities of life. The great doctrinal controversies of the past are described as "dead battlefields" and the deeper the oblivion in which they are buried the better.

This is a view with which no student of doctrine can sympathise. There is no past controversy in which he does not detect tendencies of thought which have their representatives in his own times. He could easily label opinions within and without the various Christian Societies with the names of famous heresies, which had their champions—their parties, their "schools"—of old as they have today. Always in the past he sees the *communis sensus fidelium*, the great Catholic Church of Christ in the larger sense of the title, refusing to accept definitions of the Faith which would ignore the religious experience of the past in favour of a temporary phase of opinion and a narrower range of experience; and though he sees it also sometimes refusing adequate recognition of new experience, as long as it is new and limited to the few, he sees the new interpretations winning their way into the body of Christian doctrine and forming part of the floating stream of the river of truth, though the Creeds themselves remain inviolate, just because the new interpretations, so far as they are true to the real facts of life, are found to conflict with none of the definitions of the Church. And just because he is always surrounded by heretics in mind who are Christians at heart, he finds the study of the history of the developement of Christian doctrine so full of living interest, and at the same time so instructive, so necessary for any one who would form a true appreciation of the movements of thought and tendencies of his own times.

It disturbs him less to see an Ebionite or a Gnostic, an Arian or an Apollinarian, occupying perhaps a prominent pulpit in a Christian Church in the twentieth century, as an accredited teacher of the Christian faith, when he realizes how often partial and onesided and positively erroneous views of Christian doctrine have been preached in the past, in defiance of the definitions of the Church; and he is emboldened to believe that the primitive faith in Jesus as at once both God and man, the revealer of God and the Saviour of men, will survive all attempts to interpret Him exclusively in the terms of this or that age, this or that partial and limited mode of thought or expression.

The primitive faith in Jesus as at once both God and man:—it was just this faith for which Nestorius contended, the faith which he found expressed in the Gospels and believed to have been always the faith of the Church, faith in a Person who was both God and man, very God incarnate. For this faith he felt himself called to do battle against new teaching which seemed to him to be a denial of the doctrine of the Incarnation, inasmuch as it seemed to do away with the real manhood of the Lord. In days like our own, when a merely naturalistic conception of the Person of Jesus is gaining ground in unexpected quarters, however much for the moment it may be disguised, even for some of its chief exponents, by a religious haze which is the product of the old belief, it would not have been the manhood of the Saviour of men that Nestorius would have been constrained to defend. He would have entered the lists against all who denied the reality either of His Godhead or of His manhood. The champion of a *kenotic* theory that eliminates the Divine consciousness of the incarnate Son of God; the emotional preacher who confuses the Divine and the human and gets rid of God or of man (we cannot tell which); the mystic whose doctrine of the immanence of God threatens to crowd out the recognition of His transcendence, imperatively demanded as it is by the deepest religious instincts and experience of the Saint of every age; the thinker of any school who thinks that the facts of human life and history "don't matter", or that the only criterion of truth is its working value at the moment:—all these, no less than those who frankly denied the Godhead of Jesus, would have found in Nestorius a formidable opponent. For the question which underlies the whole of the controversy is just the question of the relation between God and man, between Godhead and manhood. Is there, or is there not, a real distinction between them? Crude assertions of the humanity of God or of the Divinity of man would have seemed to the school of thinkers to whom Nestorius was opposed as ill-considered and unmeaning as to Nestorius himself. But the Christian philosophy of life, metaphysical and ethical, is summed up in the doctrine of the Incarnation; and for Christians their theory of the Person of Jesus is their statement of the relations between God and man, and in every age their theory must be consistent with the actual facts of His life in the world as well as with their own individual religious experience and the religious experience of Christians of earlier times. The authors of our first three Gospels, in giving, or at all events professing to give, a simple narrative of incident and teaching, and reporting the impression which Jesus made on the first generations of disciples, shew us a Person with a double consciousness; to whom the Divine communion He enjoyed was as real as the human life He lived. It is a Person who has a unique sense of His own relation to God in the midst of all the activities of His life on earth, that they exhibit to us:—if technical terms must be used, a Person whose uniqueness is quite as much a metaphysical as an ethical or a psychological problem[1]. And later reporters

[1] I am aware that many modern scholars would not allow these statements to pass unchallenged. I can only say here that they are made after

of their own experience, and interpreters of the early record, when they came to formulate their theory of this Person, in the terms of contemporary philosophical conceptions (only the terms, not the theory, being new), spoke of Him as having two "substances", two "natures", the one "Divine", the other "human". That Godhead and manhood were two distinct realities no one doubted: but no more did any one know how two distinct realities could be combined in a single Person. And almost all the "heresies" as to the Person of our Lord are connected with different attempts to solve or to evade this problem. In circles of Christians in which the conception of the transcendence of God in the strictest monotheistic ("Deistic") sense was dominant, either the Godhead of Jesus was conceived as a mere power not really His own, or the manhood was regarded as a delusion: He was thought of as a man, miraculously endowed with Divine attributes, or else either as a Divine Person who only seemed to have a human form and live a human life, or as a Spirit who simply used the person of a man as a medium through whom to make His revelation. And later on Arius and Apollinarius were at one in the conception of Him as a kind of demi-God,

careful study, to the best of my opportunities, of recent work on the sources and historical character of the Gospels, and express my conviction that no fresh investigations of this kind have in any way invalidated the traditional belief of the Church that our Lord made claims on the allegiance of His followers to Himself personally which are inconceivable on the part of one who was not conscious of possessing authority and power which were at once Divine and His own. No fresh knowledge which results from the literary and historical criticism of the Gospels, in my judgement, affects the evidence that the historical Jesus based His teaching on Himself. The more reason we see to doubt the historical accuracy of some of the narratives and some of the readings of incidents given in our Gospels, the more irresistibly are we forced back upon the old "apologetic" position as to the personal claims which our Lord made as the only available explanation, the necessary presupposition, not only of the beliefs about Him of St Paul and the author of the Fourth Gospel, but also of the early history of the Christian Church as a whole.

either not truly Divine, or not really human. When all these views had been decisively excluded from the Church, as incompatible with the plain facts of the Gospel history and the experience and institutions of the Church, the problem still remained. The faith of the Church demanded the recognition of the full Godhead and the full manhood of her Lord. But what was the nature of the union? where, so to speak, was its centre to be found? In what sense was the "one Christ" both God and man? Was it that the distinction between Godhead and manhood was done away with, so that the two became one? or was the one-ness to be sought elsewhere, the two remaining still distinct? These were latent questions which the controversy between Nestorius and Cyril brought to the fore. The Church agreed upon a form of sound words by way of answer, which had at least the merit of recognizing all the facts that had to be explained. But the questions are perennial. If there is still among us some professedly Christian thought that practically annihilates the manhood of our Lord, there is also much that tends to eliminate His Godhead, and Christians of the twentieth century who have the patience to review this ancient battlefield may find themselves repaid[1]. Nestorius and Cyril are with us still: though dead, their spirits yet speak. Only with one voice they would cry out against "solutions" of the problem which, professing to recognize the spiritual or religious "uniqueness" of the Lord, reduce Him to the level of the first of "Christian" saints, and therefore only push the problem farther back. Nestorius at all events would have made short work of "solutions" such as this—a Christian saint without a Christ. And both of them would have repudiated any teaching to the effect that man is "consubstantial" with God.

The only question that I have set myself to consider is the

[1] The subject is in part incurably technical, but I would venture to invite particular attention to the more general considerations which are set out in the concluding chapter of this study.

question whether the teaching of Nestorius was "orthodox" or not; but it is clear that in determining this question we shall be implicitly passing judgement on the claims of many schools of thought to rank as orthodox. The further question, whether teaching may be Catholic or orthodox and yet unchristian and untrue, I leave to others.

But the study of the Nestorian controversy brings before us also another question which is of immediate moment. We are able today to read the past history of the Church with less prejudice than was possible in former times. We can see that the "heretic" and the "schismatic" often had scant justice done them, and that free enough play for differences of temperament and individual and racial environment was not allowed in the Church. And the question is forced upon us whether any society of Christians has the right to perpetuate divisions among Christians which had their origin in circumstances and conditions alien from those that prevail today. The reunion of the separated Churches of Christendom is, doubtless, for ecclesiastical statesmen a delicate problem, for the solution of which the time is not yet ripe. To those who have no sympathy with any Church, be they Christian at heart or "enemies of the cross of Christ", the divisions of Christendom are the strongest argument against cooperation or belief. But to the moral consciousness of every Christian they are an outrage. Μεμέρισται ὁ Χριστός:—it is Christ Himself who is divided, Christ who is torn asunder in the schisms of His Body.

With one of the members of this Body, one of these separated Churches, commonly known as "Nestorian", the Church of England, not of her own seeking, has been brought into exceptionally close relations. A reconsideration of the teaching of Nestorius and the circumstances in which he was banished from the Church of his day may perhaps help to determine the nature of those relations in the future.

The main lines of the enquiry were laid down before I was able to make any use of a new and as yet unpublished source of information—the Syriac version (under the title of the *Bazaar of Heraclides*) of an account of the whole controversy written in Greek by Nestorius himself. This comprehensive and interesting account fully confirms the conclusions to which I had come from a fresh study of the documents which are independent of it, while it is invaluable as a revelation of the mind and character of Nestorius himself, and of the highest importance in determining several of the historical and doctrinal questions connected with the controversy, to which, without its help, we could give no certain answer. I have used it freely for this purpose.

The first public announcement of the discovery of the Syriac MS containing this work was made by a German scholar, Dr H. Goussen, in an incidental allusion in a book which escaped general notice (*Martyrius Sahdona's Leben und Werke*, Leipzig, 1897). It was again referred to by another German oriental scholar, Dr Braun, a few years later (*Das Buch der Synhados*, Stuttgart, 1900); but students of the history of doctrine seem to have remained unaware of the discovery till Dr Loofs (*Nestoriana*, Halle, 1905) drew attention to it and published a short note from Dr Goussen on the contents of the MS. It is to Dr Loofs that I owe my own first knowledge of the existence of the book.

From Dr Goussen I ascertained that the preparation of an edition of the text with a French translation had been entrusted to Father V. Ermoni of Paris, who in reply to my enquiry informed me that he had been at work on the MS some time but could not name a date at which his edition would be ready for publication.

Meanwhile, however, I learnt from Mr O. H. Parry, the head of the Archbishop of Canterbury's Mission to the Assyrian Christians at Urmi (to whom I am much indebted for other information as well), that the members of the Mission had long been acquainted with the book, and that several copies of it had been made. Mr D. Jenks, a former member of the Mission (1892—1899), was the first to learn of the MS and to procure a copy of it. A copy was also obtained by Dr Rendel Harris in 1899. (This copy is now, I understand, at Harvard.) Mr Parry himself has had a copy by him for the last seven years, and has made a translation of part of it. All three recognized the importance of the discovery, but have been prevented by other duties and engagements from making any public use of the book or preparing an edition of it. Mr Jenks, now a member of the House of the Sacred Mission, who was the first to have a copy made, brought it back with him to England in 1899 and has kindly placed his copy at my disposal for use in this fresh examination of the teaching of Nestorius.

A friend, who is an expert Syriac scholar, has been good enough to make a translation of it for me, and it is his translation which I have used whenever the book is referred to or quoted. He has also supplied the very valuable Appendix on the history of the use of the Syriac terms, about the meaning of which there cannot, in future, be any doubt. I cannot express too strongly my sense of gratitude to him for the time and pains which he has bestowed on the work of reading and translating the MS, the text and the language of which are often obscure, and for all I have learnt from his wide knowledge of early Syriac literature. So much of any fresh interest that the subject may have is dependent on his work that I should have wished his name to appear on the title-page. But his standpoint in matters concerning the Church and the history of Christian Doctrine is not the same as mine. He would not treat the subject as a whole as I have treated it, nor would he wish to associate himself with all the inferences which I have drawn from the fresh evidence which is now available. As, therefore, his share in the book is strictly limited to the translation of the *Bazaar of Heraclides* and the Appendix on Syriac terms, and he has no responsibility for anything else that is contained in it, I can only make this general acknowledgement of what is due to him here. The choice of extracts too has been my own, though he allows me to say that he thinks the selection fairly represents Nestorius's presentation of his case. I must add on my own account that my endeavour has been to make it as thoroughly representative as possible of Nestorius's whole position, and that I believe I have quoted his most typical and hardest sayings. I can indeed conceive that some readers of the passages which are cited will find in them abundant justification of the judgement which the Council of Ephesus passed on Nestorius.

I regret that the circumstances which I have named above (p. xiv) seem to preclude us, for the present at all events, from publishing the whole of the English translation, and that we can only herald the complete edition of the text which we hope will be given us as soon as possible by Father Ermoni.

J. F. BETHUNE-BAKER

CAMBRIDGE
23 *August* 1907

CONTENTS

CHAPTER VIII.

CHAPTER IX.

CHAPTER X.

CHAPTER XI.

CHAPTER XII.

CHAPTER XIII.

ERRATA

p. 44 n. 2 line 2 for *θεόφορος* read *θεοφορος*

p. 58 n. 2 line 6 for *protótokos* read *prototókos*

p. 74 transpose lines 3 and 4

CHAPTER I

INTRODUCTION

THERE are few more interesting figures on the great canvas of the history of Christian Doctrine than that of the learned, eloquent, and austerely religious abbot of the monastery of Euprepius outside the city of Antioch, called unexpectedly to the see of Constantinople, like a second Chrysostom; eagerly setting to work to make the Christian faith a reality in the life of the capital of the Empire; suddenly charged with heretical teaching and involved in a merciless doctrinal controversy; deposed from his bishoprick, excommunicated, deserted by friends who really shared his beliefs, banished to a remote spot in the deserts of Egypt, dying in exile.

It is a figure that seizes our attention and wins at least some measure of admiration and compassion. Such learning and enthusiasm in the cause which he firmly believed to be a life and death struggle for the doctrine of the Incarnation; so staunch a determination to accept no theory which seemed to him to obscure the true humanity of the Lord of human life, the Saviour—as he says—not of angels but of men; such a firm grip on the human appeal of manhood to men; so eager a desire to expound without fear or favour the teaching of Gospels, Epistles, and Creeds, and to make the doctrine of the Bible and the Church intelligible to men:—and yet such a fate.

It is certainly an edifying picture which ecclesiastical history has painted for us; and, if its colours had become somewhat dim through the lapse of time and we did not see its details very clearly, we might well be loth to attempt to touch it up or restore it in any way, lest we should only spoil it. But, as a matter of fact, many of the details have really become more clear to us than they were to most of those who played their various parts in the drama, and some of them seem to belong to another picture. They rouse the suspicion that the artist of the traditional picture has exercised the license, which all artists claim, to leave out some of the details which do not compose well with their interpretation of the subject before them, and to heighten or lower the tones in order to produce the effect they want.

The tale of the controversy has been told so often and so fully that there is little to add to the received account of the various stages through which it passed or of the incidents which took place. It is rather the inner history that needs rewriting. Nearly all that we know has come down to us through the medium of those who were hostile to Nestorius at the time or concerned to maintain the ecclesiastical tradition in later times, without any attempt to form an independent judgement and usually without the means of doing so, had they had the wish.

The external history, so far as it concerns us, can be very briefly told. The questions of doctrine that arise must be examined at greater length.

Nestorius when we first hear of him was a member of the monastery of Euprepius near Antioch in priest's orders. Of his earlier life we know nothing except that he was a native of Germanicia, in the Euphrates district, within the patriarchate of Antioch. To Antioch evidently he belonged by theological lineage and point of view. By his zeal for careful biblical exegesis, his insistence on the recognition of the full manhood of our Lord, by his dread of any mode of thought or expression which might obscure the reality of the human experiences of the historic Christ, by his desire to make the doctrine of the Church intelligible to men's minds, he shews his kinship to the leaders of the theological school for which Antioch was famous. At Antioch where the disciples were first called Christians, where the Gospel was first preached to Gentiles, which had been the centre from which the evangelization of the Empire had begun, which early in the second century had had as its bishop the Ignatius who had insisted with such passionate earnestness on the reality of the human nature and experiences of Jesus, who had made his appeal above all else to the actual facts of the Gospel history—at Antioch the historical tradition had never been allowed to fade. Theosophy never had a chance of success where the influence of Antioch could reach. Paul of Samosata and Lucian and the Arians who were an offshoot of his school, so far as they diverged from the Trinitarian doctrine of the Godhead, were probably led into heresy by their conviction that at all hazards they must maintain the distinction between the human and the Divine. They could admit no doctrine of the Deity of Christ which would in any way obscure the fact that He lived upon earth the life of men. They started from the one quite certain fact that He lived as a man among men[1]. They reasoned from the known to the unknown. They tried to find some means of reconciling the traditional faith in the Godhead of Jesus with their conviction that God was one, and they did it in terms that seemed to endanger the traditional faith. The definition of Nicaea prevailed and the Trinitarian conception triumphed. The full Godhead of Jesus was recognized, and the oneness of the Godhead in three modes of being. So far the question had been theological, it was the definition of the doctrine of God that had been at stake.

[1] This, I think, is true of Arians, in spite of their Christology that excluded a really human soul; and though they thus made the historical Person a demi-god.

But the same interest in the recognition of the distinction between man and God was seen again in the Christological question which the theories of Apollinarius brought to the fore. Again the theologians of Antioch shewed their native bent. In the discussion of the problem of the relation between the Godhead and the manhood in the Person of our Lord they would tolerate no teaching that seemed to merge the one in the other. Again they started from the manhood; again they laid stress on all the passages in Scripture which seemed to emphasize the human consciousness of the Lord. At all hazards they insisted on the recognition in His Person of a genuine human element—by whatever term it was described, in virtue of which a genuine human experience was possible. They did not for a moment call in question, or fail to recognize, the equally genuine Divine element, in virtue of which Divine experience and power was His. They did not doubt that the historical Jesus Christ was both God and man. They took their stand on history, on the primitive record, on apostolic testimony and interpretation.

Theological traditions such as these were the inheritance of Nestorius. There is no reason to suppose that he intended at any time to introduce new doctrines or to make innovations of any kind. In an eloquent passage in his book he deplores the attack that was made on Diodore and Theodore, who had been held in the highest esteem as Fathers by all the Church, until it was found that he was only teaching what they had taught before. Basil and Gregory and Athanasius and Ambrose must all, he declares, come under the same condemnation[1]. And he joins himself with Athanasius and Eustathius and numberless others who 'were deserted by those who were 'really orthodox'[2]. It is indeed as the champion of a great

[1] *Bazaar of Heraclides* pp. 330 ff.
[2] *ib.* p. 150.

religious and historical tradition that he figures[1]. And we shall altogether misjudge him if we fail to realize his strong religious interest and his fervent pastoral spirit. It was as one who had consecrated himself to the religious life, a monk of unusual devotion, and an earnest preacher in the cathedral church of the great city of Antioch, with its teeming masses of men and women with souls to be saved from the temptations of life in a great centre of the world's traffic, that he first won fame. The *ex tempore* preacher whom men crowd to hear is exposed, no doubt, to subtle spiritual risks. He is liable, moreover, to slips of the tongue and the peril of the "telling" phrase that seldom tells the whole of the truth, but once uttered cannot be recalled and is never forgiven by those at whose views it is aimed. Nestorius was a master of the art of speaking, as the art was taught and practised in his days; and the pulpit was the recognized medium of theological instruction and discussion. The twentieth century, weary of controversy, is disposed to claim for the pulpit a kind of *trève de Dieu*; but daily papers and magazines and journals of every kind are at the disposal of the disputants. In the fifth century the sermon afforded the chief, and certainly the readiest, way to the public ear, and Nestorius used it with conspicuous ability and great success. He had a fine voice, a keen dialectical mind, and a vigorous personality: he could present his views effectively, and his views were hard to refute: he could hit hard, and he did so freely, with all the rhetorical tricks that met the taste of the time—the taste which permitted a congregation to punctuate a preacher's points by loud applause, so that on one occasion, when Chrysostom had declaimed against the custom, the congregation shewed their admiration of his eloquent rebuke by a spontaneous outburst of the same applause. His opponents brought the usual charges against

[1] It was, of course, commonly the case that "heretics" claimed the support of tradition for their doctrines. Each case must be judged on its merits.

him. He was too fond of his own voice; he was proud of his powers of speaking: he mistook fluency for learning and rhetoric for argument[1]. These charges must be judged by the standards of the time. The same kind of thing is said of men today. Nestorius was at all events transparently honest and all in earnest. His opponents used, according to the measure of their powers, the same means to promote their own ideas; and they used many other means to which Nestorius never resorted.

His sermons at Antioch were no doubt taken down by shorthand writers and collections of them published. The "innumerable tracts on various subjects" which we are told[2] he composed at Antioch were probably these sermons revised for publication. Some of them must have reached the other great cities of the Empire, and in securing him as bishop the Church of Constantinople thought they had found another Chrysostom. A graphic picture is given, in the Emperor's address to Dalmatius recorded by Nestorius, of the difficulties which were experienced in finding a bishop who would be acceptable[3].

[1] Socrates *H. E.* vii 32 professes to give an impartial judgement. He has read his writings and repudiates the view that he held the doctrines either of Paul of Samosata or of Photinus (popularly understood to be that the Lord was a mere man): he says, however, that he was naturally fluent and puffed up by his own eloquence and anxious for applause, but unwilling to study the ancient teachers and ill-informed and ignorant, though he thought himself well educated, and so he made a "bug-bear" of the term *Theotokos* which abler men than himself had freely used in the past. Socrates also (*ib.* vii 29), on the evidence of his first utterance at Constantinople, speaks of him as superficial, impetuous, and vainglorious.

[2] Vincent of Lerinum, who was contemporary with the Council of Ephesus, (*Comm.* i 11) speaks of his daily discourses on the Divine Scriptures in public; and Gennadius (*de viris illustribus* liii) writing fifty years later, says 'he composed innumerable tracts on various subjects in which with subtle malice he distilled the poison of his heresy—which betrayed itself afterwards, though for the time his high moral character hid it'.

[3] 'The Emperor said to him [sc. Dalmatius]: I find no evil in this man [i.e. Nestorius], nor any cause deserving of deposition. I testify to thee and to all men that I am innocent. For I have no love for this man

Not a breath of suspicion of unorthodox teaching had touched his fame, though discussions had already taken place at Antioch

through any human inclination that I should act thus and be criticised and condemned as one who withstands God and arrogates to himself the rights of the priests. Never did I insist upon his ordination that punishment and vengeance should be exacted (of me) because of his election, but through the concurrence of you all I of necessity introduced this man, though he was much beloved in his own country and among his own people. You were the cause of this and not I. Thee thyself, Dalmatius, I begged to undertake this office, and I besought thee with many words not to refuse the ministry of God. But thou didst refuse, and didst beg of me in turn saying: "compel me not for I am an ignorant man." And another also of the monks, a man who was thought to be somewhat and was well esteemed for his religiousness, did I entreat, and he also refused as not knowing how to conduct this ministry because he was unlearned. Then you said: "Constantinople requires a bishop who for his words and his conduct shall be agreeable to all, who shall be a teacher in the church and a mouth to every one in all things." But when you refused for these reasons, did I do aught by my own authority? Did I not again beg of you to choose one of this character? Did I not implore of the clergy of Constantinople to choose one who was fitting? Did I not speak these same things to the bishops, saying: "It is yours to choose and to make a bishop"? And you also I implored in like manner. Did I not leave the matter in your hands all this time, being patient in order that you should choose quietly, lest through haste some mistake should be made as to him who should be chosen? But did you choose and I not receive your choice? Dost thou wish me to say something against you? Shall I speak of their violence and bribery and presents, and their promises and oaths, and how they sought to turn the whole affair into a sale. Which of these men did you wish to be bishop? But I pass on: which choice did you wish should be made? Was it to be thyself, or that other of whom I spoke, or yet another? For some chose one, some another; not according to fitness did they choose, but rather those that were unsuitable. Every one recommended his own choice and spoke ill of him whom others chose, bringing damaging charges against him. You could not agree upon one man; but whom the people agreed upon you would not accept. I read before you what the people said of each one that was selected. What then ought I to have done that I did not do? You, the monks, did not agree with the clergy: the clergy were not of one mind: the bishops were divided: and the people in like manner disagreed. Each was contending for a different man. Yet not even so did I assume to myself the authority, but I left the choice to you. But when you as to the propriety of the term which became the battle-cry of his opponents, and its use had already been denounced by Theodore, the accepted representative of the best theological thought of Antioch.

It was, indeed, as an impetuous opponent of heresy of every kind that he first impressed himself on the people of Constantinople. 'Give me' he said on his reception by the Emperor: 'Give me, Emperor, the world free from heretics, 'and I will give thee heaven in return: help me to destroy the 'heretics and I will help thee to destroy the Persians!' Finding that the Arians still had a chapel in which they met, he at once began to pull it down. They themselves set fire to it, and burnt down with it many of the adjacent buildings. The odium aroused by this conflagration was turned on to Nestorius, and within a week of his consecration as bishop the nickname of "Incendiary" or "Firebrand" was invented for him. It seems unjust that, because the Arians set fire to their own church and destroyed the property of their neighbours, Nestorius should be called a firebrand. It was an omen of the future. But the energy with which he combated the laxity of life as well as the errors of thought which were rife in his diocese naturally made him enemies as well as friends, and many were ready to take advantage of any opening for attack that he gave. His reception of the Western bishops exiled on the charge of Pelagian heresy, when they came to Constantinople, and the

were all at a loss you came to me and deputed me to choose whom I would. And even then I scarcely consented, though you all begged of me. Now I considered that it was not right to appoint any one from here, lest he should have to contend against enmity and opposition, for every one hated, and was hated by, the others, as though each were covetous of the office; so I sought to find a foreigner who should be unknown to those here and should not know them, one who should be a clear speaker and of good morals. And I was told that Nestorius of Antioch was such a one. Him I sent for and took, thereby causing sorrow to his whole city, and I brought him hither for your advantage—since this I held to be of more importance than that of the others. But when he was appointed this was not your estimate of him' (*Bazaar of Heraclides* pp. 279—281).

letters which he wrote to the bishop of Rome asking for information about them, as a bishop to a brother bishop, alienated at once the sympathy of the chief ecclesiastic of the West. *Roma locuta est*, and her decisions ought to have been received without question. And Rome was already affronted by the growing power of the upstart see of the *Nova Roma* of the East and the canon of the Council which had placed it on a level with the great and ancient apostolic sees. Official prejudice was reinforced by personal displeasure. When the controversy broke out, the representative of the West was in the mood to think and to believe the worst that his opponents could say of the bishop of Constantinople: his discomfiture would be a personal satisfaction as well as an official triumph for the bishop of Rome. Nor, if he ever got into trouble, could he hope for an unbiassed judgement from the leader of the Church of Alexandria. A certain rivalry had existed from old time between the sees of Antioch and Alexandria, and the theological schools connected with them. The mystic tendency prevailed at Alexandria, the practical and historical at Antioch; and these different tendencies shewed themselves in different methods of study and different ways of expounding Scripture and presenting doctrine. At the same time, though the Church of Alexandria had her own battles to fight with the Church of Rome, and was not averse on occasion from soliciting and accepting the support of Constantinople, she really shared to the full the prejudice of Rome against the new Eastern see. She would gladly have played in relation to other Churches in the East the dominant rôle that Rome aspired to play in the whole of Christendom; and she had at this time a bishop who, if he had few equals in theological insight and learning, was surpassed by none in official arrogance and unscrupulous use of means to compass his ends. To satisfy a personal animosity, Theophilus, Cyril's uncle and predecessor as bishop of Alexandria, had fomented the scandalous attack on Chrysostom which resulted in his deposition from the bishoprick of Constantinople. Cyril had worked at Alexandria in close association with Theophilus, and the fierce and domineering spirit of his uncle lived in him. It was only after a tumultuous contest that he was enthroned as bishop, and his episcopate was inaugurated by deeds of violence and unsparing use of the great powers which the patriarch of Alexandria could put in motion. He was urged not to perpetuate a private feud under the pretext of piety, but he could scarcely be induced to atone for the great wrong that had been done to Chrysostom, and to place his name on the diptychs of his Church, though all the rest of Christendom had made such reparation as it could, and only on these terms could communion with Rome and the West be reestablished. Was it likely that a successor of Chrysostom, both at Antioch and at Constantinople, would meet with fair treatment at the hands of a bishop of Alexandria of Cyril's type? "History repeats itself." A painful family likeness can be traced in all controversies about religion: we see in them all the same zeal for the truth as each side understands it, the same inability in all the disputants to conceive the possibility that they may be mistaken, the same mixture of the highest with the lower aims and motives. And in many ways Cyril's treatment of Nestorius recalls the attack of Theophilus on Chrysostom. Without in the first instance addressing enquiries or protests to Nestorius himself, he circulated reports of the erroneous teaching of the bishop of Constantinople, and by letters to the Emperor's sister and other ladies and officials of the court—and handsome presents such as are customary in the East, whether they be regarded as bribes or not—had won over to his side many of the most influential of the Emperor's advisers. The bribery then and later (for whatever Cyril's apologists may say, no one who reads the letter of Cyril's archdeacon and chancellor to the patriarch, who was appointed in place of Nestorius after the council[1], can doubt that it was

[1] The letter of Epiphanius to Maximianus preserved in the *Synodicon adv. trag. Iren.* ch. 203 (Mansi *Concilia* tom. v p. 987 and Theodoret *Opp.* Migne *P. G.* lxxxiv. 826).

bribery) was on so extensive a scale that the archdeacon declares the expenditure had reduced the clergy and Church of Alexandria to poverty. Cyril, moreover, had sent to the capital a large body of Egyptian bishops and monks, who appeared as a kind of guard set over against Nestorius to terrorize him, so that Nestorius could say that they had actually seized his church. 'I,' he says, addressing Cyril (*Bazaar of Heraclides* p. 106), 'who was patient with heretics, 'was to be scared and chased out; and thou, being bishop of 'Alexandria, didst take possession of the Church of Constanti-'nople, a thing that no bishop in any city would put up with.'

There is of course no intellectual discipline which is more exacting than the discipline which makes it possible to enter into another person's point of view, whose antecedents and training and environment, moral or intellectual or theological, are widely different from one's own. Even to-day members of one school of thought are seldom able, assuming that they have the will, to be quite fair to opponents; and in the times we are considering the will and the power were rarer than they are today. Partizanship is an infirmity even of noble minds. It so easily disguises itself as loyalty to tested truth and a great religious tradition. We need not blame Cyril and his school too harshly if we recognize that something of the lower nature entered into their treatment of the questions at issue, and that they were not free from the desire to seize an opportunity of humiliating a rival school of theological thought and a chance of crushing the bishop of a see, which from the mere accident of its being the see of the new capital, the seat of government, was threatening to usurp the position of their own ancient Church of apostolical foundation, with its glorious literary and theological heritage from the past. We need not blame them too severely:—but we shall fail altogether to understand the controversy if we do not clearly recognize the facts and allow them their full weight.

And yet again, though speech can be a veritable sword of God, sharper than any two-edged sword of man, laying bare the secrets of the mind and heart, it too often also does the Devil's work. A phrase may sum up the experience of a life, the loyalties of a people, the aspirations and eternal hopes of men. It may serve to make ideals real, to give stability to the elusive visions of a larger life, to guard a truth once won from the loss and change which all things human suffer. But a formula may become a mere party-cry, the rejection of which is treated as proof of blasphemy—political or social or religious.

Every society of men who are banded together for common aims must define their beliefs, must have a Creed, acceptance of which is one of the conditions—indeed the very reason—of membership: and from time to time new terms to express the aims and beliefs of the Society may be devised. The Church has never been exempt from this experience; and as each new term has been fashioned there has always been a stage in which the Church has been divided as to its real meaning and its correspondence with the old faith and the main lines of primitive and patristic interpretation. If the term which was new, or newly brought into prominence, and proposed as a test of a sound belief, was really only a summary expression of the genuine convictions of Churchmen, it was accepted on its merits as such by the Church at large after due discussion; and many who had suspected it at first acquiesced in its use. Such a term was *homoousios*, "consubstantial", round which the Arian controversy had been fought. The term itself was not new: its Latin equivalent had been in use in the West for a century at least, and before the time of Arius and Athanasius it had been the subject of discussion between the bishops of Alexandria and of Rome, and the former had admitted that, though he could not find the word in Scripture, the sense of it as expounded by his brother bishop he found and believed. But the term could easily be used in a sense that was not scriptural, and it took fifty years to convince the Easterns that no other word would suffice to exclude the Arian theories and to safeguard the reality of the Godhead of the Son.

Another such term was the title of the Virgin Mary which Nestorius feared and Cyril championed. The term *Theotokos*, "Mother of God", was free no doubt from the philosophical refinements and ambiguities that made *homoousios* as objectionable to some of the learned as it was unintelligible to the many: but it, too, could easily be understood in a sense which seemed to violate the plain and obvious meaning of Scripture and to be inconsistent with the ancient faith of the Church.

Yet though the two terms have so much in common, neither of them being a scriptural or primitive term, yet each expressing the scriptural and primitive doctrine of the Godhead of the Son, there is one great difference between them. *Homoousios* never was, and never could be, a popular term: it bears upon it the mark of the school; it is the philosopher's mintage; and though it was not actually coined to define what men would fain have left indefinite, it was imposed on the rank and file by a "superior" act, in order to keep them in orthodox paths. It belongs to the province of technical theology, and it had to live down the prejudice which always attaches to learned and technical terms: opposition to it was sure of popular sympathy. On the other hand *Theotokos* belongs to the language of devotion[1]. There is an emotional and personal ring about it, which *homoousios* could never have: it makes its appeal to the heart, and popular sentiment was outraged when she who gave birth to the Lord was denied the title that expressed the distinctive glory of her motherhood. Piety would in this case have been pledged to the phrase that

[1] Rabbûla, bishop of Edessa, a strong champion of the term, in a sermon preached at Constantinople expressed his regret that he was compelled to speak in public of things which ought to be honoured only in the silence of faith. See *infra* p. 56 note.

summed up the unreflecting religious feeling of the Church, even if exact theologians had cause to shrink from its use. It expressed in a single word the reverence that Christians felt for her who stood in the closest of human relations to the Son of God, the Saviour of men. Objections to it were merely technical.

The use of the term may have denoted a growth in the tendency to exalt unduly one who was only a woman, because she gave birth to One who was more than Man. How should it not be so, when no one denies her meed of reverence to the mother of one who is great among mere men? It was an age in which the tendency, present in the Church from early days, to pay extravagant honour to martyrs was assuming even less defensible forms, that would have been repugnant perhaps to primitive Christian feeling; though it may well be argued that the spirit which canonizes great doctors of the Church is the same as the spirit that in the age of the persecutions admitted as Saints those only who bore witness by death to the Faith. Indications are not wanting that this natural human tendency, which has its origin in the noblest of human instincts, and some of its fruits among the things that "enrich the blood of the world", needed restraint in the ages succeeding the last great persecution. But there are very few signs that this aspect of the question had much influence with Nestorius and his school. They saw in the term a danger that struck far deeper into the Christian faith, as delivered once for all to the saints, a danger affecting the Person of the Lord Himself. That His Mother should be given a title that was quasi-divine mattered little. But the danger that under cover of such a title an unhistorical conception of the facts of the Gospel should grow up, and a false doctrine of the relations between the human and the Divine be encouraged,—this was a subtle danger that needed to be exposed. So Nestorius was forced into the position of one who brings technical objections against a popular term.

To Athanasius no doubt rightly belongs the credit of having seen clearly from the outset the real significance of Arianism, and the need of a resolute stand against it, at a time when few understood the issues and most were prepared to accept a compromise which would have allowed the Arian teaching to go on unchecked. By his undaunted defence of the term *homoousios* and his persistent refusal to recognize the Arians as Christians he saved the Christian doctrine of God.

And Cyril is commonly credited with similar insight. With no less clearness than Athanasius, he is said to have grasped the real point of the controversy from its very beginning. Had he yielded to the arguments alleged against the title *Theotokos* the true doctrine of the Incarnation would have been lost. He well deserved the name of a second Athanasius which his admirers bestowed on him. He too was the true conservative, and in defending the term he was defending the deepest religious instincts and convictions of the people against a merely rationalistic mode of thought: the Christian consciousness of all ages sides with Cyril against Nestorius. This view undoubtedly has strong support in the later history of the Church. For my own part I cannot doubt that popular piety, and the phrases and forms in which it clothes itself, are the truest tests of the genuine spirit of religion; they sum up the real religious experience of ordinary men and women. But the popular phrase more often than not corresponds to a cry of the heart, in an hour of need or a moment of rapture, that ignores a wider range of feeling and thought: and it needs to be balanced by other terms that express equally genuine experiences. It is in adjusting this balance that "technical" theology has its province; in reflecting on religious experience on the largest scale and securing, so far as language allows, an interpretation that shall do justice to all the facts that have to be included. Nearly all "heresies" have arisen from over-valuation of a single aspect of the facts to be explained. If it be true that *pectus facit theologum*, and that no one can interpret religious feeling aright unless his own heart has been touched and he has some religious knowledge of his own, it is none the less true that something other than ordinary religious experience enters into and fashions the formulas of theologians. We have in them the product of reflexion, and sometimes the appeal which they make to the mind deprives them of all religious value for any but trained theologians, and the few who can make their somewhat repellent language really their own. There is a restraint about theological terms that may chill rather than guide and quicken devotion.

Such a word as *Theotokos* corresponds to the warmth of St Thomas's cry "My Lord and my God!" It might seem that, though it expressed only a half-truth, it might have been allowed to pass. But Nestorius found in it a technical flaw; and, challenged on technical grounds, Cyril at once took up its defence and claimed not only high ecclesiastical authority for its use but theological correctness for the term itself, as an expression which must be admitted by all who were sound in the Faith.

Let me quote Nestorius's own words as to the state of things which stirred him to action, in his first letter to Celestine, bishop of Rome.

'We too', he writes[1], 'find here (in Constantinople) no 'little corruption of orthodox doctrine....It is no slight com- 'plaint, but one akin to the festering disease of Apollinarius 'and Arius. For of the union of the Lord and man in the 'Incarnation they make a mixture, which results in a blending 'and confusion of both. There are even some of our clergymen,

[1] We have only the Latin translation of his letter. Loofs *Nestoriana* pp. 166—168. I have endeavoured to give here and elsewhere the exact sense, though not always what is commonly called a "literal" translation. And I have not marked omissions of words which add nothing to the sense. But where terms or turns of expression have technical importance they are added in a bracket.

'some of them merely ignorant, but others with conscious 'heretical intent, who openly blaspheme God the Word con-'substantial with the Father, representing Him as having 'received His first origin from the Virgin Mother of Christ 'and as having been built up along with His temple (sc. the 'body) and buried with His flesh. And they say that His 'flesh did not remain flesh after the resurrection, but became 'of the nature of the Godhead. So they make the origin of 'the Godhead of the Only-begotten the same as the origin of 'the flesh which was conjoined with It, and they make It die 'with the flesh; and in speaking of the "deification" of the 'flesh and its transition to Godhead they rob both flesh and 'Godhead of their real nature.

'But this is not all. They dare to treat the Virgin Mother 'of Christ as in some kind of way divine, like God. I mean, 'they do not shrink from calling her Mother of God, although 'the holy fathers of Nicaea, who are beyond all praise, said 'nothing more of the holy Virgin than "our Lord Jesus Christ 'was incarnate of the Holy Ghost and the Virgin Mary". 'And I need not mention the Scriptures—everywhere by the 'mouth of angels and apostles they proclaim the Virgin the 'Mother of "Christ", not of "God the Word".

'If however anyone justifies this title Mother of God 'because of the conjunction with God the Word of the man-'hood that was born, and not because of the mother, then I 'say that this title is not suitable for her, for a real mother 'must be of the same substance as that which is born of her: 'yet the application of the term to her is tolerable on one 'ground only, viz. that the temple of God the Word which is 'inseparable from Him was derived from her—not that she 'herself was the mother of God the Word. For no one gives 'birth to one who is in existence before herself.'

In a second letter he uses similar expressions[1], saying that

[1] *Ep.* II *ad Caelestinum.* Loofs *op. cit.* p. 171.

the men he has in view imagine a kind of amalgamation of Godhead and manhood and attribute bodily characteristics to the Godhead of the Only-begotten, and imagine some transformation of the Divine into the corporeal, confusing the Divine and the human natures which are worshipped together in the one Person of the Only-begotten because of their complete conjunction, though they remain each of them unchanged and intact. The framers of the Creed, however, were careful to use the word "Christ", which signifies both natures, in declaring Him consubstantial with the Godhead of the Father. The manhood was born afterwards of the holy Virgin and because of its conjunction with the Godhead is worshipped at the same time by angels and men.

And he gives substantially the same account in his Apology saying that he did not begin the opposition to Apollinarianism, either in Constantinople or in the East. It began before he was born, and at Antioch he had taught to the same effect and no one had found fault with him; and it was as peacemaker that he first intervened at Constantinople. Soon after he came there he was asked to decide a question which was causing dissension, and he acted just in the spirit which Athanasius shewed at the Council of Alexandria in 361.

'For a number of people who were discussing this matter 'came with one accord to the Bishop's house requiring to have 'their dispute settled and to be brought to agreement. Some, 'on the one hand, called those who spoke of Blessed Mary as '"Mother of God" Manichaeans, while those, on the other 'hand, who called Blessed Mary "Mother of man" the others 'called [Paulites or Photinians]. But when I questioned them, 'the one party did not deny the manhood, nor the other the 'Godhead. But they made confession of both in the same 'manner, differing only as to the terms. Those accused of 'being connected with Apollinarius accepted the title "Mother 'of God", and those connected with Photinus the title "Mother 'of man". But when I learned that in their quarrel they were 'not heretically minded, I said: Neither these nor those are 'heretics—for the one party knew nothing of Apollinarius and 'his doctrine, nor did the others know aught of Photinus or of 'Paul. And I tried to bring them out of their controversy and 'quarrel saying: If without separating or severing or denying 'either the Godhead or the manhood they employ those ex-'pressions that are used by them, they do not sin; otherwise 'let us employ that expression which is more guarded, I mean 'the expression of the Gospel—"Christ was born", or "the 'book of the birth of Jesus Christ", or any such like. We 'confess Christ to be God and man; for of the two was born '"Christ in the flesh, who is God over all". Do you then call 'Mary "Mother of Christ" in the union; and do not say that 'this and that are rent asunder in the Sonship, but employ 'the unexceptionable expression of the Gospel, and put away 'this dissension from amongst you, using the title that makes 'for concord. When they heard this they said: Before God 'our controversy is settled. And exceedingly did they praise 'and glorify God.'[1]

Nestorius does not for a moment dream of denying the full Godhead of the Son. Indeed, though some misunderstood his position at the time (see *infra* pp. 42 ff.), the chief point that he makes in his letters to Celestine is that the teaching which he attacks was derogatory to the Godhead; and that is why he calls its champions Arians. If the Godhead of the Son had its origin in the womb of the Virgin Mary, it was not Godhead as the Father's, and He who was born could not be *homoousios* with God; and that was what the Arians denied Him to be.

[1] *Bazaar of Heraclides* p. 108. He goes on to attribute the outbreak of the controversy to the action of those who had been disappointed over the bishoprick election, and the agents of Cyril who wanted money and got no support from him, and wanted to discredit him in connexion with the case of certain Alexandrines who had brought complaints of Cyril's wrong-doings to Constantinople.

On the other hand Apollinarius expressly denied the completeness of His human nature, in the normal sense, in teaching that the Word of God took the place of the human soul in His Person, so that a kind of deification of the human nature resulted and He was neither really Divine nor really human; and Nestorius attributed this mixture of two things which were distinct into a third, which was neither the one nor the other, to those who used the title *Theotokos*.

At Rome and in the West, if anywhere, he might have expected support on the doctrinal question. For though Rome and the West had but little mind for speculative theology, they had the Catholic genius for keeping the balance between contrasted points of view and rival schools of thought. If logical reconciliation seemed impossible, it was always easy to frame a statement in which ideas that seemed to be exclusive of each other and incompatible were simply set side by side as complementary truths, which found their unification on the higher plane of faith. The best example of such a statement is perhaps the "Athanasian Creed" (which embodies the spirit of Latin theology), and Leo had no difficulty in composing one, that gave full recognition to the standpoint of Nestorius and was accepted by the Church at large, without employing the disputed term[1]. But the personal and political accidents, to which reference has been made, threw the sympathies of Rome at the moment entirely on to the side of Cyril.

It is not necessary to review the whole course of the controversy, or to tell again the history of the Council of Ephesus. It is a singularly painful story, even in the annals of con-

[1] "Mother of the Lord" is the term Leo uses in the *Letter to Flavian*, which was endorsed by the Council of Chalcedon. In the Definition of the Faith accepted at the Council it is true the term *Theotokos* slips in, but the Definition as a whole is certainly not conceived in the spirit or expressed in the language of the chief champions of the term. See *infra* p. 205.

troversies and of Councils. All that need be said at the moment is that the circumstances in which the decisions of the majority were reached were such as to preclude the possibility of an unbiassed consideration of the questions in dispute. Nestorius and his friends never had a hearing. The "Council" was, as Nestorius says, Cyril; it simply registered his point of view.

A council attains the rank of ecumenicity by the subsequent acceptance of its decisions by the Church at large; and those of Ephesus received such acceptance at Chalcedon and afterwards. The *sensus fidelium*, however, though a finely sensitive Court of Appeal in really religious issues, is a less satisfactory judge of questions of fact: and one who accepts the positive affirmations of Ephesus as a final authority in the sphere of doctrine and faith may yet be permitted to doubt whether Nestorius taught or intended to teach the doctrines attributed to him and condemned as his.

This only is the question which I proceed to consider in the light of some fresh discoveries and a reexamination of old evidence which has lately been made more easily accessible than it has been hitherto. First of all the evidence must be described.

CHAPTER II

THE SOURCES OF OUR KNOWLEDGE OF NESTORIUS AND HIS TEACHING

On dit que Dieu est toujours pour les gros bataillons. In no case is the power of majorities more overwhelming than in the case of ancient heresies. The majority took all the measures they could to prevent the views of the minorities, when once condemned, from ever troubling the peace of the Church again. The heretic himself, if he held any official position, was deposed and sent into exile; his followers were not allowed to meet together in a religious association of their own; and his writings were carefully collected and burnt, or, if they survived to later times, no one would waste his time and defile his pen by copying them again. Our knowledge of heresies, and of the controversies which they caused, is usually derived only from the orthodox writers who undertook their refutation. They give us, of course, sometimes the heretic's own words and some of his arguments: but a *catena* of extracts, isolated from their context, and arranged in a manner designed to set them in the most unfavourable light, is not the kind of evidence on which we should wish to condemn a man today. The great St Denys, the ablest theologian and administrator of his time, used many of the very phrases which became the watchwords of the Arian party; and a list of them was sent to his namesake, the bishop of Rome, that he might check the blasphemies of his colleague. But Athanasius himself, the chief opponent of the Arians, undertook the vindication of his memory and preserved for us the words in which he described the tactics of his accusers. The phrases impugned, he says, were only cursory illustrations, good enough so far as they went: but he used besides them many others more apposite in other connexions. 'These and the like written statements', he says, 'they pretend not to see, and try to pelt me with two expressions separated from their context like stones flung from a distance.'[1] If we possessed all the writings of heretics, the suspicion we sometimes cannot help feeling, that the refutation scarcely does justice to the argument and the doctrines which are impugned, might be confirmed. The extract which looks so damaging might seem less decisive in its place in the passage as a whole, and the unfortunate phrase flung back in the heretic's teeth might recall the "stones from a distance" of which Dionysius complained.

A collection of the sermons of Nestorius seems to have reached Alexandria soon after Nestorius entered on his office of bishop[2]. So incisive a speaker as Nestorius gave many openings for attack, and the dissentients at Constantinople, when they complained to Cyril, would of course select the sayings which caused the chief offence. Such a selection of sayings and sermons was sent by Cyril to the bishop of Rome with a covering letter, and translations in full of all his own writings on the subject; and on the strength of Cyril's extracts,

[1] Athanasius *de sententiis Dionysii* 18.

[2] It is quite possible, as Mgr Batiffol points out (*Revue biblique* vol. ix pp. 329 ff.), that sermons preached at Antioch before his elevation to the episcopate (10 April 428) had reached Egypt and been circulated in the monasteries, and that it was not only the sermons of 428—429 that were known in Egypt and prompted Cyril's letter to the monks early in the year 430. According to Gennadius the sermons preached at Antioch were just as heretical as the later ones at Constantinople. But a bishop's first utterances no doubt attracted particular attention in those days as in our own, and so diligent a preacher as Nestorius must have supplied plenty of material in the first year of his episcopate.

without more ado, Nestorius was called upon to abjure the heretical propositions which were attributed to him. It was on the strength of extracts such as these, and of the inferences that could be drawn from them, that he was condemned at Ephesus, and they have formed down to the present day the chief source of our knowledge of his teaching.

Besides these extracts, which are mainly extracts from sermons, and all of them selected by personal opponents at the time and preserved in official documents or the writings of contemporary and later anti-Nestorians, we have a few letters from his own pen, preserved in the collections of the works of those to whom they were addressed—a commendable practice of former days for which we often have cause to be grateful. And to the happy accident that Marius Mercator, an African layman with theological interests, was engaged in business in Constantinople at the time of the controversy, and made or procured for his own use Latin translations of some of the sermons of Nestorius, we owe it that we have the full text in Latin of several sermons of importance and can read some of the Greek fragments in their original connexion. Moreover, one sermon at least, which throws a good deal of light on one of the more obscure details of the controversy, has lately been discovered in a collection of sermons ascribed to St Chrysostom (see *infra* pp. 105 ff.). And extracts from other works of Nestorius have been recovered in Syriac from manuscripts, not yet published, containing works of writers of the school that gave frank expression to the tendencies which Nestorius believed the champions of *Theotokos* encouraged.

The first collection of the extant writings of Nestorius was made in the middle of the seventeenth century by the French scholar, Garnier, in an edition of the works of Marius Mercator[1]. Garnier, however, allowed himself too free a hand

[1] Paris, 1673: reprinted in Migne's *Patrologia Latina* vol. 48.

in dealing with his texts and in supplying their deficiencies from other sources[1]. Fresh materials too have been made accessible since his time, and a new collection was published by Dr Loofs in 1905. In this volume, entitled *Nestoriana*, we have, accordingly, the fullest collection of the *ipsissima verba* of Nestorius that could be made, and we are enabled to read them under conditions more favourable to a fair judgement of the questions in dispute. The publication of this new collection carries with it an invitation to a fresh study of the question, even though the greater part of the evidence has been accessible to every student of the history of Doctrine or of Councils. Here, in a single volume, in some hundred pages of moderate size, can be read the remains of those innumerable writings to which Gennadius alludes. We can turn from page to page, and compare one passage with another, and correct or confirm the inference suggested by an ambiguous phrase or a passing comment. This volume is likely to remain the most useful source of information as to the teaching of Nestorius. The evidence which it furnishes is amply sufficient on all the main points, as soon as it is investigated without the personal *praejudicium* which is always fatal to a frank enquiry, and the unhistorical assumption that theological terms conveyed to all who used them at any given moment, any more than at long intervals of time, one and the same fixed and definite sense.

But for the moment this volume of *Nestoriana* is overshadowed in interest by the discovery of Nestorius's own account of the whole controversy and his statement of Cyril's position in relation to his own, under the title of the *Bazaar of Heraclides*. Written under this pseudonym, or safeguarded[2] by it from the destruction to which the works of heretics were doomed, it doubtless owes its preservation in a Syriac

[1] See Loofs *Nestoriana* pp. 1, 2; or *Journal of Theological Studies* October 1906 (vol. viii, no. 29, p. 120).

[2] See *infra* pp. 33, 29 note 2.

version to some member of the Eastern Church in the Euphrates valley where the exiled "Nestorian" bishops found a home. There we hear of it just before the cataclysm which Tamerlane's invasion brought upon that famous Church. Ebed Jesu, the learned Nestorian, who died in the early part of the fourteenth century (1318) mentions as works of Nestorius still extant (that is, of course, in Syriac), the *Tragedy*, the *Book of Heraclides*, a *Letter to Cosmas*, a prolix *Liturgy*, one book of *Letters* and one of *Homilies and Sermons*. Another list of his writings[1] names, besides the *Book of Heraclides*, the *Theopaschites*, the *Tragedy*, and another with the title *Historica*. It is possible that *Historica* was a general title that covered the Letters and Sermons, some of which, as we have seen, remain; but it would exactly fit the "Book of Nestorius" which Evagrius congratulates himself on coming across, and describes as containing his "defence of his blasphemy" and the "history" of his fortunes after his condemnation. Information as to this Evagrius could not find in the historians, and had he not lighted on this book, he says, all knowledge of the facts would have vanished and been swallowed up by time, leaving not even hear-say behind[2]. The *Liturgy* too, which may perhaps have been the work of Nestorius, is still in use in the Nestorian Church. Of the *Theopaschites* fragments are extant, and the *Tragedy*, unless it is really the work of the Count Irenaeus, may be the writing of which a passage is cited as from a "book on the history". Of the *Letter to Cosmas* nothing is known. It is not impossible that some of these lost works may still be recovered. Meanwhile we have already the "Book of Heraclides", in a Syriac version, in a MS in the Patriarch's library at Kochanes.

[1] In the translator's Preface to the *Book of Heraclides*.

[2] Evagrius *H. E.* i 7.

The Bazaar[1] *of Heraclides of Damascus*

To the words of Nestorius himself the translator has prefixed a preface in which he gives the reason why the book was published under such a title 'lest since his own name was a bugbear to many, they should be unwilling to read it and be converted to the truth'. It was written, he says, 'that it might be a remedy to restore the health of souls that were labouring under the offence of prejudice and sunk in the deep of impiety. For great in truth was the schism which Satan brought into the body of the holy Christian Church, so as to lead astray, if it were possible, even the elect. And so this correcting and health-giving antidote was needful for the disease of their mind....It enlightens the eyes of our soul with teaching concerning the Christian dispensation; and it is in truth an excellent system of teaching concerning the Godhead; for by its means we avoid both the blasphemies concerning the Divine nature and those concerning the Incarnation; and by God's abundant mercies we draw near to knowledge.' Heraclides 'was a certain man, had in honour for his way of life, and yet more for his learning; and he dwelt in Damascus. And for his eminence in these ways he was celebrated even at the Court, for his faithfulness and right speaking; for, being superior to all passions that separate from the truth, he acted in all things without respect of persons.'[2]

[1] The Syriac word is *Têgûrtâ*, which means the "business of a merchant" or "merchandise", and the translator says that the book is indeed a *têgûrtâ* of spiritual knowledge. The Greek word was probably ἐμπόριον (θησαυρός would have been rendered *Gazzâ*). "Mart" or "store" or "magazine" suggest themselves as renderings, but *Bazaar* perhaps has the best claim to represent the title.

[2] This statement may be the invention of the translator. He prefaces it with the words 'but who Heraclides was, is not clear. But this, O Reader, may be said by way of throwing light on the subject.' It was the best he could do by way of explanation. I cannot find that any Heraclides of

The translator proceeds to describe the contents of the book and to give a list of headings of the various sections. He says it was divided into two books, the first book into three parts and the second into two parts: as follows—

BOOK I

Part I 'of all the heresies opposed to the Church and of all the differences with regard to the faith of the 318.'

Part II 'against Cyril...of the exactions (*or* examination) of the judges and the charges of (*or* against) Cyril.'

Part III 'his own apology, and a copy (*or* comparison) of their letters.'

BOOK II

Part I 'an apology, and a refutation of the charges (against him), dealing with those matters for which he was excommunicated.'

Part II 'from his excommunication till the close of his life.'

The MS was much damaged at the time of the Nestorian massacre of Bedr Khan Beg some sixty years ago, and there are many *lacunae*, sometimes more than twenty pages in succession being wanting. Altogether about one-sixth of the whole—in particular most of Part II of Book I—is missing; but for doctrinal purposes the loss is probably not important. The transcriber of our copy (which is in the regular Nestorian book hand) appears to have made an exact reproduction of the MS, copying it line for line, leaving blank spaces and pages (numbered) to correspond with the original before him, and adding notes stating that the MS is defective in those places. We therefore refer to the book by the pagination of our copy.

Damascus is known to history. There were Nestorians at Damascus apparently from an early time (a metropolitan had his seat there certainly in the eighth century and probably much earlier), but it is not probable that it was at Damascus that the pseudonym was invented.

The only clue to the time at which the translation was made is to be found in a part of the Preface of which several lines and words are missing. It is apparently the dedication of the translation to one who had 'undertaken the toil of a long journey from East to West, to illumine the souls which were sunk in the darkness of the Egyptian error and were intent on the blasphemy which originated with Apollinarius.' We know that bishops of the "Nestorian" Church were more than once sent by kings of Persia on embassies to the West. The term "Egyptian error" need have, of course, no specially localized sense: there were Monophysites nearer at hand in Armenia. But Egypt was the real home of Monophysites, and on the way from East to West. Perhaps one of these bishops, whose interest in his mission was more theological than political, may have seized the opportunity of doing a little work on his own account of an evangelistic kind. And though we must infer, from the words of the Dedication, that this part of his mission was not successful in the way which he wished, and that he did not bring the "Egyptians" over to the sounder faith of his own Church[1]; it is not impossible that he found in Egypt, the land of literary resurrections, a copy of the great work of Nestorius (which had been written in Egypt and is said to have been addressed to an Egyptian), and brought the book back with him to the East and set one of his chaplains to translate it. If so, we at least must hold that his mission achieved a great success. The fact that the translator expresses his firm confidence in the power of his patron's prayers to support his "incapacity" in the work before him favours this view of their mutual relations[2].

[1] The translator can only claim that his patron had the best of the argument, not that his reasoning carried conviction ('even though...they were not persuaded, they were refuted and exposed by the error itself').

[2] We can, however, possibly fix the time of the translation more closely. The famous Catholicos of the Eastern Church, Maraba, in his earlier life, between the years 525 and 533, made such a journey as

The translator's preface is followed by the heading 'Beginning of the Book (that is to say the Saint's own words begin here)'. Then comes the title, which is apparently the translator's own composition and shews the esteem in which Nestorius was held in his circle: 'The Book of the holy Mar Nestorius, bishop of Constantinople, and Standard (κάνων) of orthodoxy.'

There is first a short introduction:

'It is right, as I think, for one who sets himself to enquire

is referred to in the Dedication, and with a similar purpose. After studying at Nisibis, he was seized with the desire to visit the holy places and to hold discussion with one Sergius, described as an Arian strongly tainted with paganism, in the hope of converting him to the true faith. At Edessa he met with a Syrian named Thomas who taught him Greek, and together they visited first Palestine and then Egypt, and from there took ship to Constantinople, staying at Corinth and Athens on the way. He did not fail to make a pious pilgrimage to the famous solitudes of the Egyptian desert, where thousands of monks were living the ascetic life. At Alexandria he expounded the Scriptures in Greek, and is said to have made a translation of them, and also to have brought back with him from the West a translation of the works of Theodore of Mopsuestia, in which he was helped by his friend, Thomas of Edessa. That he failed to convert Sergius, the most learned person of his time, famous as physician and philosopher alike, may be regarded as certain. He probably had more to learn from him than he had to teach him. His reputation, already high, was increased by his austerity of life and his work as teacher at Nisibis or Seleucia; and soon after his return to the East he was unanimously elected Patriarch (see J. Labourt, *Le Christianisme dans l'empire perse*, pp. 163 ff.). It might well have been he who found the work of Nestorius in Egypt, or even in Constantinople, and had it translated into Syriac on his return. (On the other hand, the copy which was used by Evagrius, who did not write his history till forty years after the death of Maraba, was probably found by him at Constantinople, where he held the office of Master of the Rolls, and was apparently in Nestorius's own name; whereas before it was translated into Syriac it already went under its pseudonymous title. It is not, however, impossible that the rare copy on which Evagrius lighted was a survival of the "first edition" of the book, and that in the time of Maraba it was already current in Greek Nestorian circles under the title which would convey nothing to others as to its contents.)

'with all diligence into the truth and would treat his subject 'without anterior bias, to bring forward all those opinions that 'are opposed to the truth and examine them: even as money 'testers separate the true gold from the base, and, by com-'paring the two together, demonstrate the difference to the 'view of those who would as soon have the counterfeit as the 'true, or even prefer it. For many choose evil rather than 'good, and falsehood rather than the truth; for both are alike 'to them; and they attach more importance to contending 'against and worsting one another than to establishing the 'truth. And whereas some confess Christ after this fashion 'and some after that, clinging merely to the name—though 'some even quarrel about the name itself—it is right that we 'should set forth the views of the various heresies with regard 'to Christ, that so the Faith may be recognized in contrast 'with the heresies, and we ourselves may not be perplexed 'and perhaps fall into one or other of them, like men devoid of 'vision.'

Then follows a brief statement of various heresies, after which the book suddenly assumes the form of a dialogue between Nestorius and one Superianus (or Soprinus or possibly Severianus)[1], probably an imaginary person, who puts objections and arguments from the point of view of each heresy as it comes in turn under examination, as its 'advocate and helper': and the discussion is carried on in that form throughout the first part of the book, though at times the writer's feelings run away with him and, dropping the literary device, he speaks of himself in the third person, or addresses himself directly to his friends or opponents, with impassioned appeal or ironical cross-examination, as he does in his extant sermons. In the

[1] The Syriac form is *Sôperyânôs*. At the end of the book, by an apparent play on his real or imaginary name, he addresses him as *sôphrônâyê* in the phrase 'chief of holy and *prudent* men'. Perhaps an Egyptian name is transliterated (if the "certain Egyptian" of Evagrius is more than a guess), or it may have been simply Σώφρων.

latter part of the book, too, there is a duel between Cyril and Nestorius. Cyril is introduced as speaking in his own person, while Nestorius replies: and there is a good deal of simple narrative all through. The argument thus proceeds in stages with a good deal of repetition, and its effect is cumulative. The method has its drawbacks. Nestorius's own views are often conveyed through criticism of other views; and on some points it is at first sight easier to understand what his objections were to the views he criticizes than to be sure what his own positive statement of the doctrine was. I think, however, that the passages which I have selected fairly represent his conceptions on all the points which were at issue: there are many others like them, and all his criticisms of other opinions point in the same direction. It has been difficult to know where to begin and where to leave off in making selections, especially in view of the fact that the whole work is to be published with a translation in French (see Preface p. xiv).

I have only aimed at selecting some of the passages which seem to be most characteristic and to supplement most usefully the evidence of the Greek and other fragments that are to be found in the collection of Dr Loofs.

This is, I think, the chief value of the long and sometimes (it must be confessed) rather wearisome arguments which it contains. There is a pathetic human interest in it as the work of a man of unusual mental vigour, banished in the prime of life, and growing old as an exile in the Egyptian desert, giving his own account of the matter, justifying himself and criticizing his opponents. They had no mercy on him, and he has none on them. He hits as hard as ever, and exposes the weak spots in their armour as shrewdly as an old man often can. He is anxious to shew the ambiguities and sophistries and inconsistencies of which they were guilty. What is it that they really mean? He still believes that he is right and they are wrong; and he states his case as fully as possible, partly perhaps to unburden his mind and encourage his friends, but partly, we may believe, in the hope that some day justice would be done his memory. And there is, I think, no doubt that the book reveals the strength and the weakness of his position. If it did not add much definite information to our store of his arguments and illustrations, it would be of value as putting them all in a new setting and a more systematic form. It will, however, be seen that it does contribute materially to a truer appreciation of the controversy than has been possible before, and it reveals to us the personality of Nestorius in full light. We know the man himself as he has never been known perhaps outside the circle of his own adherents; and knowledge of the man opens the way to understanding of his teaching.

That it is the genuine work of Nestorius himself, translated from the original Greek, would be clear from the style and the personal ring as well as the argumentation of the whole book, had the translator's preface which states the fact and the reason[1] for its publication under a *nom de guerre* been lost. The personality of Nestorius is unmistakeable, and it is one and the same person who speaks to us throughout this book and in the other remains of sermons and letters and tracts that are undoubtedly his. There is indeed no trace of anonymity or of any attempt at disguise in the book itself. It is probably the "other treatise" (other than the "history") which Evagrius says he wrote "in dialectical fashion (in the form of a dialogue) to a certain Egyptian" on the same subjects (viz. the history of the proceedings and defence of his own teaching), but at greater length[2]. Evagrius gives no hint that the authorship of this book was in any way concealed, and the pseudonymous title may well have been the device of an adherent to save the Master's *apologia* from destruction. In any case it goes back

[1] 'Lest on account of his own name many in their loathing for him would be unwilling to read it and to be turned to the truth.'

[2] Evagrius *H. E.* i 7.

to a Greek edition of the book, as the Syriac translator found it in his copy.

The place at which he wrote was the desert where he had long lived in exile (probably as a monk and perhaps in connexion with some monastery), till it had become a second home to him[1]; for though he had been bitterly assailed by Schenute, the great hero of the Egyptian monks, he seems to have won respect from others and to have had some friends. His personal holiness and devotion to the religious life, as it was counted in those days, must have been appreciated on its merits.

The time when he wrote is fixed within narrow limits. The date of his death has been regarded as uncertain. A Coptic life of Dioscorus[2] says that he was summoned to the Council of Chalcedon but died before the summons reached him; and Evagrius, in mentioning the statement of the historian Zacharias Rhetor that he was summoned to the Council, rejects it only on the ground that the Council anathematized him, not on the ground that he was already dead[3]. This two-fold evidence now receives at least chronological justification. Nestorius gives a full account of the second Council of Ephesus, the "Robber Synod" of 449. The barbarians have attacked Rome once, and are about to do so again[4]. Theodosius (†July 28, 450) is dead. There is no

[1] See the last words of his book *infra* p. 36.

[2] Discovered at Fayum and printed in the *Revue égyptologique*, 1880—1883.

[3] Evagrius *H. E.* ii 2.

[4] The statement occurs in the concluding section of the book, in which the writer alludes to "prophetic" announcements of his in former times. Leo, he says, shall deliver over to the barbarian with his own hands the sacred vessels of the sanctuary. This prophetic reference to an attack on Rome and Leo's action suggests the actual facts of the year 452, when Attila's threatened advance was turned aside by Leo's embassy and (doubtless) gifts. But no great prophetic insight was needed to foresee in the

direct mention of the Council of Chalcedon, but the orthodox faith—the faith of Flavian and of Leo which Nestorius regards as his own faith—has already triumphed, and Dioscorus has betaken himself to flight 'as a means of avoiding deposition 'and being driven into exile'. But Dioscorus was at the Council of Chalcedon, still endeavouring to brave out all that he had done, and if he took to flight it can only have been after the Council had already condemned him and before their sentence had been ratified by the Emperor, in the hope that his friends might secure more favourable treatment for him. The Council sat from the 8th of October to the 1st of November, and the formal deposition of Dioscorus was pronounced at the third session on the 13th of October. On the 7th of February of the following year the Emperor published an edict confirming the doctrinal decisions of the Council, but the decree condemning Eutyches and Dioscorus to banishment was not issued till the 6th of July. Nestorius therefore wrote the concluding portion of his book after the Council (apparently before the Acts of the Council had reached him) and before the news of the imperial edict which sent Dioscorus into exile had travelled so far up the Nile. The earlier parts were probably written at a much earlier time:—they breathe more of the spirit of battle and give no indication of the *dénouement*; it seems to be only to a distant future that the writer looks for the vindication of his doctrine. The attack on another bishop of Constantinople—done to death at another synod at Ephesus by another bishop of Alexandria, as he says he might himself have been had he gone to Cyril's meetings—seems to have led him to take up the pen again, rejoicing to hail this time a bishop of Rome as champion of the Truth.

year 451 (or even early in 452) the situation which actually occurred (Alaric's capture of the city in 410 and the Vandal invasions shewed what was coming), and the Old Testament parallel, when Hezekiah bought off Sennacherib's attack with the gold of the Temple (2 Kings xviii 13—16), would naturally supply the sacred vessels in the prophet's vision.

He has already dealt fully with all the doctrinal questions involved and a few supplementary pages are all that are needed to bring the history up to date and to point its moral. As he writes the last lines of his book he feels that the hand of Death[1] is already on him, but he can say his *Nunc Dimittis* in peace.

'As for me, I have borne the sufferings of my life and all 'that has befallen me in this world as the suffering of a single 'day; and I have not changed, lo, all these years. And now, 'lo, I am already on the point to depart, and daily I pray to 'God to dismiss me—me, whose eyes have seen His salvation.

'Rejoice with me, O Desert, thou my friend and mine 'upbringer and my place of sojourning; and thou, Exile, my 'mother, who after my death shalt keep my body until the 'resurrection cometh in the time of God's good-pleasure. 'Amen.'

These are for us his last words, and the Egyptian desert no doubt received his bones, and three hundred and fifty years

[1] There is no indication in the book of a lingering illness. We know that he was, in common with all Egypt, exposed to the dangers of attack by the nomad tribe, the Blemmyes, who were formidable enemies of the Empire in Africa, and that he was for some time their prisoner, and that by taking him from the Oasis and setting him free in the Thebaid near Panopolis about the year 450 they exposed him to further persecution from Schenute. He was old and ailing, and in a letter to the governor, explaining how it was that he had left his place of exile, he says he had broken his hand and a rib; and he was hurried about from place to place (Evagrius *H. E.* i 7). But the report that he died of cancer of the tongue, which is related with *gusto* by Evagrius (*ib.* "his tongue was eaten by worms and so he passed to the greater and immortal House of Correction"), was probably due to a misunderstanding of Schenute's remark quoted *infra* p. 43. The words "whose tongue swelled and filled his mouth" were probably metaphorical (cf. τὸ στόμα αὐτῶν λαλεῖ ὑπέρογκα Jude 16) and have an analogy in a modern popular phrase. (It was because of his reputation as an orator that he was summoned from Antioch to the capital, and he writes compassionately of Flavian as one who, though he was sound in the faith, could not express himself clearly.)

after his death men thought they knew where they were laid. A Nestorian who had been on a journey to Egypt at the beginning of the ninth century brought back the news that the Jacobites were insulting Nestorius and throwing stones on his tomb. A certain Gabriel, one of the many famous physicians whom the Nestorians numbered in their ranks, was indignant at the report and procured a letter from the Caliph to the Sultan of Egypt, ordering him to send the bones of Nestorius in a casket to Bagdad, that they might be deposited in the church of Kochanes. But a certain Nestorian hermit, wishing to ward off this reproach from his communion and to shew that it was not really Nestorius whom the Jacobites had outraged, said that one of the holy Apostles had appeared to him in a dream and told him that it was a mistake—they were not really the bones of Nestorius, as was commonly believed, for his place of burial was unknown to mortal men. So Gabriel the physician ceased to press for the translation of his remains from Egypt, and the Desert of the land of his Exile still keeps his dust 'until the resurrection cometh in the time 'of God's good-pleasure'[1].

The latter part of the work with its graphic picture of Eutyches, the real ruler of the Church of Constantinople,

[1] The account is given in an extract from a Syriac writer, quoted in Assemani *Bibl. Orient.* ii p. 316 (I owe the reference to Dr Salmon's article "Nestorius" in *D. C. B.*). We might be tempted to suppose that Gabriel, disappointed of his purpose, brought back, instead of the bones of Nestorius, his long-lost book the *Bazaar of Heraclides*, and so to date the translation at this time. But from Assemani's Latin translation of the passage I understand that the hermit was not an Egyptian (as indeed he hardly could have been) but a Nestorian living in Persia, and that his vision saved Gabriel the trouble of the journey to Egypt. Yet the traveller who brought back the news may have been he who brought the book, if it had not been already, as suggested above, long known to the Church of the East.

'who constituted himself a bishop of bishops', and 'used 'Flavian as a kind of deacon' (p. 333), and its account of the second Council of Ephesus, is full of personal and historical interest, and of value as shewing how Nestorius conceived his teaching to stand in relation to that of Leo. But it is in the earlier part that the doctrinal questions are really threshed out.

The fact that a number of bishops assembled in Council had condemned a bishop and his teaching would have weight with many who would make no enquiry into the merits of the case—the many of whom Nestorius speaks as 'those who 'merely believe and do not investigate' (*Bazaar of Heraclides* pp. 183, 184). Nestorius, therefore, is at pains to discredit the proceedings of the majority at Ephesus. He has no difficulty in shewing, from a simple narrative of the facts, with quotations from the protest of the imperial commissioner appointed to superintend the arrangements, the Emperor's letters, and Cyril's replies, how utterly disorderly the conduct of the case had been; how Cyril had succeeded in imposing his own will on the Council, many of whom were reluctant to act before the arrival of the oriental bishops; and how he had been at once accuser and judge.

'Was it', he asks (*Bazaar of Heraclides* p. 151), 'the Synod 'and the Emperor who summoned it that heard my cause, if he '(Cyril) was ranked among the judges? but why should I say '"ranked among the judges"? He was the whole tribunal; 'for everything that he said was at once said by all of them as 'well, and they unhesitatingly agreed with him as the per-'sonification of the court. Now if all the judges were 'assembled, and the accusers were set in their ranks, and the 'accused also in like manner, all should have had equal liberty 'of speech. But if he was everything—accuser and Emperor 'and judge—then he did everything, ousting from this authority 'him who was appointed by the Emperor and setting himself in 'his place, and assembling to himself those whom he wanted, 'both far and near, and making himself the court. And so I 'was summoned by Cyril, who assembled the synod, and by 'Cyril who was its head. Who is judge? Cyril. And who 'the accuser? Cyril. Who the bishop of Rome? Cyril. 'Cyril was everything....Who would believe that these things 'were so, were it not that God had constrained them to speak 'and to write and send them to the whole world? But 'everyone of his (sc. Cyril's) party who reads these things is 'incredulous and mistrusts even his own senses: for the things 'that happen in dreams are more credible than these. If then 'these things are so, and in fact they did actually happen, where 'was the need of the synod? for this man was everything.'

And, again, he speaks of 'a rabble of idlers and country 'folk assembled by Memnon, bishop of Ephesus' filling the streets, with the bishop at their head 'parading them armed 'through the city, so that we were obliged to flee, each and all 'of us, and to hide ourselves and employ a guard' (*ib.* p. 153).

'They acted in everything as if it was a war they were 'conducting, and the followers of the Egyptian (Cyril) and of 'Memnon, who were abetting them, went about in the city girt 'and armed with clubs, men with high necks, performing strange 'antics (lit. who were leaping over their hands, ?leaping along 'beside them) with the yells of barbarians, snorting fiercely with 'horrible and unwonted noises, raging with extravagant arro-'gance against those whom they knew to be opposed to their 'doings, carrying bells about the city and lighting fires in many 'places and casting into them all kinds of writings. Every-'thing they did was a cause of amazement and fear: they 'blocked up the streets so that everyone was obliged to flee 'and hide, while they acted as masters of the situation, lying 'about drunk and besotted and shouting obscenities. And there 'was none to interfere or lend assistance' (*ib.* pp. 273, 274).

In order to prevent these ruffians from setting upon him and murdering him, Nestorius was obliged to ask for a guard of soldiers round his house (*ib.* pp. 153, 154).

The whole account which Nestorius gives is singularly graphic: but, as the facts are not disputed, more of this part of his narrative need not be quoted, racy reading as it is. The proceedings may have been disorderly, scandalously uncharitable and partial, such as no court of judges would allow. There is, indeed, no doubt that they were. They violated at every point the Emperor's instructions, which were the authority under which the Council met. Nestorius's refusal to appear before the body that Cyril called the Council[1], and to plead his cause in the absence of all the bishops of the province of Antioch, was abundantly justified.

And yet the decision may have been right, though the method of reaching it was wrong. Nestorius is well aware of this.

'But perchance some may say:' he writes (*Bazaar of Heraclides* p. 149), '"Do not mind so much about all this, 'but shew us from your own writings and from those of Cyril 'how it was that you were unjustly deposed. For even if a 'full examination had been held, how would you have been 'benefited?...What we really have to enquire is what opinion 'it is right for us to hold; and we must not stray from the 'orthodox position either through a prejudice in favour of this 'man (sc. Cyril) or through sympathy with you".'

He wishes no favour, but only simple justice to his views, and even this not because they are his, but because the Faith is at stake. Grievous as were the proceedings of the Council, he could let them pass as a merely personal wrong: but the issue is more solemn.

'Who could refrain from weeping when he remembers the 'wrongs done at Ephesus! And would God it were against me 'and against my life they were done, and not in a wrong cause! 'For then I should have no need of these words on behalf of 'one who was meet to be punished; but on behalf of our

[1] In the Emperor's own words 'assembled for the purpose of giving only a half judgement', *Bazaar of Heraclides* p. 282.

'Saviour Jesus Christ, the just Judge, for whose sake I have 'undertaken to endure patiently, that the whole body of Christ 'may not be accused—for Him I must speak' (*ib.* p. 154).

Was Nestorius, then, misrepresented, or at all events misunderstood? Well, in the first place we have his own complaint that his sayings were garbled by Cyril; a complaint which he supports by chapter and verse: secondly we have some definite instances of misrepresentation by others than Cyril: and thirdly we have enough of his own writings to enable us to judge for ourselves what his real teaching was, what he meant by expressions which were ambiguous and how far they justify the charges commonly brought against him.

It will be convenient to state those charges and examine in some detail the evidence of his writings with regard to them. If there is any dearth of evidence, of one thing we may be sure: we have before us all the evidence that tells against him. His opponents took care that we should know the worst that could be said of him: we have their *dossier* complete. It may be that "ordinary optics" will fail to find a defence, and that to discover a case for him we "must dive by the spirit-sense". That too we must try to do. We may need to look beyond the mere words, and to endeavour to penetrate to the shadowy region where tendencies dwell, before we can account for the course the controversy ran. The process has been already indicated: we must not ignore the political and ecclesiastical considerations and the personal aspects of the question. And the verdict of the moment must be considered also in the light of the later history and beliefs of those who held that Nestorius had been unjustly judged and clung to his teaching, regarding him as Doctor and Saint.

CHAPTER III

THE DOCTRINES ATTRIBUTED TO NESTORIUS AND THE TERMS WHICH HE USED

THE controversy was precipitated by Nestorius's protest against the use of the term *Theotokos*, "Mother of God", as a title of the Virgin Mary. Mary must not be called Mother of God. We must examine the meaning of this protest of Nestorius in all its technical bearings. But before doing so we may clear the ground a little by considering the less technical charge which was immediately brought against him. It was said that he taught that He who was born of Mary was only a man: he denied that Jesus Christ was God. It was perhaps natural that such a cry should be raised by the people, and that, when once they had got hold of the belief that Nestorius denied the Godhead of our Lord, they should never let it go. But the clergy of Constantinople also joined in the cry, and a statement which they composed[1] containing the charge was one of the incriminating documents read at Ephesus on the evidence of which he was condemned. The document is headed "a deposition put forth in public by the clergy of Constantinople and published in church, to wit that Nestorius is of the same opinion as Paul of Samosata who was anathematized a hundred and sixty years ago by the orthodox bishops". It gives a list of sayings of Paul and of Nestorius,

[1] Mansi *Concilia* tom. iv pp. 1008—1012.

placing them side by side, to shew that Nestorius agreed with Paul in regarding Him who was born of the Virgin as a mere man, and that he taught that the Lord Jesus Christ was not at once the Only-begotten Son of the Father, born before all ages, and also born of the Virgin Mary, but that the Only-begotten Son was one and He who was born of the Virgin another. So some at least of the clergy attested the popular charge, and Socrates[1] could say that the general opinion was that Nestorius held that the Lord was a mere man, bringing into the Church the doctrine of Paul of Samosata and Photinus.

The charge was supported by quoting, as his, words which he never used. One instance is furnished by Schenute of Atripos who wrote[2]: 'Nestorius too, who was called a bishop... and others like him—he whose tongue swelled and filled his mouth and who died in exile, said [of the Virgin Mary] "She who bore a good man, who was like Moses and David and others".' To get the expression at all Schenute had to change one of the letters in the word Nestorius used, replacing an *iota*

[1] *H. E.* vii 32.

[2] The remark of Schenute is quoted by Loofs *Nestoriana* p. 291 note from J. Leipoldt *Schenute von Atripe* Texte u. Unters. xxv, n. F. x 1, 1903 p. 46. This Schenute (or Schnoudi) was one of the Egyptian monks who went to the Council of Ephesus. According to the account of his disciple and successor, Besa (an account, however, which is not quite consistent with the accepted tradition that Nestorius refused to appear at "Cyril's Council"), he distinguished himself by his outrageous violence against Nestorius, seizing the book of the Gospels which Nestorius brought with him and hurling it at him. Nestorius protested against his presence at the Council, being 'neither a bishop, nor an archimandrite, nor a provost, but merely a simple monk', and Cyril removed the objection on the spot by investing Schenute with the rank and robe of an archimandrite and so enabling him to act as one of the "judges" of Nestorius. He became the most celebrated abbot of the Pachomian monasteries after Pachomius himself, and all through the life of Nestorius (and, as we see, after his death) remained his bitter enemy. He was as violent a champion of Dioscorus as he had been of Cyril, and refused to accept the decisions of the Council of Chalcedon. See *D. C. B.* art. "Senuti".

by an *eta* and so converting "anointed" (*christon*) into "good" (*chrêston*). But even that was not all. For again and again in the sermons that are extant Nestorius insists that, though the terms "God" and "Christ" (i.e. "anointed"), and the like, are used in Scripture of Moses and others, yet they are applied to the Incarnate Word in an altogether different sense. 'It is the 'community of names that is alike, the honour (*or* rank) is not 'the same.' 'Community of names does not constitute com'munity of honour or equality.' 'The one, I have said, is God 'by nature, consubstantial with the Father, and Creator and 'Maker of all; but not the other.'[1]

Socrates himself, however, though he has a poor opinion of the intelligence of Nestorius, and thinks he simply made a "bug-bear" of the term *Theotokos*, acquits him of this charge and gives it as his opinion that Nestorius was no follower of Paul or of Photinus. The charge that he denied the Godhead of our Lord no doubt did much to rouse prejudice against him among those who could not enter into the meaning of his argument, but it may be dismissed without investigation. The only basis for it is the fact that he objected to the title "Mother of God", and it is refuted by almost every word he said or wrote[2]. The

[1] *Bazaar of Heraclides* p. 223, where he definitely repels the misrepresentation of his words and adds that Christ is 'something to which there is nothing corresponding in those things which were spoken of', that is, in the case of the great men of the Old Testament.

[2] The saying of Nestorius 'on account of Him that bears I worship him that is borne' gave rise to the phrase ἄνθρωπος θεόφορος as a concise description of his theory of the Person of our Lord. The compound might be either active or passive in sense. If active, the phrase would mean that our Lord was "a God-bearing man", that is to say a man who was vested or clothed with God, or who carried God about with him; and so it would express the view of a double personality in which the actual initiative would be human rather than Divine. It is in this sense that the phrase has commonly been understood. If the compound be passive, the phrase means "a man who is borne by God", uplifted, inspired, controlled by God; and so the active personality would be Divine. In any case the phrase is not Nestorius's own, but his opponents' epigram; and

charges which the theologians brought against his teaching were much more recondite and call for careful examination. These were that he so distinguished between the Godhead and the manhood of our Lord as to treat them as separate personal existences, as though a man and God were joined together, so that our Lord was not one Person but two Persons and no real union of God and man was effected in Him. It was supposed that he held the Word to be a Person distinct from Jesus, and the Son of God distinct from the Son of Man, and that therefore he avoided the term which expressed the real union of both and preferred to speak of a "conjunction" between them. And so some of the old charges against the Gnostics and Paul of Samosata were raked up again and he was said, in teaching "two Sons", to introduce a fourth person into the Godhead, and to transform the Trinity into a Quaternity.

Teaching such as this is obviously destructive of the whole conception of the Incarnation. It was on the charge of such teaching that he was condemned and it is this teaching that is known to history as "Nestorianism". It would surely have been condemned at any period in the history of the Church. We must keep these charges in view in our examination of his actual words. And we must bear in mind his anxiety for clearness of expression in matters of the faith. The interlocutor in the dialogue would let some difficult points alone. But 'No!' says Nestorius:

'I could wish that you would not pass them over, but 'examine them with all care, so that matters of faith may not 'be treated lightly and left without discussion, but rather may 'be clearly known to all—circumscribed, as it were, with defi-'nitions and illustrated with suitable examples, and not 'pourtrayed in shadowy images which hint at different things

in all his sayings which could be held to justify it the active agency is attributed to "the God", not to "the man". It would be God, not man, who would be the dominant partner, if the phrase may be allowed, in the dual alliance which Nestorius is supposed to have imagined.

'(these and those) till they are represented as the same' (*Bazaar of Heraclides* p. 14).

He is only 'one of those who knock and ask at the door 'of Truth, if only it be the truth' (*ib.* p. 15). He knows it may be said to him 'Things which ought to be accepted by 'faith, you, by accepting them on the ground of human reason, 'reduce to impossibilities; and, indeed, you sever us from the 'Christian Faith like the heathen and the Manichaeans who 'stumble at the cross of Christ' (*ib.* p. 17). He knows the difficulties which he must confront, but he knows also that great moral issues are at stake, and he will not shrink from the use of all the powers of reason in the effort to reach the truth.

In dealing with views other than his own he wishes that no argument in their favour should be ignored. To the interlocutor in the dialogue, who shrinks from adducing one line of reasoning, he says:

'Say what it is with all confidence and without fear, using 'all their arguments persistently and exhaustively even as they 'would themselves; for one cannot deliver battle effectively 'against half an opinion' (*ib.* p. 26).

He is well aware that heresies embody elements of truth, and he is anxious to give credit where credit is due—even those who confess Christ to be a mere man must have their meed of praise for recognizing a fact which some theologians in his day seemed to ignore.

'Let us divide up their heresy...that we may not run away 'from the things which have been well said by them on account 'of those that have been ill said without recognizing the 'difference. For to confess Christ to be man, and truly and 'naturally man, is correct and is attested by the truth; and on 'this count one has no fault to find with them. But their 'rejection of the Divinity, which is His in truth and by nature, 'causes them to be rejected as undoers of the incarnation of 'God the Word' (*ib.* p. 39).

He was certainly sometimes misunderstood, and he was in

consequence sometimes misrepresented as using words and expressions which he did not use. "Half the controversies of the world would never have happened if the disputants had at the outset defined their terms" is a saying the truth of which is always more obvious to the onlookers of a later age than it was to the disputants at the time. But in this case it is we of a later age who need to be on our guard that we may not import into the terms which Nestorius employed the sense that they bore in later ecclesiastical usage. No one who reads his writings as a whole could make the mistake, but single passages might prove to be pitfalls even for the wary. For one of the chief terms used had already acquired in the time of Nestorius, in other connexions at least, a sense which is different from that in which he employs it. The term in question is *hypostasis*, and Nestorius always maintained that there were in the Person of our Lord two *hypostases*. The Chalcedonian definition of the Faith, on the other hand, uses the expression "one *hypostasis*", and this expression ultimately ousted all others, so that to say "two *hypostases*" became impossible. To understand the use of Nestorius we must look backwards[1].

The history and meaning of the terms

To express any kind of real existence two terms were in common use among Greek thinkers, viz. *ousia* and *hypostasis*: the former the noun of the verb "to be" ("being"), the latter the noun of a verb of similar sense "to subsist" or "to exist" ("subsistence", "existence"). Subtle shades of difference of meaning may be detected in these two terms; but in practical use they were synonymous, and Greek writers who well knew the values of words declared them to be so. Their equivalents

[1] Only a summary statement can be given here. For fuller particulars I may refer to *Texts and Studies* vol. vii no. 1, or to my *Introduction to the early history of Christian Doctrine* pp. 231—238, and to *Journal of Theological Studies* vol. iv no. 15 p. 440, vol. viii no. 29 p. 124.

in Latin were *essentia* (or *entia*) and *substantia*, "essence" (or "entity") and "substance": but the equivalents of *ousia* were never domesticated in the Latin language; *substantia* alone was taken into use, and "substance" is thus the English representative of the original sense of both the Greek terms. We must be on our guard against attaching any "materialistic" sense to this word "substance". And if the term is not now commonly used in discussions as to ultimate realities and the objects or process of cognition, and if "modern philosophy" tends to repudiate the idea that anything exists or can be known "in itself" apart from, or in any other way than in virtue of, its relations to other things and the perceptions of minds or persons—we must yet remember that throughout the period in which Christian doctrines assumed their form a very different conception of existence and of knowledge prevailed. According to the dominant theory there were ultimate realities, whether they could be fully known or not, and whether they were conceived as in some sense material or as immaterial. And to these realities the term which we render "substance" was applied. Everything that existed was a "substance".

To this "substance" attached all the attributes or characteristics which as a whole were always associated with it, though some of them might characterize other substances as well; and these were called, by a general term, the "nature" of the thing. Different substances might have attributes in common, and so their natures might be similar; but they themselves remained distinct, and in thought at least could be distinguished from their natures: while the natures, too, of different things might have much in common with one another, but yet remained distinct, and could be spoken of almost as if they were real existences in themselves. This however was only a loose mode of speech—the reality was always the "substance" to which the nature belonged. The "nature" was not conceived of as being the "substance", nor the "substance" as being the "nature". "It" was not "it's nature", nor was it's nature "it".

It was usually, no doubt, quite enough to speak of the "nature". It was the more popular term and expressed all that was wanted. The idea of the "substance" was more technical and could be left to experts, whether in philosophy or in theology. So it is that in popular usage we commonly speak of our Lord as "of the same nature" as the Father and as taking "our nature" upon Him, though we still retain the accurate rendering of the Greek and Latin terms in the clause of the Nicene Creed "of one substance with the Father" and the very un-English "consubstantial" of our hymns; while the translation of the Athanasian Creed carefully preserves not only "substance" but also the corresponding words "Godhead" and "manhood" rather than "Divine" or "human" nature. There is such a thing as "Godhead", and there is such a thing as "manhood", and there is a real distinction between them. If we use only the vague term "nature", we run the grave risk of confusing two distinct realities, because they may have some attributes in common. In the interests of clear thought, and of the practical moral issues that ensue, it is earnestly to be desired that exponents of the Catholic faith would use the genuine English words "Godhead" and "manhood" rather than "Divinity" and "humanity" of our Lord. Nestorius knew very well what he was doing when he insisted on the recognition of the "substances" as well as the "natures" in the Person of our Lord. To express the conception "substance" he used either of the two Greek synonyms *ousia* and *hypostasis*, the latter more frequently than the former; and, inasmuch as the term "substance" is almost as strange in this connexion to English ears today as are the Greek expressions, we have usually kept in the translation the original terms. The Syriac translator himself simply transliterated *ousia*, except in a few cases in which the Being of God Himself (rather than the Godhead) is meant; and in these he used a Syriac word (*îthûthâ*) which was commonly employed of Divine beings. But *hypostasis* he always rendered by a native Syriac term (*q'nômâ*). For "nature" also he had a Syriac word at hand (*k'yânâ*). In speaking of two "substances" in the Person of our Lord Nestorius was employing an expression which had been recognized in ecclesiastical usage from the times of Melito in the East and Tertullian in the West—that is to say from the earliest days of formal theology. The phrase was simply the technical expression of the Christian faith in the Godhead and manhood of the Lord, and its constant recurrence in the passages cited from the writings of Nestorius calls for no further comment.

In like manner, in treating *ousia* and *hypostasis* as equivalent terms, Nestorius was simply carrying on the old traditional use of the words, reflected in the anathema appended to the Creed of Nicaea, in which the two terms are placed side by side, and in the assertion of Athanasius in one of his latest writings "*hypostasis* is *ousia*".

But in connexion with the Being of God, in order to express the Christian conception of Trinity in Unity, a new and artificial sense had been put upon the word *hypostasis* by some of the chief Greek theologians in the latter half of the fourth century. The word had been narrowed down from its wider meaning "substance" and forced to do duty for the conception of the particular "modes of existence" of the one God which constituted God a Trinity. In connexion with the doctrine of the Trinity this use of the term had probably won wide acceptance by the time of Nestorius. He himself recognizes the usage[1]. But it must be doubted whether this conventional sense had established itself universally even in regard to the modes of existence implied by the three names Father, Son, and Holy Spirit; and I am not aware of any clear evidence that such a usage had been extended to the Christological problem or that this sense of the term would have seemed at all natural in a discussion of the relation of the Godhead and manhood of our Lord. Cyril's own use of the term *hypostasis* (and its adjectival

[1] See Loofs *op. cit.* p. 225 and *Bazaar of Heraclides* p. 39.

form *hypostatic*) is certainly not consistently, if ever, the same as that which became established at a later time. Marius Mercator in translating Cyril renders it sometimes by *substantia* ("substance") and sometimes by *subsistentia* ("subsistence") as if he felt some shade of difference in its significance in different connexions[1]; but he never renders it by the natural Latin equivalent of its Trinitarian usage, viz. *persôna* ("person"). And if it seems incredible that a word which had acquired a definite value in the statement of the doctrine of God should be used in a different sense in the statement of the doctrine of the Person of Christ, it may be well to remember that this very word "person" of ours cannot possibly bear the same sense when we apply it to the three Persons of the Trinity as it has when we speak of the Person of the incarnate Word, both God and man.

At all events it does not appear that exception was taken to Nestorius's use of the word *hypostasis* as practically synonymous with *ousia*. The difference between the controversialists went deeper than technical terms: it was concerned with the manner in which the union of Godhead and manhood was conceived. The word *hypostasis* in this connexion did not mean to Cyril exactly "person", as it certainly did not to Nestorius.

To express the idea of personality Nestorius always uses *prosôpon* (which the Syriac translator transliterates *parṣôpâ*)--a word which has the same history as the Latin *persôna* ; meaning originally an actor's mask, or face,—the part which an actor played, the *dramatis persona*—rôle or function in life in general —the character or aspect in which some one is conceived--and so some one regarded in a particular relation, a person. The

[1] It may be this shade of difference, akin to that between the general and the particular, which made it possible to agree to speak of the one *ousia* and the three *hypostases* of God, that underlies Nestorius's use of *ousia* as well as *hypostasis* in speaking of the Godhead and the manhood of Christ. If so he would use *ousia* of Godhead or of manhood regarded, so to say, in themselves, and *hypostasis* of the particular mode of the existence of the same Godhead or manhood in the Lord Jesus Christ.

words were current simultaneously in all these senses: no one of the possible meanings drove out the others. Latin theologians used the phrase *tres personae* of the Trinity and *una persona* of Christ, though more often they seem to have avoided the word and to have been content to speak of "Three" (*tres*) and "One" (*unus*). Neither in Latin nor in Greek was a defining noun needed as it usually is in English. For Greek theologians the word *prosôpon* was tainted by the Sabellian use of it to express the conception of the One God assuming different rôles and playing the part now of Father, now of Son, and now of Holy Spirit; and therefore they had no unequivocal term to use in this connexion (of the doctrine of the Trinity) until the conventional distinction between *ousia* and *hypostasis* was established. But though they avoided the term *prosôpon* in stating the doctrine of the Trinity, they do not seem to have shrunk from using it of the incarnate Son in connexion with the doctrine of the Incarnation. And when Nestorius insisted that he believed our Lord Jesus Christ, in His Godhead and His manhood, to be "one *prosôpon*", it was not that they suspected the term *prosôpon* of any hidden heretical meaning, but that they did not believe that he really believed what he said that he believed. They, too, were quite ready to use the term to express the "Person" of the Lord, and even in the Chalcedonian definition "one person" is joined with "one hypostasis", preceding it to define the sense in which "hypostasis" was then used, just as at an earlier time in the Nicene anathema (before this new usage of *hypostasis* was recognized) *ousia* and *hypostasis* were used together as synonyms. Distrust of the term itself in expressing the doctrine of the Incarnation is of later origin than the time of the Nestorian controversy and must not be allowed to colour our consideration of it.

The problem of the union of Godhead and manhood in a single subject or being is one that perhaps defies solution. It had not been seriously faced in earlier times. Cyril was no doubt feeling after a more "substantial" unity than he thought the teaching of Nestorius allowed, and was content to guard the distinction between the "substances" in word and to ignore it in fact. To Nestorius Godhead and manhood, God and man, were much too real to be able to lose themselves in one another: the unity must be found in something other than the "substances" themselves.

A lover of epigram might be tempted to settle the question by saying that the supreme realities were to Cyril *persons* and to Nestorius *things*. But the epigram would not, I think, be true, while it certainly would have been unintelligible to Cyril and Nestorius. Nor was the one a nominalist and the other a realist. Nestorius can poke fun at Cyril because he speaks of a "nature" when the *ousia* which the "nature" presupposes is wanting[1]; but Cyril meant the "nature" to be as real as the *ousia*. As far as precision of terminology goes, Nestorius is more definite than Cyril. Cyril does not seem to have had a clear conception of the difference between the terms "substance", "nature", and "person". But he used them all, and his language is really as elusive as Nestorius found it, though it supplied the Church with phrases to which a conventional value could be assigned, so that they might become the standard expression of the Christian faith in the union of Godhead and manhood in our Lord. The fugitive phrase was captured, and acclimatized. But in reading the words of Cyril and Nestorius it must be remembered that the hunt for the proper term was still going on, unconsciously rather than of purpose; and though we cannot avoid consideration of the terms themselves, it is to the arguments of Nestorius rather than to the technical terms he uses that attention must be paid, and to these we may now pass.

As the meaning of the terms employed by the modern Syriac-speaking "Nestorians" has been uncertain, and the

[1] See *infra* p. 170 note.

Syriac translation of the *Bazaar of Heraclides* shews beyond question what the theological usage was at the time when the translation was made, and earlier writers used the words in the same sense, the English translator of the *Bazaar* has prepared a statement setting out the history of the Syriac terms as an Appendix to this volume[1].

In the citations of the words of Nestorius in these pages it must be understood that " person " represents the Syriac *parṣôpâ* or the Greek *πρόσωπον*. In translations from the Greek, *οὐσία* and *ὑπόστασις* are rendered alike either "being" or "substance": but in the translation of the *Bazaar of Heraclides*, in which *οὐσία* is simply transliterated, the transliteration *ousia* is preserved, while *hypostasis* or "substance" represents *q'nômâ*. The Greek *φύσις* and the Syriac *k'yânâ* are translated "nature", though "physical" is often used for the adjectival forms in accordance with common theological usage. The idiomatic Syriac rendering of *ὁμοούσιος* means literally "son of the nature of", and as there is no doubt about the original term it is either transliterated "homoousios" or translated by "consubstantial" or some equivalent phrase.

[1] See *infra* p. 212.

CHAPTER IV

THE TITLE *THEOTOKOS*

We have to enquire, then, first, what were the reasons that led Nestorius to object to the use of the title "Mother of God".

It would be interesting to know how far this use implied at the time with which we are concerned an incipient "cult" of the Virgin, and whether this cult had grown up in the districts in which the worship of the Virgin Goddess of pagan fame was prevalent or had its origin in purely Christian circles as the natural outcome of the same deep-seated human instincts, independent of any particular non-Christian rites. Was popular feeling roused against Nestorius because he was opposing a popular form of worship which he regarded as a pagan superstition? And was the Virgin Mother of the Lord already the patron-saint of the monastic life, and were the monks who played so threatening and noisy a part in the background of the discussions and intrigues stirred up to action by the belief that the institution of monasticism itself was the object of attack? Was any question of regular *versus* secular clergy involved?

In later ages Cyril, as the great champion of the disputed title, was held in special reverence by those to whom monasticism and the cult of the Virgin were dear.

But there is little evidence to shew that this aspect of the question had influence at the time[1]. The demonstrations of the people of Ephesus against Nestorius—the people of the city which long before had resounded with the cry "Great Artemis of the Ephesians"—the city which had been the central shrine of the worship of the Virgin Goddess—suggest some local current of feeling. The traditions of St John and the Virgin connected with Ephesus lend further support to the view that local memories and loyalties might have been enlisted against him. But feeling always ran high against a heretic, and the bishop of Ephesus was one of the strongest supporters of Cyril. There was reason enough for the violent action of the

[1] There is of course evidence that shews the high esteem in which the Virgin Mother of the Lord was held in the Church from early days. Justin and Irenaeus and Tertullian, for example, do not hesitate to contrast her and her obedience with Eve and her disobedience, in a manner analogous to St Paul's comparison of the first man Adam and the second Man from heaven, and so to assign to her expressly her share in the redemption of mankind (see Justin *Dial.* 100, Iren. *adv. haer.* Mass. v xix 1, Tert. *de carne Christi* 17). Among the Syrians I am informed the Virgin seems to have been from an early time a centre of special honour. In the works of Ephraim (fourth century) there are many hymns of praise of her, which there is no reason to doubt are genuine compositions of Ephraim, though the MSS in which they are found are not the earliest. (The hymns in question are printed by Lamy with a Latin translation in vol. ii of his edition of the works of St Ephraim. With them may be compared the certainly genuine hymns *On the Nativity* in *Nicene and Post-Nicene Fathers* vol. xiii.) And many prayers addressed to the Virgin are attributed to Rabbûla, bishop of Edessa († 435), who was contemporary with Cyril and Nestorius, a devoted friend of Cyril, and famous for his zeal against Nestorians, who named him the "tyrant of Edessa". (Yet this same Rabbûla preached a sermon on the term *theotokos* at Constantinople, while Nestorius was still bishop, in which though upholding the term he deprecated the discussion of it—see Burkitt *Early Eastern Christianity* p. 110.) The remark of Nestorius that it was sufficient honour for the "Christ-bearing" Virgin 'to have given birth to the manhood which was the instrument of the Godhead of God the Word' (*Sermo* viii, Loofs *Nestoriana* p. 247) shews that the question of the *status* of the Virgin was, as of course it must have been, deemed to be involved in the controversy; but it was not the ground on which it was fought.

mob of the town. Nestorius too had himself been a monk, with a high reputation for austerity and devotion, and as a monk he had preached against the term at Antioch. It was to please the monks of Constantinople, as the Emperor reminded Dalmatius after the Council of Ephesus[1], that he had been selected as bishop when the clergy and monks and people could not agree to elect any of the original candidates; and as a monk too, after his deposition, he gladly returned to his old home at Euprepius, and was received with welcome and honour and spent four years in peace there[2]. Cyril, on the other hand, though he had spent five years under monastic discipline in "the desert", seems to have found the restrictions irksome; he had been reproved for occupying himself, even in "solitude", with worldly thoughts and interests[3]; and he had returned to Alexandria to a more active ecclesiastical life. Though Cyril could use the monks for his purposes, it does not appear that the two parties were divided by any line of cleavage on the monastic question. The monks of Egypt were always ready to play the part of the "hooligan" of today. They did it again at Ephesus, a few years later, when Eutyches, who had been one of Cyril's agents against Nestorius at Constantinople, was arraigned for teaching what he believed to be Cyril's doctrine, and was supported by Cyril's successor at Alexandria. Eutyches, the archimandrite, might of course expect support from monks: but there is no evidence, so far as I am aware, that any question affecting the status of monks or the honour of the Virgin entered into the Eutychian controversy.

It would, I believe, be an anachronism to represent such ideas as underlying the disputes about the title *Theotokos*. Attention seems to have been fixed entirely on the question affecting the doctrine of the Person of the Lord—His Godhead and the relation between the Divine and the human in Him.

[1] See *Bazaar of Heraclides* p. 281 (*supra* p. 6 note 3).

[2] Evagrius *H.E.* i 7.

[3] Isidore of Pelusium *Epp.* i 25.

The term had been in vogue, in some circles at least, for many years. Responsible theological teachers like Origen, Athanasius, Eusebius of Caesarea, and Cyril of Jerusalem had used it incidentally, while Julian's taunt "you never stop calling Mary *Theotokos*"[1] would seem to point to a wider popular use.

Doubtless to any one with a fine sense for philological niceties the English translation "Mother of God" is lacking in precision. The Greek adjectival compound is a little less abrupt[2], and need only mean "who gave birth to one who was God" or "whose child was God". But subtle distinctions of this kind are not for the ordinary layman whether he speaks Greek or English, or lives in the fifth or the twentieth century. It was as a title of the Virgin Mary that the word was fashioned, and the sense conveyed by the only possible equivalent in English is the sense that the term must have had to most of those who used it.

The first protest, with which we are acquainted, against its use came from the distinguished Antiochene teacher, Theodore, bishop of Mopsuestia. He died in the year in which Nestorius was elected bishop, and though that most obscurantist of General Councils—the fifth held at Constantinople in 553—declared him anathema, the esteem in which he was held in earlier times is shewn by the cry often heard in the churches: "We believe as Theodore believed; long live the faith of Theodore!" 'It is madness', he said, 'to say that God is born of the Virgin,...not God, but the temple in which God dwelt, is born of Mary.' And again, 'Mary', he said, 'bore Jesus,

[1] Quoted by Cyril *contra Julianum* 262 D from Julian's Logos A *contra Christianos* (C. J. Neumann's edition p. 214).

[2] The word "God" is logically a predicate, whereas in the English phrase it is practically a subject and so includes logically the person of the Father. That is to say, the Greek term fixes attention on the Godhead of Him who was born, rather than on the glory of the motherhood of her who bore Him. "God-bearing" is the literal rendering of the Greek compound. The word is formed on the analogy of the word *protótokos* (active) in common use of one who bears her first child.

not the Logos, for the Logos was and remained omnipresent, although from the beginning He dwelt in Jesus in a peculiar manner. Thus Mary is properly the Mother of Christ, not the Mother of God. Only figuratively can she be called the Mother of God also, because God was in Christ in a remarkable manner.' We only have the version of his words as they were cited at Ephesus. According to that version he went on to say 'Properly she bore a man, in whom the union with the Word was begun, but was still so little completed, that he was not yet (but only from the time of his baptism) called the Son of God'. Now Theodore is regarded as the Father of "Nestorianism"—the *fons et origo mali.* But the thought expressed in these words, if they are his, ungarbled[1], is not "Nestorian". If the words are more than a somewhat unguarded expression of the teleological view of man's developement on which we know he laid great stress—if, that is, they mean more than the assertion of a real moral growth of the manhood of Christ; then they express not the views of Nestorius, but those which are attributed rather to Paul of Samosata, and mean that a man received in increasing measure the gift of the Word as a result of his own moral growth, and his Godhead was an attainment, the goal of endeavour. Nestorius never conceived of the Incarnation thus, and—as we have seen—it was only popular clamour that attributed to him such a conception. He expresses himself quite differently.

His account of the beginning of the controversy, which has been already quoted, can be supplemented by extracts from his

[1] I do not believe either that Theodore was "Nestorian", or that these words were his. They are not consistent with his careful statements in the passage in his work *On the Incarnation* in which he discusses the nature of the union (Migne *P. G.* lxxxvi 1 pp. 1267—1396—summarized in my *Introduction to the early history of Christian Doctrine* pp. 257 ff.); and the same interests which Nestorius had at heart account for, and I think legitimatize, other phrases or illustrations he uses which might be held to convict him of "Nestorianism" before Nestorius.

Sermons and other writings. Some of these that are not directly concerned with the term *theotokos*, though they reveal his belief about the Person who was born, will be cited later on in other connexions[1]. Here it will suffice to collect a few passages that shew his feeling about the term itself.

In the first place it may be noted that Nestorius objects to our Lord being called either "God the Word" or "Man".

'By the expression "Christ" or "Only-begotten" or "Jesus" 'or "Son", or by others which are similar to these, we indicate 'the union: but by the expression "Man" the substance which 'was assumed, and by the expression "God the Word" the 'characteristics of the substance which became man.'[2]

'They say that Christ is God alone. And see, God is the 'Trinity. So Christ is the Trinity. If however Christ is God 'alone, and the Father is not Christ, then they separate them 'in nature. Much rather is the case thus: "Christ" is not the 'name of the substance but of the dispensation [i.e. of the 'incarnate person]. And Christ is God, but God is not 'Christ.'[3]

He repeatedly insists that the terms "Christ", "Son", "Lord" are the proper terms to use of the incarnate Word, just because they are significant of the two natures and sometimes indicate the Godhead, sometimes the manhood, and sometimes both; and that in this way and in such a sense they are used in Scripture[4]. Evangelists and apostles, he protests, never said that "God" was born or died. Again and again he makes his appeal to Scripture. It is always by Scripture that he would himself be judged and judge in turn the views of others. His exegesis is of a minutely verbal kind. I should not say that

[1] See especially pp. 82 ff.

[2] Syriac fragment from the *Theopaschites*, tr. Loofs *Nestoriana* p. 211, cf. p. 254.

[3] Syriac fragment *ib.* p. 218.

[4] There are many passages to this effect. See e.g. *ib.* pp. 269 ff.

he misses the general sense of the passage, but no turn of expression escapes his vigilant eye. In his sense of the value of words he is in agreement with the extreme allegorists of the opposite school of interpreters. He will not let one go without its due share of attention. It is often in his exegesis of Scripture that his suspicious phrases are found. Here is an instance—one of the passages quoted in the Syriac collections of his "blasphemies".

'When John saw our Lord, he said "Behold! the Lamb of 'God" (See! here is the Lamb of God). He did not say "See 'the Lamb of God!" For he who is visible is the Lamb, but 'he who is hidden is God. These natures are separate....' (Loofs tr. *Nestoriana* p. 334).

This passage might of course be understood to imply two persons joined together; but as elsewhere Nestorius uses the neuter 'that which is visible' and 'that which is hidden', and says 'the visible and the invisible are one Son', and as in the immediate context he is contrasting the Godhead which could not die with the manhood which suffered death, the phrases '*he* who is visible' and '*he* who is hidden' must not be pressed against him.

In another passage the same motive is apparent: he is declaring that it was not God the Word who was killed.

'If you reflect on him who according to nature in the 'course of months was born of the Virgin, it is a man who was 'born of the Virgin, according to the words of him who was 'born, who says: Why seek ye to kill me, a man, who have 'spoken the truth among you?...One to be sure is God, one 'too the mediator between God and men, the man Jesus Christ, 'who was born of the race of David' (*ib.* p. 247).

But in the same context he goes on to say:

'But He, who was of the race of Israel as regards the flesh, 'who according to appearance was a man, who according to 'Paul's expression was "born of the seed of David", was by 'the conjunction almighty God....According to the flesh

'Christ is a man; but according to His Godhead He is God 'over all' (*ib.* p. 248).

He quotes and carefully examines other passages from St Paul, to shew his usage of titles, and that he never has the expression "as regards the flesh", or any of the terms that relate to human affections and experiences, in conjunction with the term "God", always employing instead the titles "Christ" or "Son" or "Lord" (*ib.* pp. 254, 269). And the Creed of the Fathers of Nicaea, carefully following the usage of Scripture, avoids saying that it was God the Word who was begotten of Mary, and employs the title that signifies the two natures, that is, "Christ" (*ib.* p. 295).

What he feels must be guarded against at all costs is, on the one hand, the idea that the Godhead itself was born of a woman, wrapped in swaddling-clothes, suffered and died; and, on the other hand, the idea that the manhood of the incarnate Word was not real manhood like our own.

He puts the same point clearly also in the *Bazaar of Heraclides*[1] saying that the Fathers of Nicaea were careful

[1] See also Loofs *Nestoriana* p. 226 'Pilate did not kill the Godhead, but the vesture of the Godhead'. There are many indications that Nestorius dreaded the attribution to God Himself of "the things that are proper to the flesh". The title of one of his works, the *Theopaschites* ('he who represents God as suffering')—a dialogue in which 'Orthodox' answers the champion of this view, shews his anxiety to guard against what seemed to him to be a new form of the *patripassian* heresy. And when Dalmatius, to the amazement of every one broke his life-long rule. and leaving his monastery came into the Emperor's presence and frightened him into passive acceptance of the doings of the Council of Ephesus, and as he was borne back in triumph in a litter was surrounded by the mob of Constantinople crying "God the Word died"—in that cry Nestorius sees the real mind of his opponents. 'All of them as one rose up against God 'the Word; and those who would not consent to attribute passions to the 'nature of God the Word they persecuted without mercy' (*Bazaar of Heraclides* p. 283). The same feeling is shewn by the charge he brings that they altered the *Trisagion* ("Holy God, holy Almighty, holy Immortal, have mercy on us")—believed to have been miraculously revealed as the

to speak of 'one Lord Jesus Christ', before they went on to refer to the human experiences which belonged to Him not as God but as incarnate and made man.

'We were discussing whether it was right to understand and 'to say that the proper things of the flesh and of the reasonable 'soul, and the proper things of God the Word, both belong to 'God the Word by nature; or whether we should say of Christ 'that the two natures were united in Him in a union of one 'Person. And I was saying and maintaining that the union was 'of the one Person of Christ. And I was shewing that God the 'Word certainly became man, and that Christ is God the Word 'and at the same time man, inasmuch as He became man. And 'for this reason it was that the Fathers, when teaching us who 'Christ is, about whom there was a dissension, first laid down 'those things of which Christ consists. But thou (i.e. Cyril), 'because thou wishest that the Person of the union should be 'God the Word in both natures, dost neglect these things as 'superfluous (sc. the earlier passage in the Nicene Creed), and 'dost neglect to make a beginning from them. And from this '(the human nature) thou dost apply to that (the divine nature) 'all those things which are said, with reference to the natures, 'about Christ; and as though thine was a different Christ, thou 'didst refuse to speak of the Christ of the Fathers. And yet 'thou sayest, though unwillingly, that Christ is in both natures, 'and that God the Word is not in both natures' (*Bazaar of Heraclides* pp. 176, 177).

most acceptable form of supplication. They added the words "God the Redeemer of all", he says: thus in effect repudiating the 'immortal' (*ib.* p. 358). [He also gives the form "Praise and thanksgiving to the holy and immortal God the Redeemer of all". His evidence shews that Peter Fullo's addition of "who was crucified for us" was not so original as it has been thought to be.] And again, he tells a tale that, when the barbarians were threatening Constantinople and their progress could not be checked, a crucifix was sent out against them and set up in the city, and so they were put to flight:—and the moral is that it was the body, the manhood, and not the Godhead, that suffered on the Cross (*ib.* pp. 359, 360).

The following passages also are among the most characteristic.

'Holy Scripture nowhere says that "God" was born of the 'Virgin Mother of Christ, but "Jesus Christ" and "the Son" 'and "the Lord". This, that holy Scripture teaches, we all 'confess' (Loofs *Nestoriana* p. 278).

'The Scripture speaks of the "incarnation" of the Word, 'but never of His "birth"' (*ib.* p. 287).

'They make God the Word later than the blessed Mary 'and impose a temporal mother on the Godhead that created 'time. Nay, it would be more true to say they do not admit 'that she who bore Christ was the mother of Christ. For if he 'who was from her was not man's nature, but God the Word, 'as they say, then she who gave birth was not the mother of 'him who was born. For how could any one be mother of one 'whose nature was not the same as hers? But if they give her 'the name of mother, then what was born was manhood, not 'Godhead: for the mother's offspring must be of the same 'substance as herself' (*Sermo* viii, *ib.* p. 245).

'She who bore Christ was the mother of the child whom 'she bore, not of the Godhead which is universal' (*ib.* p. 246).

'The Virgin who bore Christ bore indeed the Son of God, 'but since the Son of God is twofold in nature, she bore indeed 'the Son of God, but she bore the manhood which is Son 'because of the Son who is joined thereto....Therefore God 'the Word is called "Christ", because the conjunction which 'He has with Christ is perpetual. And it is not possible for 'God the Word to do anything without the manhood: for it 'has been brought into a state of complete conjunction with him, 'but it has not been deified as the wiseacres among our younger 'dogmatists would have it' (*Sermo* x, *ib.* pp. 274, 275).

'The form[1] that received God[2] let us honour as God

[1] Cf. Phil. ii 6, 7. Nestorius frequently in the *Bazaar of Heraclides* uses μορφή in this way, as Leo and others used the Latin equivalent *forma*.

[2] This is the term Nestorius proposed, differing in sound from the other

'together with God the Word, but the Virgin who received 'God let us not honour as God together with God. I say who 'received God, not who gave birth to God...for there is only 'one...God the Father to whom this compound word (*Theotokos*) 'applies[1]' (*ib.* p. 276).

As instructive as any of his sayings in this connexion, and absolutely decisive as to his meaning, is a passage in which he exposes one of Cyril's perversions (whether they were deliberate or unconscious) of his words:—a passage which also shews that Christians were still exposed to the heathen taunt, which Athanasius had to meet[2].

'Once, in speaking against the heathen who say that we 'declare that the Being (*ousia, substantia*) of God was created 'anew from a Virgin, I said: My good Sirs, Mary did not give 'birth to Godhead, but she gave birth to a man, the inseparable 'instrument of the Divinity. But he (sc. Cyril) by a change of 'the word "Divinity" made me say: My good Sirs, Mary did 'not give birth to God. But there is surely a great difference 'between saying "God" and saying "Godhead". For the 'latter word means the divine and incorporeal substance, not 'flesh at all (for flesh is composite and created); whereas '"God" is a term that can properly be used also of the temple

by only the difference between *t* and *d*—*Theodochos* instead of *Theotokos*—as he explains in this passage.

[1] Only God, that is, could 'give birth' to God. The argument seems to be entirely in keeping with the comment of Augustine on the saying "Woman, what have I to do with thee?", which he interprets as designed to make us understand that "in so far as He was God, He had no mother". "He who was uniquely born, had a Father without a mother, had a mother without a Father; was God without a mother, was man without a Father." "His mother therefore was mother of the flesh, mother of the manhood, mother of the infirmity which He took upon Him for our sakes." *Tract. in Joann.* viii 8, 9.

[2] See p. 92. In another passage (Loofs *op. cit.* p. 339) it is the fact that the term *theotokos* favours the Arian theory of the Person of Christ that Nestorius has in view: the theory, that is, which excluded the human soul and so emptied the manhood of ethical value.

'of Divinity which by its union with the Divine substance of 'God receives dignity, but is not changed into the Divine 'substance[1].'

If only the transcendence of God is safeguarded, and His *ousia* preserved intact, so that in gaining the Incarnation we do not lose God Himself; and if only the manhood of Christ is recognized as derived from a human Mother, so that as man He is "flesh of her flesh, and bone of her bone"—the *ousia* of His manhood one and the same as hers—He Himself as touching His manhood "consubstantial with us";—then Nestorius is content, and he does not grudge us or her the title "Mother of God"[2], for it was, he says, the Lord of the universe who came forth through the Virgin[3]. He who was born was God.

That is to say, he accepts the title in the only sense in which it is tolerable. He prefers the term "Mother of Christ" as being entirely free from ambiguity. If we say "Mother of God" we ought in strictness to add "Mother of man" as well[4]. But Mary is *Theotokos* 'because the Word was united to the 'temple...which is in nature consubstantial with the holy 'Virgin....In virtue of this union the holy Virgin is *Theotokos*'[5].

For members of the Church of England it is of interest to remember that the great divines of the Reformation period,

[1] From the *Tragedy* or the *History* of Nestorius (Loofs *op. cit.* p. 205, cf. pp. 252, 337). At the end of this passage on the calumnies of Cyril he says that he dealt with his sayings as any one might do with St Paul's, if he took his words "Behold, I Paul say unto you that, if you let yourselves be circumcised, Christ will profit you nothing", and left out the qualifying clause "if you let yourselves be circumcised"—so representing the apostle as saying nakedly "Christ will profit you nothing".

[2] 'I have already said many a time that, if any one.. delights in the term "Mother of God", I have no quarrel with the term. Only let him not make the Virgin a goddess (θεάν)' (*ib.* p. 353). Cf. *ib.* pp. 273, 277.

[3] *Sermo* x Loofs p. 272, *fragment ib.* p. 277.

[4] To this effect the whole of *Sermo* xviii Loofs pp. 297 ff. and *Sermo* xxvii *ib.* pp. 337 ff.

[5] Loofs pp. 303, 309.

of whose loyalty to the orthodox doctrine of the Incarnation there can be no question, shared the apprehensions of Nestorius as to the term "Mother of God". They withdrew it from public use in the Services of the Church[1]. The Reformers were undoubtedly anxious to bring back to the full consciousness of the Church the manhood of the Son of God, and to set Him before men as the ethical Ideal and the means of access to the Father. They thought that the Mother of the Lord and the Saints had come between men and God, and they wished to restore the supremacy of the "One and Only Mediator". But there seems to have been little discussion of the term itself. It was quietly dropped, both from the Article on the Incarnation, which in all other respects closely follows the Definition of Chalcedon, and from the place which it had come to occupy in the public prayers of the Church[2]. The invocation "Saint Mary, mother of God, our Saviour Jesus Christ, pray for us", which had been retained in Cranmer's

[1] The Lutherans and all the reformed Churches also discarded the term. The fact that the doctrine of the Immaculate Conception of the Blessed Virgin can be defended as a logical inference from the title *Theotokos* will seem to some to shew how easily the term can be understood to imply a view of the person of the Mother of our Lord that isolates her in nature, as well as in honour, from all other women, and therefore seems to impair the reality of the human nature of her Son and to carry with it the denial of the doctrine that He was "consubstantial with us".

[2] I refer only to public use of the title. It is still, of course, standard for English churchmen—not only by reason of the fact that there was no break in the continuity of the Church at the Reformation, and on the principle that every doctrine and practice of the ancient Church that has not been expressly repudiated has still such authority as it ever had, but also by explicit recognition of the doctrinal decisions of the first four General Councils—recognition made in various ways and notably in a statute of the first year of Elizabeth which was successfully pleaded in recent times before Archbishop Tait as a statute of the realm which recognized this very title *Theotokos* as in agreement with the doctrine of the Church of England, and assured any English clergyman who used it of the support and protection of the State.

Litany, was omitted altogether in the First Prayer Book of Edward VI, and of course not reinstated in subsequent revisions. "Mother of our Saviour" or "of our Saviour Jesus Christ", or "Mother of the Lord" or "of our Lord Jesus Christ" are the titles which, since the Reformation, members of the Church of England have commonly been content to use, while at the same time firmly holding the belief that He who was born of her was God as well as man. These titles are enough to secure to her all the affectionate devotion and reverence that such Motherhood inspires. The faith in the Godhead of her Son is guarded in other ways[1].

[1] In this connexion, without endorsing all the doctrinal statements and historical inferences which it contains, or all that is said of the Anglican position in general, I would refer to the interesting and suggestive survey of the doctrine of the Incarnation and the aims of the Reformers in Dr A. V. G. Allen's recently published *Freedom in the Church* (New York, the Macmillan Co., 1907).

CHAPTER V

A FAMOUS SAYING OF NESTORIUS

καὶ δὴ πολλῶν θεολογούντων τὸν Ἰησοῦν, Ἐγώ, ἔφη Νεστόριος, τὸν γενόμενον διμηναῖον καὶ τριμηναῖον οὐκ ἂν θεὸν ὀνομάσαιμι· καὶ διὰ τοῦτο καθαρός εἰμι ἀπὸ τοῦ αἵματος ὑμῶν, καὶ ἀπὸ τοῦ νῦν πρὸς ὑμᾶς οὐκ ἐλεύσομαι.

Socr. *H. E.* vii 34.

IN close connexion with the term "Mother of God" we must consider one of the sayings for which Nestorius has never been forgiven—the one which Socrates reports as spoken by him in conversation with another bishop at Ephesus. It was on one of the days when they were still waiting for the arrival of John of Antioch and the bishops of his province; and Theodotus, bishop of Ancyra in Galatia, took the opportunity to go and talk to Nestorius and convince him, if he could, of the error of his ways. All that is generally known of the discussion is the last remark of Nestorius which ended it: '*I* could not give the name of God to one who was two or three months old: and so I am innocent of your blood, and henceforth I will not come to you'[1]. There is irritation and petulance

[1] Socrates *H.E.* vii 34 gives the remark in these terms. Theodotus gave evidence at the Council and added that many others heard the same words which he repeatedly uttered (Mansi *Concilia* iv p. 1181)—*πολλάκις ἔφη, διμηναῖον ἢ τριμηναῖον μὴ δεῖν λέγεσθαι θεόν.* Acacius, bishop of Melitene, also interviewed Nestorius with the same object, and stated before the Council that he found that he had fallen into two absurdities at once. He put a question the answer to which required either a denial that the Godhead of the Only-begotten had become man or an assertion that the

in the exclamation. It sounds like the hasty utterance of a man who is getting the worst of the argument, and in his annoyance loses his temper: though it might also have come from one who had been plied by a stupid opponent with arguments that had no point and shewed no intelligent grasp of the issues, whose patience was exhausted and who simply wished to break off a futile discussion. We can all put ourselves into Nestorius's position. In any case piety was shocked. To Christian sentiment, nourished and sustained from the earliest days by the belief that found expression in St Luke's account of the Nativity and St Matthew's narrative of the visit of the Wise Men from the East to offer to the new-born Babe the symbolic gifts of gold and frankincense and myrrh, such a saying seemed intolerable. The man who could say that was not a Christian, and to play the part of a Coriolanus and say '*I* banish *you*' at the end of it was adding insult to injury. Unhappy man, what could they do with him? We can well imagine how Theodotus and Acacius hurried away and told their tale.

But Nestorius's own account of the interview (if the Syriac translator has rightly understood the Greek before him) puts a different complexion on it, and shews that even the unfortunate exclamation itself was misrepresented. His account must be given in full. He has alluded just before to the slander that he himself misrepresented the facts as to the proceedings at Ephesus in order to create a prejudice against his opponents, and so he is obliged to say what really happened and the kind of trial he had. He has said that Cyril was accuser and judge, indeed the whole court, in one; and his account of this episode opens with one of those apostrophes of Cyril which are characteristic of the style of the book, which throughout passes backwards

Godhead of the Father and of the Son and of the Holy Spirit had become incarnate with God the Word. Acacius added that not Nestorius himself, but a bishop who was with him, had interposed and said that the Son who suffered death was one, and God the Word another. Unable to endure this blasphemy Acacius made his adieus and retired.

and forwards without warning from simple narrative to impassioned personal taunt or appeal.

Nestorius's own version of the facts

'But (to resume):

'Thou didst first of all sit among the judges. And as 'there were no accusers—since they were judges—they put 'forward to accuse me Theodotus bishop of Ancyra in Galatia 'and Acacius bishop of Melitene, who was the questioner.

'First, Theodotus said that he had had a conversation with 'me; but the conversation itself he did not report; nor did 'this man (Cyril) ask what the conversation was about, so that 'they might weigh as judges what was said on either side, '(p. 155) and accept the one and reject the other as one 'who had fallen into open impiety: but the charge alone they 'heard.

'Theodotus bishop of Ancyra says[1]: I am pained indeed for 'my friend's sake: but religion is of more importance than any 'friendship, and therefore I am constrained, with much sorrow, 'to answer truthfully the questions I am asked. Yet I think 'that my testimony is needless, since his views are known from 'his letters to your piety; for the things that he there said 'that one might not say of God—i.e. of the Only-begotten—'reproaching Him with human things: the same he has said 'here in conversation, to wit, that it is not right to say of God 'that He sucked milk, or that He was born from a virgin. In 'the same way he has often repeated here the words: "I do 'not say that God is two or three months old"[2].

[1] Nestorius is evidently quoting from the Acts of the Council, as in the case of the speech of Acacius (see below).

[2] The Syriac is ܒܪ ܬܪܝܢ ܝܪ̈ܚܝܢ ܐܘ ܒܪ ܬܠܬܐ ܠܐܠܗܐ ܠܐ ܐܡܪ ܐܢܐ; that is, literally: 'a son of two months or a son of three God I do not say (to be)'. The saying is given in the same form lower down (MS p. 156 *ad init.*). The fact that the prefix *l* is attached to

'They did not as judges examine this evidence, nor yet did 'he speak as to scrutinizers and judges. But he stood as the 'witness of an accusing judge: "For the things, forsooth, that 'he there rejected, that they should not be said of God—i.e. of 'the Only-begotten—reproaching Him with human things: the 'same he has said here in conversation, to wit, that it is not 'right to say that God sucked milk or was born of a virgin. 'And he has likewise said: 'I do not say that [God] is two 'or three months old'"[1].

'And he (Cyril) received this statement without examination, 'as a hostile judge, without asking the witness any questions, 'such as: "Of what was he speaking to you when he spoke 'thus?" or: "What did you say to this? Stay, tell us in 'what it was that he was opposing you, that we may know 'in what sense he rejected these expressions, and not admit 'without cause an accusation against him in his absence, and 'that we may not give sentence (ἀπόφασις) against him without 'examination and without enquiry and before we know those 'things that ought to be accurately ascertained, namely, of 'what he was guilty. For thus neither will the accused be 'able to deny, nor will he have any ground for accusing me 'of partiality. Say, then, O Theodotus [what it was about 'which] you were talking with him. If, as you say, (p. 156)

'God', and not to 'a son,' shews that (rightly or wrongly) the Syriac translator took 'God' to be the subject described, and 'a son', etc., to be the description predicated of 'God'. This is in accordance with the regular Syriac usage: cf. below (MS p. 156 *ad init.*): 'Was it as though he did not say that Christ is God?' where 'Christ' has the prefix *l*, and not 'God'. Moreover, the Syriac expression 'a son of', followed by a number of days, months, years, does not of itself introduce the idea of childhood, but merely indicates the age. In Lk iii 23 the Syriac versions say, 'now Jesus was about a son of thirty years'. In giving a person's age Syriac employs the same idiom as Hebrew: cf. 2 Kings viii 17, xii 7, xiv 2, etc.

[1] In the MS these words are given as if repeated by Theodotus with a fresh heading "*Theodotus*", but it is clear that they are a scornful repetition of Theodotus's words by Nestorius.

'you were accurately informed as to his meaning: when you 'questioned him and he answered you that he did not say that 'God is two or three months old, was it as though he did not 'say that Christ is God—for He was two or three months 'old—was it in this sense that he said it to you? You, then, 'did you say that God was born of a woman and was two 'or three months old in the sense that His own *ousia* was 'changed into the *ousia* of a man, and that in this sense He 'was begotten and became two or three months old? or that 'He was changed in His form and appearance (σχῆμα) into 'the form and appearance (σχῆμα) of a man as regards His own '*ousia*, and that Christ is thought of as in the single *ousia* of 'God, and not in two *ousias*? And, if in both *ousias*, how? 'Are both from the one *ousia* of God the Word, or was He of 'distinct and unlike *ousias* and begotten in both of them? Or 'was it that one of these *ousias*[1] was begotten and became 'two or three months old in the sense that before it was 'begotten and became two or three months old it did not exist? 'Or was it that the *ousia* was eternal and did not receive a 'beginning so as to be begotten and become two or three 'months old, since He (the Word) did not possess that which 'they have who must of necessity be begotten? Or was He 'begotten in the birth of the flesh by 'appropriation'[2] of '*ousia*?"

'If he were thus questioned he would of necessity confess 'that which he said before the Eastern Bishops when he was 'questioned by them in writing, viz. that the Only-begotten 'Son of God created and was created—He the same, but not 'in the same sense: that the Son of God suffered and did not

[1] It is fairly clear that the Divine *ousia*—God the Word—is here meant.

[2] The Syr. word corresponds in formation to οἰκειότης, the verb οἰκειοῦσθαι being constantly used in the controversy of the Word "making His own" the things of man. The Syriac word itself means "association" or "intimacy."

'suffer—He the same, but not in the same sense. For some 'of these things belong by nature to the Godhead, but some to 'underwent by the manhood, and all the divine by the Godhead. 'the nature of the manhood. All the human experiences He 'For the birth from a woman is human, but the birth from the 'Father [is Divine]: [this is] without beginning, but that with a 'beginning: this is eternal, but that in time. About these 'things, when he was throttled by the truth, he was unable to 'hide his opinions, but was forced by the persistency of the 'examination to put them into writing; and, as a dog which is 'forcibly tied up hides his evil manners, but as soon as he 'escapes from the chain runs off (p. 157) to the kennel of his 'companions, and barks at those who held him, and dares not 'come out into the open and fight: but when he is inside 'he sets back his ears and puts his tail between his legs: 'so this man did not dare to promise that he would speak 'and vindicate himself, while confuting me, nor any such thing 'as those are accustomed to do who have confidence in their 'own case—I mean, that he should uphold his cause and 'vindicate himself from the Divine Scriptures and the traditions 'and teachings of the holy Fathers; but: "Hear", he says, '"these things". Not openly, as I speak, does he dare to treat 'of the things he speaks of, and to establish from the Divine 'Scriptures and from the writings of the Fathers what they 'have said and how they have said it. Nor has he deemed 'it necessary to be consistent and commit to writing the things 'that he has said; but, "it is right", says he, "to say what 'I consider to be the truth".

'This was the first [anxiety] that took hold of them, (viz.) 'that they (the assembled bishops) should not know the whole 'conversation nor the whole discussion that we (Theodotus 'and I) had. Since, if they related those things that were 'said against them they would have nothing to say, for this 'reason they did not write them, not even in the *Hypomne-* '*mata*,—save only this, that it is not right to say that God 'sucked milk or that He was born of a virgin in the common 'way. They enquired (only) so far as they thought fit. But 'about these matters we shall speak presently.

'After this man (Theodotus) came Acacius, and recounted 'to them a conversation that he had with me—and (the things 'he said) did [not][1] appear impossible to them! He answers 'his interrogation by detailing an accusation against me: not 'by a refutation, nor by shewing the truth of those views that 'he held: but he received the questions asked him with an 'accusation against me. And, that you may know that this 'is no fabrication of mine, hear it from their own *Hypomne-'mata.*

The speech of Acacius Bishop of Melitene

'"As soon as I came to the city of Ephesus I had a dispu-'tation with this man, who has already been spoken of; and 'when I learned that he held incorrect opinions, I used all 'possible diligence to put him right and to remove him from 'this mind of his. And he appeared to me to make a 'verbal promise to change his views. (p. 158) After I had 'dropped the matter about ten or twelve days, a discussion 'having again arisen upon some point between us, I began to 'speak up for the correct faith, and I saw that he was against 'it. And I found that he had fallen into two errors. For first 'he perversely asked a question which laid upon those who 'were to answer it the necessity of either denying altogether 'that the Godhead of the Only-begotten became man, or 'confessing—what is impious—that the Godhead of the 'Father and the Holy Spirit also became incarnate with the 'Word."

'[*Nestorius*] Some questioned, others answered that the 'things were absurd and impious. Some confessed and

[1] Unless we supply a negative I cannot make sense of this passage. It would be very easy for the scribe to omit one, for two may have stood near together in the original—thus: 'and it did *not* seem *not* possible to them!'

'accepted the expression[1] which I had proposed to confute 'them: [others rejected it][2] and were condemned by those 'who accepted it.

'Surely one would suppose that there is some mistake 'when they write all these things in the *Hypomnemata* and 'make everybody bear witness against them! For suppose 'that my dilemma (lit. "question") were true[3]: then thou '(Acacius) oughtest not to have accepted it, but rather to have 'exposed the fallacy of the alternative, lest, by accepting its 'validity, thou shouldst launch into the ford that leads to 'impiety and absurdity. But thou didst accept religiously an 'absurd alternative; then, from this, thou camest to impiety, 'so as to confess either that God the Word, the Son of God, 'did not become man, or that the Father and the Spirit 'also became man. That, therefore, which thou didst agree 'to when questioned thou oughtest to have let alone, even if 'thou didst not—treating it as someone else's—correct it. 'Grant that thou didst not, either willingly or unwillingly, fall 'into this absurdity: why didst thou not pronounce the question 'absurd on the strength of which you wished to condemn me? 'But thou didst not pronounce it so, nor did the judges require 'thee to do this. And if it was so absurd that it was left with-'out refutation, being unrefuted by your whole synod; and if 'you all left it unrefuted, and there was not among you anyone 'that was able to refute it, say, if you have even the appearance 'of being judges, that they examined an absurd alternative, and 'write the question down as fictitious (p. 159) for those who 'have sense and will have to examine your judgement. But 'through your incapacity you remained in the dark, for you 'could not see even what was obvious: rather I should say 'that God was assisting you in your examination, that you

[1] This probably means "the alternative".

[2] Some such words seem to have dropped out.

[3] i.e. that I really put it.

'should write down these things, in order that it should be 'made manifest to every man that all this was done through 'enmity and without cause.'

From this account, then, if the Syriac translator has not misunderstood the Greek, it appears that the actual words of Nestorius have not come down to us correctly. He did not say that he could not bring himself to call a babe God, but he said that he could not bring himself to call God a babe. The word "God" was the subject rather than the predicate. He refused to predicate infancy of God, rather than Godhead of an infant. The verbal difference is clear. There is really the same logical difference between the two expressions as there is between saying "Christ is God" and saying "God is Christ"[1]. And there was a real difference of intention in the mind of Nestorius. He did not intend by the phrase to deny the Godhead of Him who was born. He intended to deny that God Himself could in His own being (in His essence, substance, *ousia*—whatever it is that makes God God) submit to a human birth and become a babe. In Himself, in His own being, He remained God and ought not to be called by any other name. Nestorius had no wish to imply by the words he used any disparagement of the Holy Infant: he did wish to safeguard the Majesty on High from merely human experiences and attributes. The recovery of the setting of the words which were impeached reveals to us the thoughts and the fears that prompted them. This setting is so thoroughly consonant with the general trend of his argument elsewhere, and fits so naturally into its place in his narrative of those miserable days at Ephesus, that I am quite unable to harbour the suspicion that Nestorius—writing at a later time after further reflexion—has himself given a cunning twist to the phrase he actually used. I have quoted already

[1] See *supra* p. 60.

(p. 46) the words in which he shews that he knew that his opponents thought he was a man who propounded conundrums—subtle dialectical puzzles—in matters which were beyond reason and ought to be accepted in humble unreasoning faith. Nestorius did not take their view, and the passage just cited gives us an instance of the method which they disliked. There is the real man—"at his worst" perhaps: subtle, ingenious, unsparing and—must we add?—unanswerable on his own ground: chafing as one whose arguments are ignored, whose sense of intellectual fair-play is outraged:—himself intellectually straight as a die. It is to reason as supreme interpreter of the words of evangelists, apostles, and fathers that he appeals throughout his book, and it is an intellectual sense of outrage at the treatment meted out to his ideas, rather than to him, that makes him write: page after page throbs with this *saeva indignatio*. It is impossible to suppose that the man who reveals himself so plainly would have condescended to such a perversion of the facts. Not one respite has he had, nor any human consolation all those years; but he has not been 'cowed by hardships, nor run away from 'the contest'[1]. However outspoken he was, however onesided his phrases may seem, they are at least always straightforward. Perhaps his very straightforwardness was his bane. He is too impatient of any approach to intellectual jugglery or the vagueness of statement that shuffles this and that together till you cannot tell what either is, or which is which[2]. There is of course a sense of moral wrong underlying all the personal references to Cyril and his "judges", and the specifically moral note is firmly struck at the end of his book, when he speaks of the impending siege of Rome by the barbarians and says that it is sure to come because Leo 'although he held the faith 'aright, agreed to all the things that had been done against him 'without examination'. Such moral obliquity does indeed cry

[1] *Bazaar of Heraclides* p. 370. [2] Cf. *ib.* p. 14.

out to Heaven for vengeance, and the cry has gone up to Him who works out His moral purpose in the world by human means. But the intellectual is the dominant theme throughout his *apologia*.

Although, however, we could not entertain the idea that Nestorius himself on second thoughts slightly altered the words he actually used, there remains the possibility that his Syriac translator misunderstood the Greek. But we can turn to the Greek itself, and by this instance judge of the competence of the translator. For Nestorius evidently had a copy of the official report of the proceedings at Ephesus before him as he wrote, and quoted from it: and Theodotus's version of his saying, taken down at the time no doubt by the shorthand writers who compiled the report, can be read in the Acts of the Council. And when we turn to this official record, we find that it supports the Syriac version of the words. What Theodotus told the Council was that Nestorius said that the words two or three months old ought not to be used of God ("God ought not to be called two or three months old"). It can only be familiarity with the traditional version of the saying that has led anyone to understand the words as they stand in the Acts of the Council in any other sense[1]. It will

[1] I have cited the words *supra* p. 69 n. 1; but they must be read in their context. Theodotus has referred to expressions used by Nestorius in a letter to Cyril, and then goes on as follows: ἃ γὰρ ἐκεῖ (that is, in his letter to Cyril) ἀπηγόρευσε περὶ τοῦ θεοῦ λόγου λέγεσθαι, τουτέστι τοῦ μονογενοῦς, ὀνειδίζων αὐτῷ τὰ ἀνθρώπινα, ταῦτα καὶ ἐνταῦθα (that is, here in Ephesus) διαλεγόμενος ἔφη· μὴ δεῖν περὶ θεοῦ λέγειν γαλακτοτροφίαν μηδὲ γέννησιν τὴν ἐκ παρθένου· οὕτω καὶ ἐνταῦθα πολλάκις ἔφη διμηναῖον ἢ τριμηναῖον μὴ δεῖν λέγεσθαι θεόν (Mansi *Concilia* iv p. 1181). There cannot really be any doubt that θεόν is here the subject of the predication, as in the preceding saying that God must not be said to have sucked milk or undergone birth. The words διμηναῖον and τριμηναῖον are ordinary adjectives (used e.g. of corn that ripens in two or in three months) and without the article (which Socrates inserts), or a noun like βρέφος, could only be predicates. Θεόν on the other hand could be used with or without the article, indifferently, as subject. No Greek scholar, I am sure, would read

be noticed that Nestorius makes no complaint here, as he does elsewhere, that his actual words were distorted; and his other sayings at the same time, which he says were repeated by Theodotus, and all the questions which he suggests should have been put by his "judges" in order to discover his real meaning, have reference to the attribution of human experiences to God, and imply that God was the subject, rather than the predicate[1], in the particular saying which has ever since been quoted as proof of his unorthodoxy. The Syriac translator has thus restored to us the words Nestorius really used, and opened our eyes to the fact that the Greek Acts of the Council shew that Theodotus reported them fairly. The perversion of them, with which we are familiar, is due to misunderstanding or malice on the part of his opponents. The word was passed round that Nestorius said he could not call a baby God, and Socrates, no doubt, in his account of the saying, is reporting what people believed he had said.

Perhaps even at Ephesus they understood his actual words to mean what the traditional version of them has seemed to mean. In any case the main contention of Nestorius is that they did not stop to ask what he really meant. They isolated the words from their context, and made no enquiries as to the subject under discussion. His words as reported to the Council

the passage in any other way. Our Syriac translator evidently knew the language. (It ought to be noted also that the words would apply to a child before birth as well as after birth.)

[1] There is, so far as I can see, only one passage in Nestorius's imaginary cross-examination of Theodotus in the *Bazaar of Heraclides*, quoted above p. 73, which may seem at first sight to favour the other version of the saying: the passage 'When you questioned him and he answered you that he did not call God two or three months old, was it as though he did not call Christ God?' As "God" is predicate in the principal clause, the logical balance of the clauses would be more exact if "God" were predicate also in the saying itself. But the lack of exact correspondence in such a case could only turn the scale if the other evidence was much less cogent than it is.

were to his "judges" simply another of his "blasphemies", quite in keeping with his arguments against the term *Theotokos*; and all that has been said as to the real meaning of his objection to this term applies to the saying that he could not bring himself to call God a three months' child. As a matter of fact he does not shrink from saying 'the Babe is 'God in His own right''[1].

Even if he had said that "a child two or three months old ought not to be called God," it would be clear that he did not intend in any way to question the Godhead of our Lord. What he was anxious to maintain was the Catholic doctrine of the relation between the natures in the Person of the Incarnate Son of God, the doctrine commonly known by the term *communicatio idiomatum.* In view of other, ancient and more modern, teaching which conceives of the Godhead and the manhood of our Lord as so completely identified that what is true of the one is true also of the other, it is perhaps well to remind ourselves that the Catholic doctrine (admirably expressed by Tertullian and Athanasius and others, and lucidly summed up by Leo in his *Letter to Flavian*), while maintaining that all experiences, whether of Godhead or of manhood, are rightly predicated of the one Person Jesus Christ, whether He be styled Son of God or Son of man,—yet forbids us to ascribe human experiences to the Godhead or Divine experiences to the manhood: the special properties of either nature belong to it and to it alone, though the Person who is both God and man is the subject of them all. All Catholic teachers have always repudiated the idea that God in His own being was capable of human affections (πάθη).

[1] See the passage cited *infra* p. 85.

CHAPTER VI

"TWO PERSONS" NOT THE TEACHING OF NESTORIUS

NESTORIUS did not hold the belief commonly attributed to him that in Jesus Christ two persons, the person of a God and the person of a man, were mechanically joined together, one being Son by nature and the other Son by association, so that really there were two Sons and two Christs. He is as explicit as possible on this point. He knows that such ideas have been held, but he regards them as absurd and entirely incompatible with Scripture. Writing of the followers of Paul of Samosata, who come near to regarding Christ as only a man and distinct from God the Word, he describes them as saying that there is a division into two Sons, so that some things may suitably be attributed to the one and some to the other, in such a way as not to be absolutely incompatible with each other nor yet in mere semblance (σχῆμα). 'They speak of 'a double son and a double Christ, both as to persons and as 'to substances; and even as the saints received the indwelling 'and image of God, so they say [it is with Christ]' (*Bazaar of Heraclides* p. 40).

This view Nestorius proceeds to refute, by special reference to the prologue to St John's gospel, insisting that there is but one Word and Son of God and that He assumed flesh and made it His own without any change of *ousia*. And to those that receive Him and believe in His name He gives authority to become the sons of God (which they could not do before). 'He is "full of grace and truth", not as one that has been 'changed, but as being that which He was, even the beloved 'Son. Such as they received Him and believed Him to be 'such also they saw Him revealed in the flesh—Him, and not 'another God, nor another Word, nor another Life, nor another 'Light, nor another Only-begotten, but Him, the same, that 'was revealed in the flesh. "And of His fulness we have all 'received" as those who had nothing. And we received "*of* 'His fulness", and not "His fulness", for this is a fulness that 'lacks nothing, as God. Therefore He, "The Only-begotten 'who is in the bosom of His Father", has declared to us God '"whom no man hath ever seen"; not another, but He "that 'is in the bosom of His Father"; and He came and became 'flesh and dwelt in us. And He is in the bosom of His Father, 'and is with us; since He is what the Father is, and has '"declared" unto us—though plainly He did not shew the 'infinity and incomprehensibility of His *ousia* as He is in the 'bosom of His Father. As one who knew our nature, in the 'same nature of ours He "declared" unto us Him "whom no 'man hath ever seen".

'How then can we understand this to be one Son, and 'Christ to be another Son, and one that is man only? For He '(Christ) keeps the equality and the honour of sonship in 'the image of Him whom you deny to have been sent and to 'have dwelt among us; who, while He is in the form[1] of God, 'dwells as a divine indwelling. And so it is that the Evangelist 'clearly begins from God the Word and leads us up to God the 'Word. And he knows nothing of any Word or any Only-'begotten Son of God apart from God the Word—but Him 'only, the same with His flesh' (*Bazaar of Heraclides* pp. 43, 44).

Nestorius thus forcibly refutes the idea that there are two

[1] i.e. μορφή.

persons, though he persistently maintains that there are two substances, in the one Christ, who is the one Son and Word of God. He also argues at length (*ib.* pp. 300 ff.) that the charge might equally fairly be brought against all who believe that Christ was in two natures.

Many other passages equally explicit might be cited. Here are a few of them.

'God the Word and the man in whom He came to be (ἐν 'ᾧ γέγονεν) are not numerically two. For the Person of both 'was one in dignity and honour, worshipped by all creation, in 'no way and at no time divided by difference of purpose and 'will' (*Fragment* Loofs *op. cit.* p. 224).

'The unity of the natures is not divided; it is the *ousiae* of 'the natures that are united that are divided. This division 'consists not in the abolition of the union, but in the idea of 'the flesh and the Godhead. Hear this plainly stated. Christ 'is indivisible in His being Christ, but He is twofold in His being 'God and His being man. He is single in His Sonship; He is 'twofold in Him who has assumed and him who is assumed. 'In the person of the Son He is a single (person), but, as with 'two eyes, He is different in the natures of manhood and God-'head. For we know not two Christs or two Sons or Only-'begottens or Lords, not one and another Son, not a first and 'a new Only-begotten, not a first and a second Christ, but one 'and the same, who was seen in the created and the uncreated 'nature' (*Sermo* xii Loofs *op. cit.* p. 280).

'He who is one is Himself twofold...in nature' (*ib. ib.* p. 281).

'Our Lord the Christ is God and man' (*ib. ib.* p. 284).

'The natures must remain in their own properties, and so 'one glory must be understood and one Son confessed in virtue 'of the wonderful union which transcends all reason...we do not 'make two persons one person, but by the one name "Christ" 'we denote the two natures together' (*Letter* xi *ib.* p. 196).

Again and again he insists that He who was born of Mary,

our Lord, the Christ, was one Son, the Son of God, but twofold in His Godhead and in His manhood.

'I say this that you may learn how close a conjunction of 'the Godhead and the Lord's visible flesh existed even in the 'babe. For the same person (ὁ αὐτός) was both babe and 'Lord of the babe. [At this the congregation seem to have 'applauded, for Nestorius goes on] You approve the expression, 'but do not applaud it without seeing what it means. For 'I said: The same person was babe and inhabitant of the 'babe' (*Sermo* xv Loofs *op. cit.* p. 292).

If the babe and the Lord of the babe are one and the same person, the suspected phrase 'inhabitant of the babe' must be simply intended as a safeguard against identification of the Word with the flesh. So Mary is *Theotokos*—

'because the Word was united to the temple...which is in 'nature consubstantial with the holy Virgin....It is in virtue of 'this union that the holy Virgin is called *Theotokos*' (*Sermo* xviii Loofs *op. cit.* pp. 303, 309).

'The Word of God was not separated from the nature of 'the temple' (*ib. ib.* p. 308).

'I call Christ perfect God and perfect man, not natures 'which are commingled, but which are united' (*Fragment ib.* p. 332).

'The visible and the invisible are one Son' (*ib.* p. 299).

On the text "Jesus Christ yesterday and today, the same for ever" (as he reads it) he says:

'He himself [sc. the one and the same person] is new as 'man, but as God before the ages' (*ib.* p. 270).

'Great is the mystery of the gift: for this babe that can be 'seen, this fresh appearance, this that needs swaddling clothes 'for the body, this that in the visible substance is newly born, 'is in respect of that which is hidden eternal, the Son who 'made the universe....Yes, and the babe is God in his own right '(θεὸς αὐτεξούσιος). So far is the Word of God from being 'subject to God, O Arius!...We acknowledge therefore the 'manhood and the Godhead of the babe....We maintain the 'singleness of the Sonship in the nature of manhood and of 'Godhead' (*Sermo* xx Loofs *op. cit.* pp. 327, 328).

And another passage must be added here in which he expressly repudiates the inferences which were drawn by Cyril and Acacius from "cuttings" from his writings:

'Neither hast thou (sc. Cyril) properly understood those 'cuttings (from my writings) which thou hast written down, (e.g.) 'that I say "we learn from the Divine Scriptures that God 'passed through the holy Virgin, the mother of Christ", as 'thou hast written that I say. How then dost thou cry out 'that I speak of God the Word who was born of the Father as 'one Christ apart, and of another Christ who was born of holy 'Mary? Of which dost thou consider that I said "God passed 'through her"? It is obvious that I said it of God the Word, 'who was born of the Father. How then do I speak of another 'Christ apart from God the Word who was born of the Father? 'I said that He (the Word) also passed through blessed Mary 'inasmuch as He did not receive a beginning by birth from her, 'as is the case with the body which was born of her. For 'this reason I said that God the Word "passed", and not '"was born", because He did not receive a beginning from 'her. But the two natures being united are one Christ. And 'He who "was born of the Father as to the Divinity", and '"from the holy Virgin as to the humanity"[1] is, and is styled, 'one; for of the two natures there was a union.

'And it is right for us to say against thee also, Acacius, 'that the two natures unconfused I confess to be one Christ. 'In one nature, i.e. the Godhead, He was born of God the 'Father, and in the other, i.e. the manhood, of the holy Virgin. 'How then canst thou style her Mother of God, when thou

[1] These phrases are borrowed from the *Confession* of John of Antioch and the Eastern bishops which was accepted as orthodox by St Cyril. Throughout this passage "born" is to be understood in the sense of "begotten"—a distinction which cannot be expressed in Syriac.

'hast confessed that He (God) was not born of her? If thou 'hast said that the Godhead was born of the holy Virgin, she 'will be called Mother of God from the (Divine) nature being 'born of her; but if thou also confess that the Godhead was 'not born (of her), how canst thou—confessing that It was not 'born—confess her to be Mother of God? And how canst 'thou accuse me of speaking of two Christs, when thou thyself 'dost confess that Christ is of two natures, one nature of the 'Godhead, which is called Christ, and one of the manhood, 'which thou also stylest Christ? Dost thou confess two Christs '(p. 300) because the natures are different[1]—one, the manhood 'which was born of the holy Virgin, and another, God the 'Word who was born of God the Father? Or dost thou say— 'as he (Cyril) says—"One in the union", and nothing more? 'Why then hast thou gone to such extremes, and brought 'others with thee, against a man who has also said this?' (*Bazaar of Heraclides* pp. 299, 300).

In view of the many expressions and arguments of which these are only typical, it is impossible to doubt that Nestorius was clear in his own mind that his doctrine of the Incarnation safeguarded absolutely the unity of the subject. He did not think of two distinct persons joined together, but of a single Person who combined in Himself the two distinct things (*substances*) Godhead and manhood with their characteristics (*natures*) complete and intact though united in Him. (Indeed at a later time his worst enemies themselves bore witness on this point. For when the charge of "Nestorianism" was flung by the Eutychians at their opponents, and Flavian and his friends defended themselves by saying that Nestorius believed there were "two Sons", whereas they taught "two natures" only, and not two persons; the Eutychians declared that he never taught

[1] The text has 'in one variety of natures'. The above translation is based upon a trifling and obvious correction of the MS.

"two Sons" and was condemned simply because he taught "two natures" in the Incarnate Word—though, they added, two natures could only mean two persons[1].)

But the question arises, Was it a real union? Did he not constantly use phrases and turns of expression that rob his strong assertions of the unity of the Person of all their value, and shew that he was either radically unsound in his doctrine or hopelessly muddle-headed? He used the terms "the God" and "the man" and spoke of them as "joined together" and as "worshipped together", and of the relation between them as one of "good-pleasure", and he had some very suspicious phrases about "the person of the Godhead" and the "person of the manhood". What kind of "union" was it that he had in mind?

These phrases must be examined. We need not dwell long over the first. The language which Nestorius spoke and wrote is responsible for some of the ambiguities of his expressions. Ordinary usage in Greek allowed the concrete to stand for the abstract, "the God" for "Godhead", "the man" for "manhood". The use of the concrete may perhaps convey a shade more of personalized significance than the use of the abstract would; but I can find nothing in Nestorius on this count that could not be found in other theologians of untarnished reputation. The conception that one nature is the sphere of one set of experiences passes insensibly into the conception that it is in some sense the particular subject—or almost the agent—of them. Leo, in his letter to Flavian, uses expressions that are at least as strong in this respect as any that Nestorius used, in the way of personalizing the two natures[2].

[1] See *Bazaar of Heraclides* pp. 366, 367.

[2] e.g. "Agit utraque forma cum alterius communione quod proprium est."

Men whose own language was Greek might, of course, be expected to understand such ambiguous expressions. But it is clear that the opponents of Nestorius were determined to put the worse sense on his words and never to give him "the benefit of the doubt". We have seen already that one of the passages which Cyril garbled has reference to this very point. Nestorius had actually used the word "Godhead" and Cyril replaced it by the word "God". Frequently in decisive connexions Nestorius speaks of "the Godhead" and "the manhood" rather than of "the God" and "the man". Athanasius[1] employs the phrase "the man" in his discussion of the same problem which Nestorius handles, both by itself and in direct antithesis to "God the Word". For example, in explaining the terms "humbled" and "highly-exalted" of Phil. ii 5—11, he says that they have reference to the manhood and the assumption of flesh, in consequence of which the exaltation was necessary: "for *the man* was in need of this on account of the lowliness of the flesh and of death"[2]. And elsewhere he uses the same or similar phrases. He has no scruple in speaking of the "union of God the Word with *the man from Mary*"[3], and with regard to the title "Christ" he represents the Word as saying "I the Word am the unction, and that which is anointed by me is *the man*. He would not be called Christ apart from me, but because *he is with me* and *I am in him*"[4]. Athanasius also has the same term, "the man", qualified by the addition "belonging

[1] I turn to Athanasius for parallels the more readily because he is commonly regarded as a chief representative of the orthodox school of thought farthest removed from "Nestorianism"—the school of thought, that is, which sees in the Incarnation a real re-creation of the human race or deification of mankind, the whole race *solidaire* in sin and alienation from God receiving in Christ actual, real, redemption.

[2] *Or. c. Ar.* i 41, cf. i 45, ii 45.

[3] *ib.* iv 35.

[4] *οὐ χωρὶς οὖν ἐμοῦ χριστὸς κληθείη ἄν, ἀλλὰ σὺν ἐμοὶ ὢν καὶ ἐμοῦ ἐν αὐτῷ* *ib.* iv 36. This passage furnishes other notable parallels to the language of Nestorius. See also *infra* p. 92.

to the Lord" or "of the Saviour"; and by a barbarous word-for-word rendering of the former phrase as "the lordly man" (instead of "the Lord's manhood") scholars have been able to convince themselves that the tract in which it occurs could not have been written by Athanasius[1], though St Augustine's Latin equivalent of the phrase (*Dominicus homo*) has not, I believe, been called in question[2]. The Pauline expressions "the second man, from heaven", "the heavenly (man)" (1 Cor. xv 47, 48)—if we agree that they cannot be allowed to support the conception of a preexistent manhood of a celestial character, attributed to Apollinarians—must be given a sense which covers the Athanasian use of "the man". And if we do not find a doctrine of "two persons" in Athanasius[3], we need not attribute such a doctrine to Nestorius merely on the evidence of his use of these phrases.

But what of the term "conjunction" (συνάφεια), which Nestorius used to express the relation between the God-head and the manhood? In the first place, the translation "conjunction" scarcely does justice to the term: it expresses a closer connexion than the word "conjunction" necessarily implies and might be rendered "contact" or "cohesion". In

[1] The phrase ὁ κυριακὸς ἄνθρωπος, as well as τὸν ἡμέτερον ἄνθρωπον, occurs twice in the *Expositio Fidei* (part of which is printed in Hahn *Bibliotek der Symbole*[3] p. 137). The phrase ὁ ἄνθρωπος τοῦ σωτῆρος in the *Sermo major de fide* 24, 30 has contributed to throw doubt on the Athanasian authorship of that treatise too. The fact seems to be that, a *prava interpretatio* having been put on Nestorius's expressions, a *praejudicium* has been established which has blinded the eyes of literary and historical critics.

[2] It is rendered "Divine Man" in the translation in *Nicene and Post-Nicene Fathers* series i, vol. vi p. 40 b.

[3] It is true that in *Or. c. Ar.* iv, where the phrase is so frequent, it is constantly the phrase of the heretics whom Athanasius is combating, and that in the opening sections of the book it bears the sense of mankind in general (we all receive exaltation in the exaltation of the incarnate Word), but plenty of instances remain to shew that Athanasius had no objection to the phrase itself in connexion with the doctrine of the Incarnation.

the second place, we are accustomed to contrast the Nestorian use of this term with the Catholic use of the term "union" (ἕνωσις). But Nestorius himself had no such antithesis in mind. He uses the terms "united" and "union", much more frequently (in the *Bazaar* at all events) than those which we render (following the Latin translation) "conjoined" and "conjunction". His choice of the latter terms was in antithesis to words like "mixture", "commingling", "blending together", "confusion"[1], and to all ideas which would merge the two substances and natures of Godhead and manhood in one: it was determined by his resolution to maintain the doctrine that the Redeemer of men was at once really God and really man. In his own words he had 'one end only in view:—that 'no one should call the Word of God a creature, or the man-'hood which was assumed incomplete'[2]. He denies altogether that he means any placing side by side of dignity or honour.

The same resolute purpose accounts for his use of the expressions "worship-together" or "glorify-together"—'I separate 'the natures, but I conjoin my reverence', that is 'the worship 'I pay them is joint and one'. In the minds of his opponents the compound verb which he used in this connexion, the "with" or "together", was clear proof that he thought of two persons who were only brought into an external relation to each other. This, they said, is evidently what he means. But it was not what Nestorius meant; and he makes much play with them for pretending to think it was. For he does not believe their charge is honest[3] and he has no difficulty in shewing that they

[1] κρᾶσις, μίξις, σύγχυσις and the like.

[2] *Sermo* xviii *Nestoriana* p. 313. See also further on this point *infra* ch. x.

[3] He is so clear that the charge cannot with any show of reason be laid to his door on the ground of his language about "uniting the worship", that he tells his accusers that anyone knowing the facts would say to them 'O men, you have been drinking mandrake!' (*Bazaar of Heraclides* p. 209). More-

themselves used similar expressions[1]. Cyril, indeed, in the very sentence in which he repudiated the Nestorian phrase, spoke of the Word's flesh or body "with which He is seated with the Father". It is true he used a different preposition[2]: but Nestorius insists that, if his own phrase implies duality of persons, Cyril's cannot escape the same—as Nestorius thinks—absurd inference. "Consession" implies at least as much difference of person as "co-worship", and Cyril's statement that "the difference of the natures was not destroyed by the union" meant, Nestorius says, as much division of natures as he wanted, 'as when the fire was united with the bush and the bush with 'the fire, and they were not confused'.

Athanasius may again be cited[3]. The Arians brought the charge against the Nicenes that they worshipped the human nature of Christ, a creature. Some sought to repell the charge by saying "we do not worship the Lord *with the flesh*, but we separate the body and worship *Him alone*". But Athanasius does not approve of this denial that "the flesh" (the manhood) has any share in the worship paid to the incarnate Word. "Let them know that in worshipping the Lord in the flesh, we are not worshipping a creature, but the Creator clothed with the created body....We neither divide the body, as such, from the Word, and worship it by itself; nor, when we wish to worship the Word, do we set Him far apart from the flesh; but knowing... that 'the Word was made flesh' we recognize Him as God also after he has come in the flesh." And he speaks of "the Creator of the universe dwelling in a created temple" and of "the Lord who is in the flesh as in a temple".

over the actual word he used was not "conjoin", as Marius Mercator has it, but "unite"! This is shewn by the Greek extract from the Sermon itself (Loofs p. 262) and by the Syriac in a passage of the *Bazaar of Heraclides* in which the saying is referred to. See *infra* p. 169.

1 *Bazaar of Heraclides* pp. 184—186. See the letter of Cyril read at Ephesus, and *infra* p. 175.

2 μετά instead of σύν.

3 *Ep.* lx (*ad Adelphium*) 3, 5.

Here again the language of Athanasius is very close to that of Nestorius. It is true that the words "We worship the Lord *with* the flesh" are not the actual words of Athanasius, but he would not meet them with a negative; he would not see in them any denial of the unity of the Person; and no expression which carries full recognition of the place which the manhood occupies in relation to the worship paid to the one Person seems to come readily to his lips.

Yet again, Nestorius, following in this as in other respects the teaching of Theodore, spoke of the method of the Incarnation as an "indwelling" of the Godhead in Christ by the divine complacence or good-pleasure (εὐδοκία). He is therefore supposed to have meant that a man became the habitation of God the Word, and that the relation between them, however intimate and close, was yet only moral and conditioned by the exceptionally holy character of the man[1]. In earlier times the term had been used in connexion with the doctrine of the Incarnation:—the Son was said to be begotten by the Father's good-pleasure, or will, or purpose or design. The Arians used the latter phrases to justify or cover their teaching as to the subordinate rank and being of the Son, and the phrase of Nestorius might hide or reveal the conception that the relation between the Divine and the human in Christ was similar in character to the relation of God to ordinary men. But Nestorius uses it in another way. He does not represent a man as the recipient or object of the divine complacence;

[1] In the *Bazaar of Heraclides* p. 217 he complains that he is wronged when he is said to teach 'that the *ousias* are distinct in the sense of being locally apart, and that only by cohesion and love do they participate one in the other, by agreement and not by nature'. He declares that he says the opposite—'for I unite the *ousias*, and from the union of *ousias* I speak of one person, asserting one equality in everything that pertains to the person; and in this the *ousias* are separate, not by severance and putting apart, but in one and the same person'. See also the passage cited *infra* p. 168.

nor indeed, if it may be said without implying any tritheistic conception, is it God the Father who is the subject of the "good-pleasure", but God the Word. The thought is not that God bestows Himself or His favour on a man, or that He is present by any kind of mere sympathetic benevolence in a man: but the term is used to safeguard the voluntariness of the condescension by which He who was God became man. God the Word of His own good pleasure becomes incarnate, and so the idea that His being or nature was changed into the being or nature of man is excluded. The Incarnation is the outcome and free and unconstrained expression of God's love for man: remaining what He is in being and in nature, he takes to Himself in the Person of the Word the being and nature of man[1].

There remain to be noticed his expressions about "the person of the Godhead" and "the person of the manhood". Phrases of this kind occur several times in the *Bazaar of Heraclides*, and must be considered in their context. The following passages seem to be fairly representative of the thought of Nestorius. The first of them furnishes, I think, the clue to his real meaning; it occurs in his statement of his own opinion in relation to Cyril's, and must be considered in its context. As the passage is quoted in full later on[2] I give here only the chief sentences:

'It is by person that He (the Son) is distinguished (from 'the Father). But it is not so in regard to the union of the 'Godhead and the manhood. He is not by the union in 'all those things that the person by its nature is, so that in the 'one person He should become another *ousia*. For He took 'man's person, not the *ousia* or the nature, so that it should be 'either *homoousios* with the Father or else another Son altogether 'and not the same Son. For the manhood is the person of

[1] See *infra* pp. 152 ff. [2] See *infra* p. 163.

'the Godhead, and the Godhead is the person of the manhood: 'but they (the manhood and the Godhead) are distinct in nature 'and distinct in the union' (*Bazaar of Heraclides* p. 79).

Again:

The union was 'into the Person of the dispensation which 'was for us (i.e. the Incarnation). For the natures bear the 'person one of the other: wherefore the one nature employs 'the person of the other nature as its own—not by both 'natures employing either the one or the other person in-'differently, nor yet by a compounding into one complete 'nature, like soul and body into the nature of man; but one 'nature employs as its own the very same person as the other' (*ib.* p. 303).

Or again:

'Therefore Christ took upon him the person of the nature 'which was in debt, and by means of it as Adam's son paid the 'debt' (*Sermo* ix Loofs p. 255).

And again:

'Just as a king, when he assumes the garb of soldierhood 'and is a soldier, does not become a double king, nor yet is he 'king without the soldier, for the reason that he is in the 'soldier; nor is he worshipped without that in which he is 'made known and in which they[1] have known him and been 'delivered: so God also adapts His own person to the con-'descension of poverty and shame, even unto the death of the 'cross, for our redemption; and in this person He was exalted 'unto honour and glory and worship. In that wherein He 'suffered reproach, in the same He was glorified. But the 'standard of redemption and victory is one of honour, and not 'of disgrace; and He received no addition of *ousia*[2], since the

[1] sc. the other soldiers.

[2] With this may be compared Athanasius's discussion of the passage Phil. ii 5—11 in *Or. c. Ar.* i 40—45 (see esp. 45). Indeed the argumentation of Nestorius constantly recalls that of Athanasius.

'*ousias* remain unchanged[1]. If that which is different in *ousia* 'should receive identity of *ousia*, that would be an addition of '*ousia*[2]. Nor is there any addition to the person when He takes 'man to His own person and not to another[3]—not with 'a distinction (sc. of persons) but with a union into His own 'person of that also in which He became man. And in this 'way his (? man's) person also is in Him and not in another: 'for He put on the form[4] of a servant and thereby emptied 'Himself; and He clothed the servant with His person and 'lifted him up to His "name which is above all names". In 'the person of the Godhead therefore He is worshipped, and 'not in that of some other. One therefore is the person and 'the name of the Son' (*Bazaar of Heraclides* p. 22).

Now in considering these statements we must of course bear in mind the main argument of Nestorius to the effect that any view of the Incarnation which does not recognize the continued existence of the *ousia* of the human nature is not a real incarnation. If the human nature was seized upon by the Divine nature as by fire and so transmuted into the Divine nature itself that no addition to the Trinity resulted (for the upholders of this view were obliged to repudiate the charge that they meant an addition to the *ousia* of Godhead) then there was no incarnation, but a sheer abolition of the incarnation: 'for that which results in the abolition of the human 'nature and not in its preservation—this does not effect an 'incarnation' (*Bazaar of Heraclides* p. 24). A theory which changes the *ousia* of man into the nature of God is no better than one that changes God into the *ousia* of man. In the

[1] i.e. His own *ousia*—His own Godhead—is not altered in any way. For any depreciation of the Divine *ousia* would be defeat, not victory.

[2] i.e. if the human *ousia* were identified with the Divine, there would be an addition made to the Divine.

[3] Or, 'and not (sc. does not take) another (person)'. This is to guard against the introduction of a fourth person into the Trinity.

[4] μορφή.

latter case the Divine nature lapses, in the former human nature is sublimated. Unthinkable and impossible results follow on either theory. Nestorius puts the theories to elaborate dialectical test to shew this, and that the union must be found somewhere else than in either the *ousia* or the nature of either God or man, and he finds it in the "person".

But what does he mean by the "person"? His use of the word in these passages is undoubtedly puzzling. The phrase "He took man's person", if isolated from the context, would convey the idea that the Incarnation was a conjunction of two persons. We can sympathize with those who thought that this was his meaning, in spite of all his asseverations that it was not. But the rest of the passage shews unmistakeably that whatever he meant, he did not mean this. Nor can we put on the word "person" the sense of *rôle* or function or part played:—this sense is equally excluded by the context. "The manhood is the person of the Godhead, and the Godhead is the person of the manhood":—these words are quite inconsistent with the idea of the coexistence of two separate and distinct persons side by side; they come near to eliminating "personality", as we understand it, altogether, or at all events they suggest the merging of one personality in the other, each in each. This in fact seems to be the meaning of Nestorius. He is in search of the real centre of union, and he finds it here. He uses the term "person" to express that in which both the Godhead and the manhood of our Lord were one, even while remaining distinct from one another, each retaining its own characteristics. The Godhead becomes the subject of human experiences by taking to Itself that which is the centre of human experiences; and the manhood becomes in turn the subject of Divine experiences by being taken up into the centre of Divine experiences. But the Subject is nevertheless one.

There is a passage in which, in arguing with Cyril, he refers to the words he has used 'as a brother to a brother' saying: 'We do not sever the union and the person which results from 'the union; nor do we begin from God the Word as the 'person of the union, but from Him (sc. Christ) from whom 'the Fathers (sc. of Nicaea) began, who were wiser than thou 'and better acquainted with the Divine Scriptures'[1]. By themselves these words might suggest the conception of a personality which only began at the Incarnation: *the* person was one who was both God and man, and that person did not exist before. It was a new Person (Christ) who was formed, not a new divine-human nature. The strong interest of Nestorius in the historical person, who lived the life of man, would favour this interpretation. But his reference really is to the words of the Nicene Creed and the order in which its clauses are placed, "beginning" with the "one Lord Jesus Christ"; and elsewhere he is strong on the point that it was the pre-existent Word of God, consubstantial with the Father, who became man.

The later orthodox phraseology (by eliminating altogether the human centre, and declaring the human nature of the Lord to be impersonal in itself, but personal in Him only[2]) secures perhaps a clearer expression of the unity of the subject: one Divine Person, the subject of Divine experiences, becomes also at the same time the subject of human experiences—He exists in both substances and in both natures. But the words of Nestorius seem to be an attempt, by no means unworthy of respect, to express the same conception, and the ambiguity of the expression must be settled by other passages to the effect that it is in the one Person that the two substances and natures—the Godhead and the manhood—have their union[3]. Will it not at all events be time to condemn them as

[1] *Bazaar of Heraclides* p. 179. Cf. pp. 196—199.

[2] More accurately perhaps, the 'human nature of the Lord' is never impersonal, because it has His personality from the first.

[3] See further his statements *infra* ch. xi pp. 177 ff.

incompatible with a sound belief in the Incarnation when we have found a solution of all the problems metaphysical and psychological by which the orthodox doctrine is beset? For if the human mind is so constituted that we must discuss these questions, and our Lord Himself is truly represented as moving His disciples to the enquiry by the words "But whom say ye that I am?", we shall not forget that after a bitter controversy it was decided that, though our Lord's human nature had no personality of its own (but only the personality of the Word), He had nevertheless a human will, and that the chief opponents of this doctrine—the "orthodox" doctrine—were the descendants of the opponents of Nestorius, and that they denied also the reality of the human nature of our Lord. We have got a form of sound words; but is not "will" one of the chief notes of "personality"? If "man" without individuality is conceivable, can we say the same of "will"? Or can we feel security in the old theological explanation that the will belongs not to the "person" but to the "nature"? Theology, like all other sciences, may fairly claim a language of its own, but when that language is incapable of being translated into the language of intelligent and well-informed men and women, it ceases to fulfil any useful function beyond that of registering an *impasse*.

After subjecting different theories of different thinkers, and the chief passages of Scripture which bear upon the question, to an elaborate examination, Nestorius concludes his discussion of the relation between the Godhead and the manhood with the words—'Wherefore by no other line of reasoning than this '[which I have followed] can the words of the Divine Scripture 'be made consistent with Christ; but, as we have tested and 'found, they all favour, not a union of mixture, but a natural 'and hypostatic[1] Person' (*Bazaar of Heraclides* p. 70).

The adjectival phrase a 'natural and hypostatic' Person

[1] The words are the adjectival forms of *k'yânâ* and *q'nômâ*.

can only mean a single Person who is characterized by the natures and hypostases of God and man—who is the subject of the two "natures" and the two "substances", to whom both alike belong. The phrase expresses what has always been the orthodox doctrine.

CHAPTER VII

THE HIGHPRIESTHOOD OF CHRIST

It was, as we have seen, as a monk of exemplary life who was also a great preacher, that Nestorius was called from Antioch to occupy a more prominent pulpit and a position of wider influence in the counsels of the Church; and it was by incessant sermons ("he never stops talking" was Cyril's complaint) that he expressed and propagated his views, alike at Antioch and afterwards. Of these sermons only the few that the Latin translation of Marius Mercator has preserved have come down to us as the sermons of Nestorius. It is, however, well known that works of heretics were often, after their condemnation, issued under the name of some older writer of unblemished reputation in order to save them from destruction. The works of Nestorius were so diligently sought out and burned that very few remained, and his followers were obliged to content themselves in later times with the writings of other representatives of the School which bred Nestorius. (It is worth noting, by the way, that they served their purpose equally well.) But some of the "infinite number of homilies" to which Gennadius refers may well have escaped and survived in collections under other names. To one such sermon, which is certainly genuine, a fresh survey of the teaching of Nestorius must give particular attention. It illustrates so well his method of exegesis of Scripture and one of the more obscure points in his teaching. But notice must first be taken of a number of other sermons, culled from various collections, which have recently been attributed to Nestorius[1].

Mgr Batiffol's Nestorian Sermons

In the year 1900 Mgr Batiffol published an interesting article in the *Revue biblique*[2] in which he proposed, on grounds of internal evidence only, to father on Nestorius no fewer than fifty-two sermons, which have passed under the names severally of Athanasius (three), Hippolytus (one), Amphilochius (three), Basil of Seleucia (thirty-eight), and Chrysostom (seven). Some of these sermons present close parallels of thought or expression or mannerism with what we know of the ideas and the words and the pulpit-style of Nestorius. But there is one important demurrer which I should make at the outset, and it amounts to a *praescriptio* such as Tertullian urged. To whom do the early Fathers and ecclesiastical writers belong? In a very true sense, of course, to the Churchman, the systematic theologian of a later time, for whom all the hard work of the making of Christian doctrine and the manufacture of formulas has been done, who only has to take up his heritage and use it as wisely as he can: but in a sense more true, I think, they belong to the student who can forget altogether the end of the great movement of thought which was in progress in those earlier days and abstain from interpreting expressions, however significant they may appear to be, by the standard of the settled terminology of a time when men no longer thought for themselves. And in this particular study it appears to me that the standpoint from which Mgr Batiffol approaches his enquiry is the standpoint of the Catholic theologian securely entrenched

[1] I mention them here partly because the suggestions of so distinguished a scholar as Mgr Batiffol cannot be ignored, and partly because—in spite of his authority—they seem to me to afford an illustration of a kind of research which is common today and is, I believe, to be deprecated rather than welcomed.

[2] *Revue biblique* vol. ix pp. 329 ff. "Sermons de Nestorius".

inside the tradition of ages. From this position of assured results, as from some lofty tower, he looks back on the centuries when these results were in the making, and anything which has a "Nestorian" ring about it he "restores" to Nestorius.

But, in spite of the earlier doctrinal investigations and definitions—in spite of the work of Tertullian with his sagacious and illuminating descriptions of the relations between the two natures in the Person of our Lord, which seem to have established a sound tradition in the West; and although almost his very words and the same illustrations were repeated by Dionysius of Rome in the third century and by Athanasius in the fourth; yet the tradition was not established so firmly in the East, and the period with which we are concerned was really a *creative* period: a period to which the later history of the Church can offer many parallels, when problems which seemed to have been already solved (perhaps they were not quite the same) again presented themselves and again demanded solution. And the scholars and divines of those days seem, as it were, to have started afresh—as they so often must—and to have made the same or very similar mistakes, and slowly, not without misunderstandings of each other's meaning and intentions, to have reached some common ground on which the *communis sensus fidelium* could find safe footing.

To this demurrer the Roman Catholic theologian in Mgr Batiffol might object; the scientific historian in him, whom we know well and admire, would I am sure, in other connexions at all events, admit its validity.

I would only add: first, so far as these sermons recall the *style* of Nestorius, we must remember that pulpit oratory was, in those days, an art that was carefully studied; and nothing so bears upon it the mark of the "school" as rhetoric (this is almost Mgr Batiffol's own phrase):—the use of the same rhetorical style is, as regards those times at least, far too precarious a test of authorship to give any sure results: and secondly, so far as these sermons offer parallels to the *thought* of Nestorius, they may fairly be claimed as evidence rather of the wide diffusion of similar ideas and as tending to shew that they were current Antiochene conceptions at the time and not peculiarly characteristic of Nestorius.

It does not appear to me, therefore, that even a *prima facie* case is made out for these sermons. We are probably too eager today to give new names and dates to our ancient Christian writings. It may well happen that a later generation of students will restore to their traditional authors, or at least to the repose of anonymity, some of the works which are being so diligently re-christened today, and then perhaps, less distracted by investigations of this kind, have leisure for more truly sympathetic appreciation of their contents. In this particular case, just as Dr Lietzmann in his recent collection of the genuine writings of Apollinarius (against whom Nestorius so often inveighs) disowns all those which Dr Dräseke a few years ago had laboriously rescued from other authors, so in like manner Dr Loofs says nothing about these sermons of Nestorius and allows them no place in his volume of *Nestoriana*.

If the sermons were genuine they would add nothing, I think, of importance to our knowledge of the teaching of Nestorius; but the moral which I have ventured to draw from Mgr Batiffol's study is so vital, in my judgement, to a true appreciation of the whole controversy, that the result of these reflexions on his method of investigation is by no means only negative, although for the present purpose we must leave the sermons in question out of account. In any case the attribution of them to Nestorius is a hypothesis that lacks all support of external evidence.

The Sermon on the Highpriesthood of Christ

The case is altogether different with regard to a single sermon which seems to have escaped the notice of Mgr Batiffol. It was first published in 1839 by Wilhelm T. M. Becher, chaplain to the military prison at Dresden, from a MS of the ninth century which had belonged to a Russian monastery and had come by purchase from a professor of Greek at Moscow to the library of Dresden. The MS contained eleven homilies ascribed to Chrysostom. Six of these had been already published. Becher edited the remaining five, adding a Latin translation of his own. Our homily is the fifth of his edition. All five were afterwards reprinted in the supplement to Migne's edition of the works of Chrysostom[1]. As genuine works of Chrysostom they were accepted, till two voices were raised almost simultaneously in protest against this attribution to Chrysostom of one of them. A Roman Catholic scholar of Salzburg pointed out[2] the fact that the sermon with which we are concerned could not be Chrysostom's, but must be the work of Nestorius on the highpriesthood of Christ already known from the extracts contained in anti-Nestorian writings; and Dr Loofs independently made the same identification in the Prolegomena to his volume of *Nestoriana*. The strongest external evidence attests this sermon as the work of Nestorius.

The apologist of Nestorius would not be slow, I imagine, to seize the point that a sermon which contains many of the characteristic thoughts of the great heretic, in regard to matters which were in dispute between him and his critics, could be

[1] Migne *P. G.* lxiv 453—492.

[2] S. Haidacher *Zeitschrift für katholische Theologie* 1905 i pp. 192—195. The only good word, however, that he finds to say for Nestorius is one of surprised recognition of the soundness of his teaching about the Eucharist, as if it were in spite of himself and his real convictions. See the passage at the end of the sermon *infra* p. 112.

identified as the work of the "golden-mouthed" preacher of his own home Antioch, who had sat in his own episcopal chair—a Saint of the Catholic Church: that this identification could have been made by a scholar of the nineteenth century and the sermon allowed a place among the genuine works of St Chrysostom in Migne's edition of the Fathers. Such an apologist would recall, perhaps, the complaint of Leontius of Byzantium that the Nestorians used to get people to read their books, without telling them the author's name, in confidence that, if only they would read them without knowing that they were Nestorian, they would see for themselves how much maligned Nestorians were. "Read first," they say, "and then learn who these men were, and how important, whose names, poor soul, you had never so much as heard of till now."[1]

One who enters on the investigation in no apologetic spirit, simply desiring to find out the facts and form his conclusions as the evidence suggests, may be content merely to note the fact. Here is a newly discovered homily, by general consent of scholars of our own time quietly attributed to Chrysostom: and yet nearly a quarter of it, the most striking doctrinal part, could have been reconstructed from materials already in our possession—in a quarry, indeed, to which we should not have looked for the wherewithal to fashion one more memorial of Chrysostom, namely the various collections of the heretical sayings of Nestorius that are to be found in the Acts of the Council that condemned him and the works of the Fathers who exposed his errors[2].

It was the exegesis of Nestorius that first roused opposition. He lived, as we have noted, before the age of theological

[1] Migne *P. G.* lxxxvi 1362 B.

[2] If it be urged that Chrysostom really was in some respects "Nestorian", I can only plead for a less anachronistic reading of history and refer to what has been said in the preceding pages.

journals, when the pulpit was the recognized medium of theological investigation. One of his sermons offers us as fair a test of his point of view and general teaching as we can get. I give a summary of this, the only complete sermon of his which we possess in his own tongue. It is an exposition of passages in the Epistle to the Hebrews.

Nestorius begins by expressing his sense of the inadequacy of human language, and his constant fear lest in his instructions he should be guilty of unwittingly belittling instead of magnifying God. Even the highest hymnody that man can direct to God is superlatively low in comparison with His surpassing glory. Yet the offering of divine praise (θεολογία) which man can make is acceptable to the Lord of the universe, for He knows man's limitations.

But heretics complain that Nestorius attributes greater honour to the Lord of the universe than He himself claims: and they examine the Scriptures as though they were the papers of some opponent in a law-suit, and make of them a tribunal for God, and treat Paul as if he were a lawyer drawing up a contract for the servitude of God the Word, as though it were this object that he had in view when he declared to everyone about Him "Consider the apostle and highpriest of your confession Jesus Christ, who was faithful to him that made him". See, they say—indisputable witness that the Son was created! The words are clear enough, but the heretics are blind. They think that God the Word is apostle and the Godhead the highpriest. It is a surprising piece of madness on their part. No one else would imagine that the terms "apostle" and "highpriest" are used of the Godhead. If the Godhead is highpriest, who is it who is served by the ministry of the highpriesthood? if he who offers is God, there is no one for the offering to be made to. Offering is from an inferior to a superior, and there is no superior to whom God could offer.

Moreover Paul's words shew clearly that a highpriest must be taken from among men, to minister on behalf of men, one who is able to bear gently with the ignorant and erring, since he himself is beset by infirmity and therefore must, as for the people, so also for himself, offer sacrifices for sin. This could not be said of Godhead which is in no need of the perfecting which comes of grace. God the Word needs no sacrifices for His own progress as the highpriests do—so it cannot be God the Word who is called highpriest. All the expressions which are used in the context are inapplicable to the Godhead. It is not the nature of angels that he takes upon him[1], but it is the nature of the seed of Abraham he takes upon him: and therefore he must needs be made like his brethren in all things, in order that he might be a merciful and faithful highpriest in the things concerning God: for in that he himself suffered by being tempted he is able to succour those that are being tempted. "Consider therefore..." and so on. This is the connexion of the phrases, and the heretics do wrong to tear them apart. But since they prefer *disjecta membra* and find it pleasant to read disjointedly, I will take, he says, the phrases one by one and shew you what violence they do to them.

Nestorius then proceeds to shew by this method that it is not to the Godhead that the writer ascribes the highpriesthood. He who is to be the highpriest takes upon him the seed of Abraham: the seed of Abraham is not Godhead. He must be made like his brethren in all things. Did God the Word possess brethren like the Godhead? It is he who has suffered who is a merciful highpriest, but what is capable of suffering is the temple (sc. the human nature) not the life-giving God of that which suffered. It is *he* who is "yesterday and to

[1] So Nestorius with all ancient commentators understands ἐπιλαμβάνεται, though Becher translates *opitulatur*. The paraphrase οὐκ ἀγγέλων περιθέμενος φύσιν occurs further on in the sermon, though elsewhere he says you must take hold of that which you want to lift up.

day"—in Paul's phrase—who is the *seed* of Abraham; not he who says "before Abraham was, I am". Like his brethren in all things is he who took upon him brotherhood of human soul and flesh: not he who says "he that hath seen me hath seen the Father". Apostle is he who is of one substance with us, so as even to be anointed to preach release to captives and recovery of sight to blind, he who says plainly "The spirit of the Lord came upon me, wherefore He anointed me, to preach good tidings to the poor He sent me". It is not Godhead but manhood that is anointed. This is he who has been made a faithful highpriest to God—he came to be, he was not eternally so before: he advanced by degrees to the dignity of highpriest.

There are still clearer words used on this point, shewing that he was gradually perfected. Nestorius appeals to the passage "In the days of his flesh having offered prayers and supplications to him that was able to save him from death with vehement crying and tears, and having been heard because of his piety, though he was Son, he *learnt obedience* from the things which he suffered, and being made perfect became to all that obey him the cause of eternal salvation" (Heb. v 7—9), receiving from God the appellation highpriest after the order of Melchisedek.

To say that he was made perfect means that he advanced little by little: and Paul's words are in agreement with Luke's "and Jesus advanced in stature and in wisdom and in favour". He is highpriest who in relation to his office as leader is compared to Moses, who is called the seed of Abraham, who is like his brethren in all things, who became in time highpriest, who was made perfect through sufferings, who in that he suffered himself by being tempted is able to succour those that are tempted, who is called highpriest after the order of Melchisedek.

Why then, says Nestorius, with the personal address which he is fond of employing, apostrophizing in this sermon even

Paul himself[1] as to his meaning—Why then, O heretic, do you misinterpret Paul and confuse the divine and the earthly and represent God the Word who cannot suffer as a highpriest who suffers?

To do this is, he insists, to do violence alike to the actual words of St Paul and to the general purpose and aim which he has in view throughout. The Epistle, he says, is addressed to Hebrews who while they professed love for Christ and faith in Him wished to retain unchanged the Law and the ancient priesthood and its ordinances. Paul, in reply to their specious reasoning and appeals, shews that the system of the Law was shaken by the coming of Christ, and that the purpose of the Incarnation was to fit him to be highpriest and so to replace the levitical priesthood by a higher order. The promise had been given to the patriarch Abraham that one who was of his seed should bring blessing to all nations. The seed had grown, but no one had been worthy. The claims of Moses, Aaron, and Elijah are briefly discussed and dismissed. Moses was too timid, Aaron too complaisant to sinners, Elijah for all his zeal lacked sympathy.

There was wanted, as the means through which the promise should be realized, a highpriest—by birth a descendant of Abraham, by dignity higher than prophets, sinless and gentle, capable of suffering, inasmuch as he was kith and kin with Abraham, but knowing how to cry to God in moments of peril "Only not what *I* will, but *Thou*". For this purpose, with this end in view Christ was born. Paul's purpose is to shew those who thought this priesthood of Christ superfluous that without it the promise of the blessing could not be fulfilled.

Anyone who carefully attends to the sequence of Paul's argument and the niceties of his expressions will see, the preacher claims, that this is no figment of his own brain, and

[1] In accordance with the prevailing opinion of the time Nestorius regards St Paul as the author of the Epistle.

he wishes to accustom his hearers to exactitude of doctrine, so that they may be a people well instructed and able themselves to teach the things of God. So he takes them through the steps of the argument again, to shew that it is all directed to the one end of establishing the fitness of Jesus to act as highpriest and mediator of the promise in virtue of his human nature and perfected experience of the temptations and sufferings which are the lot of men, remaining himself sinless through all[1]. The very fact that he suffered[2] temptation in his sinless human nature confers upon him a power on behalf of those who are his kinsmen, an unanswerable plea in their defence[3]; for the fact that not even the sinless man escaped the Devil's malignant attack shews the injustice of the power with which he assails all other men[4]. On behalf of himself and of the race he offered as a joint offering (sc. for himself and them) the sacrifice of his body[5], and so he reconciled human nature to God by means of his own sinless human nature.

The comparison with Moses is only intended to shew that there were parallels to this providential order by which one who was man could act as the medium between man and God. With a few sentences to this effect Nestorius concludes his argument.

But before he ends his sermon he has something else to say, and I venture to quote his words in full though they deal with another matter. They give us a glimpse of Nestorius in a *rôle* which we are apt to forget he played with conspicuous success, so completely has the great moral preacher and pastor of souls been lost for us in the vigorous thinker and

[1] His exact words are 'exhibiting in himself the person of human nature free from sin'. On the phrase 'the person of human nature' see ch. vi pp. 94 ff.

[2] So Nestorius understands the words ἐν ᾧ πέπονθεν.

[3] Or an irrefutable justification for them, a δικαιολογία ἀήττητος.

[4] Cf. *Bazaar of Heraclides infra* pp. 133 ff.

[5] συνεπαγόμενος τὴν...θυσίαν.

maker of phrases which the Church of his day could not conceive to be compatible with the true doctrine of the Incarnation. The subject is a familiar one—neglect of the sacrament of the Lord's Supper by the faithful. It has often, I think, been less effectively treated. He concludes his exposition of the passage in the Epistle to the Hebrews with the words: 'Let what I have 'said suffice as regards the violence which the heretics do to the 'expressions the Apostle uses.' He goes on:

'But there is something amiss with you which I want to 'put before you in a few words and induce you to amend it. 'For you are quick to discern what is seemly[1]. What, then, 'is it that is amiss? By and bye the holy rites are set before 'the faithful, like a banquet, a king's gift to his soldiers. But 'by then the host of the faithful is nowhere to be seen: they 'are blown away along with those who are not allowed to 'stay[2], like chaff, by the wind of indifference. And Christ is 'crucified in symbol, slain by the sword of the prayer of the 'priest; but, as at the Cross of old, he finds his disciples fled! 'This is a grievous fault—betrayal of Christ when there's no 'persecution, desertion of the flesh of their Master by believers 'under no stress of war! What is the reason for their deser-

[1] Such I suppose is the meaning. The Greek words are γοργοὶ γὰρ πρὸς τὰ καλὰ καθεστήκατε and Becher translates *nam honesto reluctati estis*, taking γοργοί to mean "hostile". Such a meaning is possible:—the vigorous action taken by Nestorius at Constantinople to check abuses of all kinds, and raise the tone of spiritual life in that great city, must have involved plain speaking, and we know he was not one to disguise his meaning by honied words. But the tone of this sermon, as indeed of all the extant sermons, throughout suggests that the preacher expected a sympathetic congregation, and—though he must reprove—he would hardly alienate them in this way. The noun γοργότης is used by writers of the second and the fourth centuries in the sense "quickness", "rapidity", and the use of the adjective of a horse ("spirited") is familiar. Nestorius, practised orator as he was, puts his audience "on their mettle". He has to find fault, but first he gives the praise he could. "You are", he says, "on your mettle to do what is right."

[2] The "catechumens", not yet admitted to full Church privileges.

'tion? is it urgent engagements? Why, what engagement is 'more binding than one that has to do with the service of 'God, and that, too, one that takes but little time? Is it, 'then, fear because of your sins, pray? What, then, was it 'that purified that blessed harlot? was it fleeing from the flesh 'of the Lord, or fleeing to it for refuge? Shame on us if we 'shew ourselves less compunctious than that harlot woman! 'We ought to tremble at the Master's words adjuring us— '"Verily, verily, I say to you, except ye eat the flesh of the 'Son of Man and drink his blood, ye have not life in your-'selves." We ought to be afraid of his rebuking us too and 'saying to us from heaven—"Were ye not able to stay with 'me one hour?"'[1]

And so he comes back to his doctrinal theme:

'Moreover let us beware of becoming accomplices of the 'heretics in their evil doings against Him. Let us give diligent 'heed to Paul's expressions about the Incarnation. Let us not 'dehumanize the manhood and at the same time humanize the 'Godhead[2]. Let us not confuse the experiences of the man-'hood with those of the Godhead. While we keep distinct the 'properties of the natures, let us conjoin the dignity of the 'union[3]. Let us not say that God the Word is the temple, 'but rather its inhabitant; let us not imagine that the temple

[1] *οὐχ ἰσχύσατε μίαν ὥραν παραμεῖναι μετ' ἐμοῦ;*—for *γρηγορῆσαι* of all the MSS. Dr Becher, instead of translating, gives the Vulgate *vigilare*, as our English translators of early Christian writers were wont to obliterate for their English readers any differences between their author's biblical text and the Authorized Version.

[2] The Greek is *τὰ τῆς ἀνθρωπότητος τῷ τῆς θεότητος ἀσωμάτῳ μὴ συνασωματώσωμεν* 'Let us not do away with the corporeal character of the things of the manhood along with the incorporeal character of the Godhead.' Or the meaning might perhaps be "along with (because of) the incorporeal character of the Godhead", i.e. "in our zeal for the transcendence of the Godhead".

[3] I leave the un-English expression. The meaning clearly is "let us make no distinctions of rank in the honour we pay to the Person who is one"—cf. *supra* p. 91 and *infra* p. 169.

'is He who inhabits it, but rather that which is inhabited. 'Let us remember the words which express in turn one after 'another His two natures:—"Destroy this temple", that is, 'what is capable of coming to an end; "and in three days 'I will raise it", that is, I, the God who am invisibly con-'joined with that which is mortal. His is the glory for ever. 'Amen.'

Such is the sermon. Is it heretical? It elucidates the rather puzzling tenth anathema of Cyril and the reply of Nestorius. The question of the highpriesthood of Christ is a very precarious one to handle, involving as it does the whole problem of mediation; and Nestorius was charged with so treating it as to deny the union of the natures in the Person of our Lord, and at the same time to teach that He offered the sacrifice on behalf of Himself as well as on behalf of us. The inconsistency between these two charges seems not to have been noticed. The latter could only be maintained if the former were false, for it presupposes the unity of the Person which the former charge alleges to be denied.

Read in their context, the passages which were extracted by the opponents of Nestorius can be more fairly judged, and the sermon as a whole seems to me to be an able and honest piece of exegesis[1]. Following closely the argument of the Epistle, Nestorius maintains that the expressions which are used of the characteristics of the highpriest—his initial qualifications "taken from among men", "beset by infirmity", "like his brethren in all things"—and the course through which he passes "strong crying and tears", "being tempted", "learn-

[1] If Nestorius is unorthodox in his language, it would be difficult to ward off the charge from the writer to the Hebrews: even though we have to admit that the expressions of a single writer in the New Testament must be harmonized with the language of other writers, and that genuine Scriptural language might well be "unorthodox" in the fifth century—an admission which we can only make with important qualifications.

ing obedience", "made perfect through suffering"—are all of them applicable not to the Godhead but to the manhood of the Lord. They refer, he says, to one who 'exhibits in 'Himself the person of human nature free from sin'. The whole argument, he urges, is directed to the one end of establishing the fitness of Jesus to act as highpriest and mediator in virtue of His human nature and perfected experience of the temptations and sufferings which are the lot of men, remaining Himself sinless through all. On behalf of Himself and of the race of men He offered as a joint offering the sacrifice of His body, and so reconciled human nature to God by means of His own sinless human nature. It is to the manhood that the highpriesthood and the offering must be referred: and the offering was made on behalf of the highpriest Himself as well as of all men.

The question turns mainly on the interpretation of two passages in the Epistle. The first is the passage "For every highpriest being taken from among men" (Heb. v 1). One interpretation, adopted in our Authorized Version, regards the words "taken from among men" as part of the subject, and makes them express a contrast between the highpriesthood of Christ and all human priesthood. The interpretation of Nestorius, on the contrary, sees in them the expression of one of the primary qualifications of Christ to be the Priest of men, namely that He is himself *man*. This interpretation is adopted in our Revised Version, and in his commentary on the Epistle by Dr Westcott, who says "It is unnatural and injurious to the argument to take [the phrase in question] as part of the subject". On this point at all events Nestorius gets strong support from scholars. And he has also support which in a matter of this kind is perhaps still more decisive. For it is the human qualification that men's hearts have seized upon. It is a *Brother* who is our *Highpriest*.

Difficult as is the whole conception of the highpriesthood

of our Lord, that it can be the centre of the devotional life and eucharistic worship of the Church is due to this fact, which finds familiar expression in the hymn "Where high the heavenly temple stands".

The second passage is the one on which Nestorius based his argument that the highpriest is said to offer on behalf of himself, and that, as the Godhead had no need of offering, it must be to the manhood that the priesthood attaches.

Here again it is possible to throw over Nestorius the cloak of Dr Westcott. The passage is "Who hath no need daily, as the high-priests, to offer up sacrifices first for their own sins, then for the sins of the people, for this he did once for all in that he offered up himself" (Heb. vii 27). With special reference to the last clause Dr Westcott writes: "It is generally supposed that the reference is to be limited to the latter clause, that is, to the making an offering for the sins of the people. It is of course true that for Himself Christ had no need to offer a sacrifice in any sense. But perhaps it is better to supply the ideal sense of the highpriest's offering, and so to leave the statement in a general form. Whatever the Aaronic highpriest did in symbol, as a sinful man, that Christ did perfectly as sinless in His humanity for men." Dr Westcott expresses himself guardedly, with less positive assertion than Nestorius; but the concluding sentence "...that Christ did perfectly as sinless in His humanity for men" gives essentially the interpretation of the passage that Nestorius gives, to the effect that the offering of the sinless One, in His humanity the perfect representative of men, was in some sense therefore on behalf of Himself as well as on behalf of the whole race of men whose representative He was.

It is the human nature which qualifies our Lord to act as our highpriest; it is the human nature, perfected through temptations and suffering, perfectly obedient to the Father's will and sinless through them all, that constitutes the offering. Is it dividing the natures to say with Nestorius that it is not of

God the Word that these things are said? Must not some such distinction be made, if we are to attempt to embody in accurate doctrine the profoundly edifying and ennobling conception of the highpriesthood of our Lord—a distinction which we may feel to be logical rather than real, but one that is forced upon us by the conditions under which we think and express our thought. Who is it that offers, what is the offering, to whom is it offered? if the priest is a true representative of those for whom He offers, so far as He is representative does He not offer also on his own behalf? It is easy of course for us to find orthodox words in which to answer these questions, and to say that the one Person, the incarnate Son of God, who is both God and man, offers His perfected manhood to God the Father; while we insist that it is only in virtue of His manhood that He is enabled to act as highpriest. And it may be that while the protest of Nestorius was valid as against the tendencies of those whom he suspected of Apollinarian heresy, from whose circle the frank Monophysites of later times were descended, yet none the less his own conception was at fault. Let us turn to the anathemas.

Cyril leads off: "Holy Scripture says that Christ became (*or* was made) highpriest and apostle of our confession, and offered up Himself on behalf of us to be a sweet-smelling savour to God the Father. If therefore anyone asserts that it was not the Word of God Himself who became highpriest and apostle, when He became flesh and man like us; but man born of a woman conceived of as distinct from Him (i.e. as a separate person): or if anyone says that He offered the offering on behalf of Himself also, and not rather on behalf of us only—for He who knew not sin could not have needed an offering: Let him be anathema."

Nestorius replies (according to the Latin version of Marius Mercator which is the only form in which the counter-anathemas of Nestorius are extant): 'If anyone says that the Word who was 'in the beginning was made highpriest and apostle of our 'confession, and offered up Himself on behalf of us, and does 'not rather say that the apostleship is Emmanuel's[1], and on the 'same principle divide the offering between Him who united 'and him who was united in the one Sonship[2]—that is to say, 'attributing to God what is God's and to man what is man's: 'Let him be anathema.'

Now here, so far as the actual words go, we have Cyril insisting that we must say that the Word of God Himself is highpriest, though he qualifies the baldness of the assertion by adding "when He became flesh and man like us"; and he declares it anathema to say that He offered on behalf of Himself. The verbal difference between Cyril's requirements and the argument of Nestorius in his sermon is almost absolute.

But in his reply to Cyril's anathema Nestorius only repudiates the teaching that the Word who was in the beginning (that is, the pre-incarnate Word, the Word in His own Divine substance) was made highpriest and offered Himself (that is, not the manhood but the Godhead) as a sacrifice for us; and he declares that it is the Person who is man as well as God (Emmanuel, "God with us", the Incarnate One) whose function it is to perform this act, and that in the offering itself the distinctive parts which are played by the Godhead and the manhood respectively must be recognized. What these distinctive parts are, the anathema does not define[3].

[1] That is to say, the incarnate Person's, who is "God with us", both God and man—the title which safeguards the manhood.

[2] The Latin is *ad unam societatem* (al. *communitatem*) *filii*, which represents I suppose the Greek *εἰς μίαν κοινωνίαν υἱοῦ*, and means that the union was of such a kind that He who united and he who was united became in fellowship together one Son.

[3] In an incidental illustration in another sermon he says the Lord's supper is not commemorative of the death of God the Word—'And it is not the death of God the Word we proclaim when we feed on the Lord's blood and body, for the nature of God receives sacrifice and is not itself offered as a victim in sacrifice' (*Sermo* x Loofs p. 271). Cf. also *infra* pp. 140 ff.

The sermon might seem to leave the whole act the act of the manhood, and yet it assumes and presupposes the unity of the Person, and indeed seems to be conceived quite in the spirit of Leo's *agit utraque forma cum alterius communione quod proprium est*—a dictum which was of course strongly objected to by the opponents of Nestorius. The phrases and arguments that might be suspected, so far as they are more than legitimate comment on the words and arguments of the Epistle to the Hebrews, are explained partly by the fact that he has in view teaching which appeared to attribute to Godhead itself characteristics and functions which are proper to manhood, and partly by the difficulty of the subject and the ambiguity of some of the terms. If we dealt with his opponents' phrases in the same critical spirit, we should find many which could be similarly misinterpreted, as they were, in the opposite direction[1].

The real problem whether "manhood" can exist in any other way than in an individual man was apparently not recognized on either side, and therefore—though it is the

[1] I am in no way concerned in this enquiry to question the soundness of Cyril's beliefs or to belittle such services as he rendered to the Church. But many of his expressions are at least no more immaculate than some of those of Nestorius, and we do not need to turn the microscope on them to discover flaws. He used it freely against Nestorius, and of course Nestorius retaliated. Here is one example which bears on the question before us. He is objecting to Cyril's expression "two natures, out of which (ἐξ ὧν) we say that the ineffable union was effected". 'This "out of which" sounds as if he spoke as regards the natures of the Lord of *parts* on one side and the other, which parts became one. For he ought to have said not "out of which" but, as we say, "of which" (ὧν) an ineffable union was effected. For that ineffable union is not out of the natures, but it is such a union of the natures....Here he surreptitiously confuses the peculiar properties of the natures' (*Letter* xii Syriac fragment Loofs p. 197).—It will be remembered that it was just such a phrase as this of Cyril's that seemed to justify the contention of Eutyches that our Lord was "of two natures" before the Incarnation, which Leo dubbed as impious as the assertion of "one only nature" after the Incarnation was scandalous.

crucial question for Christian philosophers today—it need not be brought into account in this connexion.

Accordingly the conclusion of this examination of the sermon as a whole and the anathemas would be that, in this particular controversy as between Cyril and Nestorius, judgement cannot be given against Nestorius.

This question of the highpriesthood of Jesus is, at its core, of ethical even more than of metaphysical interest and importance. Of the highest ethical significance too is the doctrine of the Eucharist, the Sacrament of the Body and Blood of Christ, in which He who is "at once the Victim and the Priest" fulfils His sacrificial function—the supreme illustration and example of the union of the Divine and the human and of the dual natures and functions of the One Highpriest. As such Nestorius inevitably referred to it in his sermon, pointing the moral, and inviting his hearers to realize for themselves, in the only way they could, the mystery of the ineffable union, which (as he said at the outset) words were unable to describe. How keenly alive he was to the ethical significance of the doctrine of the Person of Christ, which needs for its statement such abstruse discussions—and how barren he would have thought these discussions apart from their ethical implications—is shewn by passages in the *Bazaar of Heraclides* to which I must now ask attention.

CHAPTER VIII

THE ETHICAL VALUATION OF THE DOCTRINE OF THE PERSON OF CHRIST

No student of the history of Christian doctrine would for a moment belittle the value of a sound metaphysical theory of God and of the Incarnation. But no would-be disciple of Christ attaches importance to it apart from its moral issues. It is only so far as doctrine embodies an interpretation of human life, and so supplies a working theory of life, that it appeals with constraining power to men and women who are set here in the world to live that life. It is essentially a moral appeal that doctrine makes to the ordinary man

> "with soul just nerved
> To act tomorrow what he learns today".

Only so far as doctrine furnishes a basis for actual life, and expresses principles which can be applied to the conditions of things as they are, has it practical value for the "children of men". And the practical consequences which flow from doctrines, the principles of active life which can be deduced from them, are a sure test of their truth. They must correspond with human experience; they must interpret the facts of human life, and direct the aims and activities of men. In the doctrine of the Incarnation the whole Christian philosophy of life is summed up. Nothing else matters, for indeed it is all in all: it spreads its ramifications into every nook and cranny of human life. Jesus is to His disciples of all ages the clue to the mystery of existence: so far as they can understand Him they have the solution of all the enigmas of their being; they know what they are, and therefore they know what to do. They do not give or withhold obedience to commands imposed by an authority outside themselves: it is the law of their own being that they follow or resist. If, then, the Person of Jesus is a metaphysical "problem" which challenges the highest efforts of man's intellect, it is one in which his deepest moral interests are involved. And the moral issues of the problem have never been absent from the consciousness of His Church. That doctrinal controversies should so often seem to be a mere exercise of dialectical subtleties is not the fault of theologians. Such "subtleties" are not the monopoly of theologians, but the common property—the alphabet—of thinkers. If impeachment is to lie at all, it is the "mind of man" that must be arraigned. The Nestorian controversy is full of such subtleties: we have had to consider some of the dialectical puzzles with which the *apologia* of Nestorius abounds. But Nestorius was not the man to lose himself in a maze of metaphysics. His hold of the moral thread is as firm as the simplest believer's. As much to him as to the humblest sinner who has found salvation in faith in Jesus, Jesus is the Saviour and Example of men; and he brings the doctrine of His Person to the test of this conviction.

Does the doctrine correspond with the facts of the life of Jesus on earth as they are told in the records of Scripture? and are the results that follow from it, as affecting the life that men live in the world, consistent with the results to which the earliest interpreters and preachers of Jesus pointed?

To Nestorius it seems that the moral purpose of the Incarnation is frustrated unless the incarnate Word of God underwent a genuine human experience, and he argues against every doctrine of His Person which seems to debar Him from being a real Example and Pattern of a genuinely human life.

'If He did not become man in (*or* into) man, then He 'saved Himself but not us. But if He saved us, then in us He 'became man, and He was in the form of men, and in fashion 'He was found as a man, and He did not of Himself become 'a man'[1].

In this connexion, as illustrating the paramount interest of Nestorius in the moral issues of the questions in dispute, it is a pleasure to quote a passage in which he writes of the "obedience" of Christ and its bearing on the doctrine of the relation between the Divine and the human in Him. The two or three sentences which are obscure will be examined in another connexion. The passage as a whole glows with enthusiasm for the triumph of Manhood under a searching trial[2].

'And therefore He took the form of a servant—a lowly 'form, a form that had lost the likeness of God. He took not 'honour and glory, nor worship, nor yet authority, though 'He was Son; but the form of a servant was acting with 'obedience in the person of the Son, according to the mind of 'God; having His mind[3] and not its own. Nor did it do 'anything that it wished, but only what God the Word wished. 'For this is the meaning of "the form of God"—that the form 'of the servant should not have a mind or will of its own, but 'of Him whose the person is and the form[4]. Wherefore the 'form of God took the form of a servant, and it did not 'avoid aught of the lowliness of the form of a servant, but

[1] *Bazaar of Heraclides* p. 224—the phrase 'of Himself' means independently of human conditions, or, so as to be changed from His own nature into the nature of man.

[2] The main idea is touched upon also in *Sermo* ix Loofs p. 250 ff. and *Sermo* xviii *ib.* p. 307.

[3] i.e. aims and purpose. Nestorius strongly opposes the Apollinarian theory, that the Word took the place of the human intellect.

[4] Nestorius is speaking morally rather than psychologically.

'received all, that the (Divine) form might be in all; that 'without stint it[1] might make it[2] to be its own form.

'For because He took this form, that He might take away 'the guilt of the first man and give to his nature that original 'image which he had lost by his guilt, it was right that He 'should take that which had incurred the guilt and was held 'under subjection and servitude, together with all its bonds 'of dishonour and disgrace; since apart from His person it 'had nothing divine or honourable or independent. Just as 'a son who is still a child does not attain to be heir or "lord 'of all" independently, but through obedience; so also the 'form of a servant which He took unto His own person He 'took as the form of a servant—not unto authority, but unto 'obedience, and obedience of such a kind that from it there 'should be begotten exact obedience, even sinlessness. And 'truly He was seen to be without sins.

'Now, when a man is saved from all the causes from which 'disobedience arises, then truly and without doubt is he seen 'to be without sins. And therefore He took of the nature 'that had sinned, lest, by taking of a nature which is incapable 'of sins, it should be thought that it was by nature that He 'could not sin, and not through His obedience. But though 'He had all these things that belong to our nature—anger, and 'desire, and thought—and these things also were developing 'as He grew gradually in age; yet they were made firm in 'the purpose of obedience.

'And the response of His obedience extended to all the 'former commandments, and not to some only, that it might not 'be thought that it was through their easiness that He was able 'to continue innocent. Nor did He undertake obedience in 'the matter of those things in which there is a certain incentive 'of honour, of power, of renown, but rather in those that are 'poor and beggarly and contemptible and weak, and might

[1] i.e. the form of God. [2] i.e. the form of the servant.

'well baulk the purpose of obedience: things which have 'absolutely no incentive to obedience, but rather to slackness 'and remissness. And He received no sort of encouragement; 'but from Himself alone came His desire of obedience to God 'and of loving what God wills[1].

'And therefore He was needy in all things. But though 'He was forcibly drawn by contrary things, in nothing did He 'decline from the mind of God; although Satan employed all 'these means to withdraw Him from the mind of God. And 'Satan sought to do this the more because He saw that He 'was in no wise anxious[2]: for He was not seen at first to 'work any miracles, nor did He appear to have a charge to 'teach, but only to be in subjection and keep all the command- 'ments. While He was consorting with all men and surrounded 'on all sides by all the commandments, which shewed that 'He had the power to disobey, in the midst of them all He 'behaved manfully, using nothing peculiar or different from 'others for His sustenance, but availing Himself of such things 'as were usual, like other men; that it might not be supposed 'that He was preserved from sin by aids of this sort, and that 'He could not be so preserved without these things. And 'therefore in eating and drinking He observed all the com- 'mandments. And through fatigue and sweat He remained 'firm in His purpose, having His will fixed to the will of God. 'And there was nothing that could withdraw or separate Him 'therefrom; for He lived not for Himself but for Him whose 'own the person was[3]; and He kept the person without stain 'and without scar; and by its means He gave victory to the 'human nature.

[1] All this shews that Nestorius was not a monothelite. The human will conformed itself to the Divine—it was not sunk in the Divine will, so as to will by necessity what God wills.

[2] From what follows this would seem to mean that He was not at first anxious to display His Divinity.

[3] Or 'whose person He was'.

'And because in all things He was full of obedience, He 'received the baptism of John as a first-fruits, like all men. 'And although He had no need, as being without sins, yet in 'His entire obedience He received it as though he had need; 'for it was the first-fruits of obedience that He should not 'behave in a manner conformable to His honour and glory, 'but as under obedience to one who commands[1]; and that He 'should not only permit him to baptize, but should even 'be baptized by him as one requiring purification and in need 'of forgiveness. This is what obedience in all things means—'that He should not require or exact anything in His own 'person, but in the person of Him whose the person is, and 'that He should possess His own will, in that the person is 'properly His own; and that He should account His person 'to be His own person[2].

'One is the person; therefore the Father pointed Him out 'from above, saying: "Thou art my beloved Son; in Thee am 'I well pleased"; and the Holy Ghost came down in the form 'of a dove and abode upon Him. And it does not say that 'the Son came down, since He is the Son who has the person, 'and the things that belong to this One (i.e. Jesus) His own '(i.e. the Son's) person did, without being distinguished from 'Him (Jesus). Therefore He is one even in the birth of flesh: '"The Holy Spirit", it says, "shall come and the power of the 'Most High shall overshadow thee; therefore also that which 'is being born of thee shall be called Holy (Thing), Son of

[1] i.e. John Baptist.

[2] The pronouns refer, of course, to the Divine and the human natures; but it is difficult to assign them to their proper subjects. The following, which is, I think, a legitimate rendering, gives a better sense: 'that He (the Word) should not require or exact anything in His own person (i.e. on His own behalf), but in that of (i.e. on behalf of) him (i.e. the man) whose person He is; and that He should win his will, since He is strictly his person; and that He should account his person to be His own person': but the passage is obscure.

'God "[1]. It never said that the Son should come; since that 'which He took unto His own person is not another but the 'very same—even Him whom He gave for the dispensation 'which is on our behalf for the reasons of which we have 'already spoken.

'And because He was accounted to be a more eminent 'observer of the Law than all (other) men during His sojourn 'amongst all men...[2] 'He went forth to the wilderness alone to be tempted by 'the devil, lacking all things that are in the world, and even 'that which is accounted fatigue and privation[3]. And by 'reason of His withdrawal from all things He attained to the 'greatest eminence to which bodily power is capable of being 'exalted. And, instead of the impulses of physical delights, 'He was holding on to the things of God, as though He were 'incorporeal, not answering to His body as if it were His own, 'but as if apart from it. For this belongs alone to the image 'of God and of Him who keeps the image of God in God— '(viz.) that He should will what God the Father wills; and 'because there was nothing else[4], in all that the devil said He 'put him to shame as one who was removed from the will of 'God. He lifts Himself up to God, bringing the things that 'belong to His own will into conformity with the will of 'God, so that it should be merely the image of the archetype, 'not of itself; for an image is in itself without a form; but it

[1] Earlier in the book it appears that Nestorius adopts this interpretation of the passage. The Syriac seems to imply it here also.

[2] I cannot translate ܟܕ ܕܝܢ ܒܡܫܟ̈ܢܬܐ ܢܬܚܘܫܪ ܗܘܐ ܦܢܝܢ ܠܡܘܟܠܗ ܐܝܟܐ ܕܠܝܬ ܠܗ ܡܕܡ ܕܡܟܝܢܗ ܠܟܒܪ.

[3] The context suggests that this refers to the sublime rapture of contemplation which Christ enjoyed during the fast in the desert. But the words may be taken with the first clause: 'and [be tempted] by that also which is accounted', etc.

[4] This appears to mean: "and because no other motive could enter into the mind of Christ".

'has as its proper form that of the archetype; and both of 'them are the same, and the appearance is one. For by 'deeds He kept the form of God in bodily things from all 'bodily passions; and elected that God's will should be done 'and not that of the flesh; and made the form His own by 'deeds, so that He should will what He (God) willed, and 'that there should be one and the same will in them both, 'and one person, without division: This being That, and That 'This, while both This and That are preserved[1]. And He 'was being made firm in all things by temptations of body 'and soul—in cities and in the desert—there being no dis-'tinction[2] in His observance (of the commandments) and in 'His subjection.

'Henceforth, as one who had conquered and triumphed in 'all things, there was given to Him as the prize of His victory 'authority to preach and to announce the Gospel of the 'Kingdom of Heaven, saying, "Be of good cheer, I have 'conquered the world; now is the judgement of this world; 'now is this its ruler defeated. And I, when I shall have 'been lifted up from the earth, will draw every man unto 'myself". And, although He is the Son, through the fear and 'suffering which He bore He learned obedience, and was 'made perfect; "and He became to all who obey Him a 'cause of everlasting life". And He was sent to teach every 'one, and to work signs and wonders and cures, and all the 'rest—not that He should be stimulated and urged to obedi-'ence: but, that those things that were done for our sake should 'be believed, He employed all these things (i.e. signs etc.) to 'bring about the obedience of those who were learning. For 'until the time of His victory[3] He was striving to make firm in 'God the image that had been given to Him. But because

[1] Nestorius is now, apparently, speaking of the two natures—explaining the relation of the two wills—united in the one Person.

[2] As to the natures (?).

[3] i.e. at the temptation.

'He had now established His image in divers manners through 'all kinds of temptations, being without any shortcoming or 'defect, He was henceforth acting on our behalf, being eager 'to rescue us captives from the oppression of the tyrant, and 'to draw us to Himself and make us all sons of His kingdom—'partakers and heirs and sons of God. For the overthrow of 'the tyrant was to be without hope of recovery, when He should 'openly cast him down from his principality, and seize his 'power after He had cast him down. And His own victory 'was not to suffice for Him, after He had seized him, but was 'now to be ours also for whose sake He had fought. And 'those who obeyed Him He was henceforth bringing to Him-'self, freely, and not by compulsion. And those who come (to 'Him) He persuades to depart from him (Satan) willingly, 'and not against their will...[1].

'Wherefore, after His victory was complete, and it had 'been said from Heaven: "This is my beloved Son", He 'commenced again other battles. [And when He undertook][2] 'the leadership and the office of teaching and the working 'of wonders with authority, again He becomes obedient. And 'He did not act loftily in matters pertaining to us, i.e. in 'human and weak things: [but just as though][3] He possessed 'no authority and superiority at all—being persecuted, and 'smitten, and fearing with such fear as troubles all men, 'having no place, as even the birds and beasts have, where 'to lay His head, changing from place to place, and being 'buffeted and expelled from them all,—for our sakes, and to 'make us obedient, without compulsion from anyone, that He 'might fully teach us with all care. And He bore all temp-'tations in order to teach us. And from every place He 'was driven forth to those to whom He had not yet bee

[1] Some words are missing from the MS.

[2] A word, or words, missing from the MS.

[3] Supplying ܘܐܝܟܢ.

'announced; so that the very thing which He Himself was 'anxious to bring about was accomplished by the persistence 'of enemies who could not foresee the outcome of the matter, 'but were thinking to hinder Him by opposition. (And He 'undertook) tasks full of contempt and dishonour, and fear 'even unto death. And even after His victory, and after His 'election by God (when He said): "This is my beloved Son 'in whom I am well pleased": after He had received the 'authority of the Gospel, after He had been made manifest 'that by His own authority He was doing the works of God, 'after He had said "I and my Father are one", He was in 'all this weakness and contempt in things human—things the 'burden of which it was not thought possible that He should 'bear, but, on the contrary, that they would be irksome to 'Him, and cause Him to reject grace. And so there were 'many things that were hindering Him from announcing the 'Gospel; whence it came about that there arose against Him 'accusers, (as it were) on God's behalf—as though He (Christ) 'afforded them an excuse for disobedience in that they could 'charge Him with being contemptible and weak.

'For on all hands the dishonour that comes after honour 'is accounted the most contemptible. But Christ came in the 'flesh and, on the contrary, accepted "obedience unto death, 'even unto the death of the cross," as the greatest honour. And 'He shewed to Satan and to every principality and authority 'that it is complete obedience that is the cause of honour, 'rather than the disobedience to God through which Satan 'suffered when he made himself equal to the Divine nature 'and honour, and brooked not the obedience which belongs 'to men, since he estimated honour and dishonour according 'to the difference between his own nature and that of men; 'and on account of this ambition of his he considered that 'this obedience was not due from him to God. And he 'cast Adam into the same evil plight by persuading him not 'to obey God. And he (Adam) chose to be unthankful (to

'(God) and disobedient in all things; and, because he was 'deemed worthy of His image, when he was forbidden to 'eat of one of the trees he took it ill, where there was no 'cause for grievance, and transgressed the command of God, 'regarding God as niggardly. Wherefore, because He acted 'with entire obedience, God accounted the Second Adam 'worthy of all this honour—honour than which there is none 'higher, corresponding to obedience which nothing could 'surpass—who esteemed not Himself to be anything, but '(strove) to be conformable to the will of God, even as God 'wished that He should be.

'And so God became incarnate in a man in His own 'person. And He made his person His own person. And 'there is no condescension comparable to this, that his person[1] 'should become His own person, and that He should give 'him His person. Wherefore He employed his person in that 'He took it to Himself. But He took it, not as having made 'it honourable, but as (having left it) contemptible—that He 'might shew to all henceforth[2] that whatever exaltation there 'is comes about by (previous) condescension—and not as 'though it were abolished by the fact that He "took the 'form of a servant, and was found in fashion as a man".

'The form of a servant served this purpose according to 'His will: for He willed, according to what belonged to (its) 'nature, that He should be obedient to His person: not only 'for His own sake—that there might be no doubt about His 'being the Son of God—but also for our sake: that He might 'be led away and die for the sake of our redemption: for 'our sake, I say, not as though we were righteous or good—'for in this there would be an inducement, if one should die 'for such as these—but for the wicked: "for scarcely for the

[1] Lit. 'the person of that one'.

[2] Conjecturing that ܠܟܠ ܕܡܢܗ ܕܥܒܕܐ stands for *λοιπόν*, or *τὸ λοιπόν*. Taken literally the text yields no tolerable sense.

9—2

'ungodly (plur.) will one die: yet peradventure for the good '(plur.) some one would dare to die"[1].

'Since then in a manner unsearchable He condescended in 'all things with an incomparable condescension, (here) again 'was shewn one purpose, one will, one mind—not to be dis-'tinguished or divided—as though in One (being). And in 'might and in authority and in judgement—in all things He '(the Man) was partaker with God inseparably: (acting) as 'though from One, with one discrimination and choice of 'both; in such a way that in things human He should not, 'as human, possess aught as (peculiarly) His own, but that the 'will of God should be His will, when He had been stablished 'by works and by natural sufferings; and that in Divine things, 'in like manner, nothing should belong to Him as (peculiarly) 'His own, apart from human lowliness, but that in all things 'that which was by suffering and by its nature man should 'be a party to all the Divine things, and even impassibility; 'that, even as by depletion He employed the form of a 'servant, so also He should participate in the exaltation of 'the form of God, since He (Christ) is in both of them—'in the form of a servant, and in the form of God—and 'possesses one and the same person of the humiliation and 'the exaltation.

'Wherefore it was required that the incarnation of God 'should be into the complete nature of rational beings; that 'we should learn to share that graciousness of His, by reason 'of which, without any need, He did everything (for us), and 'did not shrink from doing even things that are despised; 'and further, that He should make man to share His image, 'that everyone beneath Him[2] should, in imitation (of Him), 'share His greatness without giving way to pride. And according 'to His power He was doing everything in the sight of God[3].

[1] Cf. Rom. v. 7.

[2] Or, 'after Him'.

[3] So text. We expect rather: 'and according to his power do everything in the sight of God'—'everyone' continuing as subject.

'Since then Satan dealt perversely with those (powers) 'which were given him by God and fell away from the mind 'of God, he did not employ the image of God (in him) as a 'model and pattern worthy of God, but with spite (he used it) 'against man, to lead him astray from God. And he caused 'man to go astray and to fall away from His image by not 'observing the Will of God; and he established him as an 'enemy and one whc fights against God, that thereby he 'might accuse God of unjust dealing, in that He shewed so 'friendly a disposition towards man, and make good his charge 'against Him when at length He should avenge His disgrace 'upon man and lay a just punishment upon him for what he 'had done against Him. For since Satan acted in anger and 'without counsel, he forgot that God might act in a manner 'contrary to what he could have wished.

'For God did not by means of death compass man's 'destruction, but brought him to a better mind, and gave him 'helps that he should not sin nor again consent to the counsels 'of the Evil One which lead to destruction.

'Nor has this become an occasion of slandering God, but 'rather (a proof of) His greater goodness, that He advanced 'man to such an honour as this when he was nothing at all; 'and that He might convict the tyrant of his treachery, who 'had thought to destroy man, and shew that He had not 'determined on his (man's) destruction, but that in His 'goodness He would save him and preserve him and be 'careful of him, so that he might return and come again to 'that which he (formerly) was. But Satan thought that if, after 'all this God's love towards man, he could make him again 'transgress the commandment of God, He would certainly be 'so enraged as to destroy him, and that man would have no 'chance of repenting and being healed. For those who had 'sinned and had been held worthy of redemption, but still 'continued in the same (sins)—though they were not as yet 'quit of the original punishment—there could be no refusal '(he thought) but that wrath should be stirred up against such 'as these, without any further possibility of their rescue. These 'things, then, that Satan determined for man's destruction he first 'thought out with himself, and he persuaded himself that he 'had rendered man liable to punishment without leaving him 'any chance of forgiveness. And because he was blinded by 'rage and spite he did not learn from his own case the 'goodness of God, by reason of which He did not destroy 'even Satan himself, deceiver as he was, but bore with his 'wickedness—(he did not understand, I say) that for the sake 'of this (His goodness) God would be patient with men also 'when they sinned and committed iniquity—inasmuch as it 'was another that had led them astray—and that He is patient 'with the folly of men, and with the boundless wickedness of 'the devil towards them, who, in the height of his malice, 'conceived the design of leading all astray, and of bringing 'all into enmity (with God), that our whole race might be 'seduced by him without any one to act as its advocate. 'And, whereas Satan displayed all this exceeding wickedness 'without any cause at all: with all this wickedness was shewn 'forth also the goodness of God. And He shewed His unspeakable goodness by doing good to all men in common. 'For with surpassing condescension He came unto him who 'had thus greatly sinned, in contempt and dishonour and 'weakness. And He did not shrink from dishonour for the 'sake of his advantage; but through His person He became 'his (man's) own person; and he became God's (person), 'fulfilling[1] all the things of God, teaching the lesson of the 'condescension; for the surpassing obedience of the humanity 'was a lesson of humility, since it sought not its own but 'God's. And it was united into one mind (with Him), 'so that Satan should have no chance at all of bringing

[1] The writer is now thinking of the Person, Christ, rather than of human nature in general.

'in[1] disobedience. And because He had singled out death alone 'to be both for defeat and for victory, finally He underwent 'this also, that, when He should be found victorious over it, 'He should utterly abolish it. And two things He accom-'plished by it (death): He convicted Satan, and He removed 'from Himself all suspicion of disobedience.

'And since many were overcome by the fear of death, 'He bore even death itself, and paid for us the penalty 'justly due by substituting for our death that death which 'unjustly came upon Himself. Wherefore, after he had kept 'all the commandments, so that He should be innocent of 'death and receive for us the verdict[2] of innocence, He again 'adopted this course of action[3] for the teaching of those who 'had erred. And He died for us erring ones; and He 'brought Death into the midst, because it was necessary for 'him to be destroyed. And He did not hold back even from 'this, that He Himself should submit to Death; for by this 'He won the hope of Death's undoing. And it was for this 'cause that He first of all underwent divers temptations also, that 'we might not die as evildoers, without the penalty being paid. 'And it was with this same hope that He undertook obedience 'with immense love—not that He Himself should be cleared 'of guilt, but that He might pay the penalty for us; and not 'that He should gain the victory for Himself, but for all men. 'For as the guilt of Adam established all under guilt, so did 'His victory (*or* acquittal) acquit all.

'And from these two (i.e. Adam and Christ) all intelligent 'powers have learned that there is no respect of persons with 'God, but the love of just judgement, whereby mankind was

[1] Reading ܠܡܥܠܢܘܬܐ ܕ, 'for the introduction of', instead of ܠܡܥܠܝܘܬܐ ܕ, 'for the loftiness of' (text).

[2] Or 'election', 'calling' (ܓܒܝܘܬܐ): but the language appears to be legal.

[3] i.e. obedience and suffering.

'cleared of guilt and Satan was convicted. And God increased 'His victory, and gave Him an honour "better than all names". 'And all intelligent powers together marvelled at His victory, 'and were kneeling and worshipping the name that was given 'Him, acknowledging that it was justly given; and every 'tongue was confessing the just dispensation which was 'wrought on behalf of all, through which peace and concord 'reigned over the earth. And in all things by persuasion He 'was bringing them near (to God), and not by compulsion.

'And God Himself carried out the dispensation, and did 'not accomplish it by the hand of another, lest, when he 'should be in contempt and weakness of this sort, His com-'mandment should be accounted dishonourable, and again 'envy should be stirred up afresh against man. But He of 'Himself accepted it (i.e. apparently, the commandment) who 'is able to bear all things. And He established as witnesses of 'the lowliness of His humanity the angels who were strength-'ening Him[1]; that no one should say that it (the humanity) 'was undergoing sufferings without pain because that He (God) 'was strengthening[2] it that it should not suffer, and hence 'there was no cause why it should not be obedient. For 'everything that could possibly be thought or said about 'Him in doubt: and those things that He knew men might 'say about Him—even though (perhaps) they did not actually 'say them, either through fear, or through obedience (to Him) '—everything He did; that He might not leave any cause at 'all for doubt. For men were not aware of this mystery: but 'it was hidden even from principalities and authorities and 'from all powers, and was revealed to them that had know-'ledge; and they were confessing, after this refutation, that 'design which overthrew all (human) designs and vanquished

[1] Pointing ܕܡܚܝܠܝܢ instead of ܕܡܚܝܠܝܢ, which would mean 'who were feeble'.

[2] Pointing ܡܚܝܠ for ܡܚܝܠ.

'them. And He shewed that His incarnation was a dispen-'sation that was universal, unto all those who, with one mind 'and with one accord, conspired with Him to oppose their 'common enemy—even him whom He had crushed and 'brought to nought, that he should no more find scope for 'his treachery and spite.

'But though overthrown he (Satan) remains, as it were for 'his own manifest condemnation and theirs who consented to 'him, since he no longer has the same power to lead astray. 'And (that he remains), it is for the sake of the victory of those 'who do not consent to him; for "no man", it says, "is 'crowned except he strive lawfully". And hence he (Satan) 'remained (as a factor) in the Christian discipline, even after 'the victory (of Christ) and the abolition of death—that dis-'cipline which had been abolished by Christ—that those also 'who are in Christ may conduct themselves after His likeness: 'not through the grace of the resurrection alone, but also by 'individual works and conduct[1]. For the former is universal, 'but the latter is for each one. And that it may not be thought 'concerning the (human) nature of Christ that it is a unique 'and peculiar creation—that it was fashioned so as to be 'without sins, and gained the victory by virtue of this (alone)—'He brings it about that he (Satan) is conquered by many 'myriads in our very nature, by means of conduct such as 'Christ's[2], even by those who strictly keep the commandments, 'and in respect of the law behave in the body well nigh with 'the conduct of incorporeal beings, and in tribulation and in 'distress and in all weakness bear the seductions of nature and 'its fluctuations, with those assaults which are from without. 'And they have so conquered in all things that the complete-'ness of Satan's defeat is proportioned to the advancement of

[1] i.e. the grace which comes by virtue of Christ's resurrection and victory over death does not remove individual responsibility, or abolish the contest. Satan has to be overcome by each and all.

[2] Lit. 'which is in Christ'.

'the commandments; whereas he had thought that it was just 'by men's conduct that their ruin would be effected most 'easily.'[1]

To the same effect is a long discussion (which follows the passage just cited) of the moral purpose and issues of the Incarnation in relation to the power which Satan had acquired over men—a discussion which seems to me to compare not unfavourably with other familiar investigations of the question *Cur Deus homo?* in connexion with the supposed rights of Satan. He who was really and fairly to overcome the Devil and break the fatal rule he exercised over mankind needed to be himself man (to have man's real *ousia*), and as man in all respects to fight against and conquer evil. Man's real nature must be appropriated, made his own, by one who can as man render perfect obedience to the will of God. No theory of the Incarnation which does not leave the victory man's victory, Nestorius argues, can avail to release men from the Devil's authority and to secure to men the mastery in the struggle in which they are engaged. No mixture of natures (which would produce a being neither God nor man) would avail, and no deification of man (a change of the *ousia* of manhood into the *ousia* of Godhead); and yet no mere man could achieve the triumph.

'How should He make His incarnation a stumbling-block 'through mixture or confusion or participation of natures, so 'as to be thought of as neither God nor man, but as one made 'from the two, and not (as He really is) simple and indivisible? 'Hence it is, then, that with the manhood He is as an 'arbiter in a cause, and in a true contest, while He has the 'manhood in His own person and it is obedient to Him in all 'things. And it is not He that contends and is judged, except 'only in so far as He has brought the manhood into an ap-'propriation[2] with His own image—but not into the *nature* of

[1] *Bazaar of Heraclides* pp. 53—63.

[2] Or 'intimate association': see above, p. 73 note 2.

'the invincible and impassible *ousia* of the Godhead' (*Bazaar of Heraclides* p. 68).

We need not, I think, consider whether the implications of the doctrine of which Cyril was in the eyes of Nestorius a champion were necessarily inconsistent with the moral interests which appealed so strongly to Nestorius. But we are concerned to note that these interests could only be satisfied, in his judgement, by a doctrine of the Incarnation which secured a real condescension of God in the Person of the Word, a real assumption to His own Person of real manhood in its own being and characteristics, so that the sphere of the struggle which He underwent was man's own sphere of struggle, and it was manhood that issued invincible in His victory—the pledge of future victories of man. His whole treatment of the question utterly excludes the idea that the protagonist in the drama of man's redemption merely played the part of man, or achieved His end by magical means beyond the reach of men. It attributes the work to a single Person and excludes any notion of a mere external alliance between an individual man and God, while it allows for the double consciousness of Christ to which many a passage of Scripture points. It draws largely, as Nestorius does elsewhere, from the teaching of the Epistle to the Hebrews.

CHAPTER IX

THE EUCHARISTIC TEACHING OF NESTORIUS

HOOKER, it will be remembered, introduces his description of the doctrine of the Sacraments by a careful statement of the doctrine of the Person of our Lord. The theory of the sacraments is that they effect union between man and Christ, and that that union is union with God in Christ. It is necessary therefore to shew that Christ is a Person able to be the medium between man and God. "And forasmuch as there is no union of God with man without that mean between both which is both, it seemeth requisite that we first consider how God is in Christ, then how Christ is in us, and how the Sacraments do serve to make us partakers of Christ. In other things we may be more brief, but the weight of these requireth largeness."[1] Our theory of the Eucharist must, if it be a reasoned theory, correspond to our doctrine of the Person of Christ; and Eucharistic experience will readily furnish analogies by which to illustrate—or even tests by which to determine—our doctrine of the Person of our Lord. In the Eucharist He gives His Body and His Blood. What is it that He gives? The answer to this question may help to determine the answer to the question Who is He that gives?

Eucharistic experience was invoked in early days to refute theories of the Person of our Lord that reduced His human nature to a mere illusion. The incidental character of the

[1] Hooker *Ecclesiastical Polity* bk. v ch. l.

illustrations from the Eucharist which occur, for instance, in the writings of Irenaeus, shew how naturally they came to his mind in combating Gnostic conceptions. The Lord's body was real, because the Eucharistic bread and wine are real and able to nourish our body and blood: they impart to us the gift of eternal life, because they become the very body and the very blood of the incarnate Word of God[1]. So against Nestorius appeal was made to the doctrine of the Eucharist, and what he has to say upon the subject is of value in the indications it gives of the difference between his point of view and that of his opponents. Their *advocatus*, Superianus, hints that there is one argument they use which perhaps it would not be edifying to mention, though by it they confidently support their view of the union of the natures in our Lord. Nestorius urges him to state it without hesitation, even as they would themselves. Superianus states it, and Nestorius discusses it at length.

'*Superianus*. The union ought to be like that of the bread 'when it becomes the body. The body is but one and the same, 'and not two; and that which is thought of (*or* the object of 'thought) is but one—but (one) in that into which it has been 'made, as having been made into it[2], and so that it is no longer 'that which it appears to be, but that which it is thought to 'be (*or* the object of thought). And for this reason it was that 'the Apostle gave a terrible sentence against those who sup- 'posed that the Body of our Lord was "of the common sort"[3], 'speaking to this effect: "If one who transgressed the Law 'of Moses was put to death without mercy when convicted 'out of the mouth of two or three witnesses, of how much 'more severe a sentence is he deserving who has trampled

[1] See Irenaeus *adv. haer.* iv 31 4, *ib.* 51 1, vii 2.

[2] This I take to be the meaning of

ܐܠܐ ܒܗܘ ܕܠܗ ܗܘܐ ܐܝܟ ܕܠܗ.

[3] Heb. x 29: *κοινόν*.

'upon the Son of God and accounted the blood of His testa-'ment, by which he has been sanctified, to be common, and 'has blasphemed the Spirit of grace?"[1] This he said against 'those who accounted the blood and body of God to be the blood 'and body of a man, and wrongly supposed that it was like 'that which is common to all men, and blasphemed that body 'and blood, whereby they had been sanctified, and the Spirit 'of grace, by not confessing it to be the Son of God, con-'substantial (ὁμοούσιος) with God the Father, but saying that 'that body of the Son of God was a human body—though 'He had taken up His body and blood into His own *ousia*, 'and did not leave them to be insulted with the reproach of 'being a human body, but willed that they should be wor-'shipped in His own *ousia*.

'*Nestorius*. Does this illustration then seem insignificant 'to you, that you should pass it over in silence? Yet they set 'great store by it; and so you should not have been so tardy 'in bringing it forward. For if this had escaped my notice 'it would have looked as though I were like those who see the 'mote but not the beam.

'Let us examine it from all points, and see exactly what it 'may import, and what it is that the Divine Scripture wishes to 'make us understand; that so we may not incur the just blame 'of God.

'And first, let us speak here of the Greek word *q'yônôn* '(*κοινόν*). It can mean (1) that which is defiled, (2) what is 'common (*or* universal), (3) participation.

'(1) In the sense of "defiled":—as when [Peter] says in 'the Acts, "I have not eaten anything 'defiled' or unclean"[2].

'(2) In the sense of "common":—as the saying that every-'thing the Apostles had was "in common".

'(3) In the sense of "participation":—as, "the cup of 'confession which we bless, is it not a participation of the

[1] Heb. x 28, 29. [2] Acts x 14.

'blood of Christ? And the bread we break, is it not a partici-'pation of the body of Christ?"[1]

'Again: "He that sanctifies and they that are sanctified are 'of one. Wherefore He was not ashamed to call them (His) 'brethren saying: I will declare Thy name to my brethren; 'in the midst of the congregation I will praise Thee; and again, 'I will rely on Him; and again, I and the sons which God hath 'given me"[2]. Therefore, since the sons participated in the flesh 'and blood, so He also in like manner participated in them[3]. 'Since then some use the word in the sense of "unclean", and '"defiled", or again, of what is "common" (i.e. universal), and 'yet again of "participation"—did the Apostle then use the 'expression, which may fall into three different usages, and, 'without first specifying against what opinion he used it, lay 'down that on this account men were trampling upon the Son 'of God? Which of the three is the correct (meaning)?

'*Superianus.* He uses it against those who think that He 'did not die on our behalf, but died His own death, like all 'men; and that, whether alive or dead, He was as one of the 'sons of men, and possessed nothing over and above: being 'ignorant that He is the Son of God, and His blood the blood 'of God and not of man.

'*Nestorius.* Do you say then that the body and blood are 'the *ousia* of the Son of God, or that the body and blood are '*of* the human *ousia*, but became the nature of the Divinity? 'For, according to what you say, the flesh is not really flesh, 'since it has been changed by means of mixture and union 'into the *ousia* of God the Word; and, forsooth, the blessed 'Apostle soundly rated those who were confessing His body 'and blood, and said that they were holding it to be something 'unclean.

'*Superianus.* He spoke these things not against those who

[1] 1 Cor. x 16. [2] Heb. ii 11—14.

[3] i.e. flesh and blood—as the Syriac shews by the use of the fem.

'altogether denied that it was in truth body; nor yet against 'those who change or destroy the *ousia* of flesh, as it were by 'fire, or make the *ousia* of flesh defiled by means of mixture[1]; 'but against those who confess the flesh and blood, but reckon 'it to be of the common sort.

'*Nestorius.* It appears to me that the opinion which you 'hold is not so much in point against these, but rather against 'those who change the *ousia* of God into the nature of flesh 'and blood, thinking that the *ousia* of the flesh and blood of 'our Lord is not of the common sort, but that it is derived 'from God the Word and not from man.

'*Superianus.* Hence we ought not to answer these persons 'except with rebuke for using contradictory arguments. But 'now discuss those who think that the flesh was from the *ousia* 'of God.

'*Nestorius.* You forget that the Apostle has not said two 'contradictory things; for what he means is this: that "He 'that sanctifies and those who are sanctified" should be "of 'one", and that they should be brethren, of one *ousia* and 'not of one and another (*ousia*), and His sons as springing 'from Him. And he speaks to this effect: "He that sanctifies 'and they that are sanctified are all of one". Wherefore that 'blood also by which we are sanctified and which was shed 'for our sake is "of one", and by this we also are His 'brethren, as of one father. But again we are His sons 'as having the same *ousia* (with Him): in which also we 'are sons. But God the Word has nothing in which He 'and we should be at one, or we be called of one form with 'Him, and so be His brethren. For we have no source of 'resemblance such as sons of the same Father have. Nor 'could we, again, become His sons, since we do not participate 'in one and the same *ousia.* He (the Apostle) then convicts 'those who will not acknowledge that the human blood (of

[1] The text of this last clause is somewhat obscure.

'Christ) is able to sanctify, and who think that it is unclean as 'being the blood of a man. And therefore they deem unclean 'the blood of the testament whereby we have been sanctified 'and saved from death by the true death of a man. This is 'what Blessed Paul says; and he hereby declares that we are '"of one" (nature with Christ's body); and he calls us His 'brethren by reason of that nature which was born of our 'fathers and also died for us. For in that He was born He 'belongs to our race, and we are all "of one". But in that 'He died for us and renewed us in immortality and incor'ruption unto that estate which is to be, we are His sons; for 'He is "Father of the world to come"[1]. Are we not there'fore all together one body? For we all receive of that one 'body, even of that in which He has made us to participate, 'with that very blood and flesh which are of one and the 'same nature (with us). And we are made to participate with 'Him in the resurrection from the dead and in immortality. 'And thus are we in regard to Him, even as the bread is His 'body. "Even", he says, "as that bread is one, so are we all 'one body, for we all receive of that one bread."[2]

'Are we then changed into His flesh, and are we His body: 'and are we no longer the body and blood of man, but His 'body? For one is the bread, and therefore we are all one body, 'because we are the body of Christ. "But you", he says, "are 'the body of Christ, and severally[3] members."[4] Is the bread 'the body of Christ by a change of *ousia*, or are we His body 'by a change, or is the body of the Son of God one in nature 'with God the Word? But if they are one in nature, it is no 'more bread, nor again is it body. The Apostle, then, says 'that they who think the body of the Son of God to be some'thing defiled trample upon the Son of God in the sense that

[1] Is. ix 6 (the readingof ℵ$^{c.a}$A). [2] I Cor. x 17.

[3] Lit. 'in your parts'. Syr. vg. has 'in your place'. Gr. καὶ μέλη ἐκ μέρους.

[4] I Cor. xii 27.

'they reject and deny it. Not of those who confess the body 'to be of our nature [did he say that] they account it as something defiled; but rather that it was given for our redemption 'because it was pure and without blemish, and preserved from 'sins, having undertaken death on behalf of all sins as an 'offering to God. But if we are not all of one (nature) we 'have not rightly been called His brethren and His sons; nor 'again are we His bread and His body. But if all these things 'truly belong to Christ, we (also) are His body and of one 'nature with Him, because we are the same that the *ousia* of 'His body also is' (*Bazaar of Heraclides* pp. 27 ff.).

And later on in the book Nestorius touches on the matter again, to illustrate the coexistence of the two natures (and their *ousias*) in Christ.

'How is it that, when He said over the bread "This is my 'body", He did not say that the bread was not bread and His 'body not body? But He said "bread" and "body" as 'shewing what it is in *ousia*. But we are aware that the bread 'is bread in nature and in *ousia*. Yet Cyril wishes to persuade 'us to believe that the bread is His body by faith and not by 'nature:—that what it is not as to *ousia*, this it becomes by 'faith' (*ib.* p. 326).

When our Lord called the bread His body, Nestorius argues, He shewed that His human nature (with its *ousia*) was real and did not simply exist in *idea* as the object of faith; whereas Cyril's doctrine of the unification of the natures in His Person would imply, he holds, the existence of the human nature merely in idea.

The view of the Eucharist which is represented as that of Cyril's school, it is evident, approximates closely to the doctrine of "transubstantiation", the *ousia* of the bread and wine becoming the *ousia* of the Word of God and ceasing to remain real bread and wine; whereas Nestorius champions the view that they remain in their own *ousia*, though inasmuch as that *ousia* is the same as the *ousia* of His human nature they are His body and blood. It is because He really has a human *ousia* that we who are human can be His sons and brethren, and that the bread and wine become means of union with Him. The Word of God as such, in His own *ousia*, has nothing in common with our *ousia*; and we, as men, have no share in the divine *ousia*. According to our own Article, the doctrine that the *ousia* of the bread and wine does not remain after consecration "overthroweth the nature of a sacrament". According to Nestorius, apparently, a similar doctrine of the Eucharist, that did away with the reality of the bread and wine, corresponds to a doctrine of the Person of Christ which, by transmuting His human *ousia* into the divine *ousia*, annihilates the reality of the Incarnation.

Precisely the same conception underlies his reply to Cyril's eleventh anathema, directed against the denial that the "flesh of the Lord" was "life-giving"[1].

[1] Cf. also passages in Loofs *Nestoriana* pp. 227—230, 355—357; and Cyril *c. Nest.* iv 3—6.

CHAPTER X

NESTORIUS'S STATEMENT OF HIS OWN POSITION POSITIVELY AND IN RELATION TO CYRIL'S

THE examination of the teaching of Nestorius which we have conducted up to this point seems to be steadily leading to the conclusion that he was the victim of much misunderstanding, that many of his sayings and arguments were misrepresented, and that the doctrines attributed to him were not his. I have said already that this is the conclusion to which I myself have been led by the attempt to understand what he really meant; and I have quoted largely from his own words. I do not think I have brought too sympathetic a mind to bear upon them, or that any isolation of them from their context (which has, however, been avoided as much as possible) could in any event be favourable to Nestorius. It was however on the evidence of extracts and of such isolated sayings that he was condemned, and his Western judges refused (as he believed) to consider what he really meant. He may be allowed now to address himself at length, without interruption, to a wider world of the West than he could ever have conceived —or at least to that small part of it that still considers the questions which to him were more than life and death worthy of an hour's attention. Let him, then, speak for himself and state in his own words his own position, and how he believes it to be related to Cyril's.

At the end of the first part of the discussion in the *Bazaar of Heraclides* Superianus asks Nestorius to pass in review briefly the theories of the Incarnation to which he is opposed, and then to state his own theory clearly so that no one can misunderstand him. The section is headed by the translator "Concerning the Faith"[1].

'*Superianus.* Since then there are many who accept the 'faith of the 318 which was set forth at Nicaea, even among 'those who hold divergent beliefs and interpret in divers ways 'the divine Scriptures, and understand the words "He was 'incarnate" and "He became man" in different senses: may 'it please your Piety to pass in review their opinions and 'notions; and do you write for my information what is your 'opinion and which view you approve as correct; that you may 'give no occasion to those who seek one for misrepresenting 'you.

'*Nestorius.* (A) Some of them say then that the incarnation 'of Christ our Lord took place in fancy and semblance only, 'to the end that He might be seen of men, and that we might 'learn about Him, and that He might give the grace of the 'Gospel to every one. And they say that just as He appeared 'to each of the saints, even so in the last times He appeared 'to all men.

'(B) Others say that the very Divine *ousia* itself became 'flesh, so that the *ousia* of flesh should be in His (God's) very '*ousia* instead of the nature of men; and that He might conduct 'Himself as a man and suffer, and set free our nature. For 'one, they say, that became man not in His own *ousia* but in 'outward fashion assuredly did not set us free, but utterly 'deceived us, since He appeared in outward fashion only, and 'seemed to suffer on our behalf, whereas He did not suffer.

'(C) Others again confess that God became incarnate in 'flesh, as a complement (*or* for the completion) of the nature—'instead of a soul—being physically incarnate in flesh, so as to 'do and suffer; and that He was suffering physically the natural

[1] *Bazaar of Heraclides* pp. 70 ff.

'passions of the body: being in His own nature impassible, 'yet passible in the physical incarnation. After the manner of 'the soul, they say, which of its nature is not susceptible of the 'passions of the body, and feels neither pain nor hunger, yet 'by a physical dispensation suffers physically the passions of 'the body while physically united to it—(so He became in'carnate) that He might act and suffer for our sake physically. 'And not in imagination or in outward show, or in a different 'nature, but in His own nature He set us free from death and 'corruption.

'(D) Others confess that He became incarnate in a body '*and a soul*, as a complement of the nature; and that God the 'Word was in the place of the intelligence: so that He should 'take the place of the intelligence in the body and the soul; 'and that He should act and suffer in the nature of man for 'our sake. For He came, they say, to do away with that 'intelligence which transgressed the commandment and was 'disobedient to God, and to be instead of the intelligence in 'the soul and body; and not in semblance without substance '(*q'nômâ*), or in a different nature, nor yet in an inanimate 'body.

'(E) Others say concerning that flesh in which God the 'Word was incarnate, that in flesh endowed with a soul He was 'incarnate; yet He (Christ) did not exercise sensation by 'means of its nature, nor did He understand by means of the 'soul; but He understood and felt by the operation of God 'the Word;—yet the soul itself also felt and understood, and 'the body too, and it was as an instrument (ὄργανον) in the 'nature. Yet we do not, they say, divide Christ into an instru'ment and an operator, for (here) instrument and operator 'operate together.

'(F) Others confess two natures in Christ before the 'union, and hold that each one of the natures is to be con'sidered as in its own nature—God the Word in the Father 'and in the Holy Spirit, and man in the flesh. But after the 'union, they say, two natures are not thought of; since they 'have been united in *ousia* and have been made one out of 'two. And they change them from one nature to another: 'so that He may strictly be man, and, He the same, God 'also; and so that God may act as man, and die for our sake 'as God, and rise by His own power.

'(G) But others[1] say that the incarnation of our Lord was 'in flesh endowed with a soul,—a rational soul, and one capable 'of knowledge and complete in its nature and in its powers 'and natural functions—and not in seeming only, nor by a 'change of *ousia*, nor yet by a physical substitution for the 'nature of body and soul or for the intelligence. Nor was it '(sc. the incarnation) a welding of two natures into one; nor 'were the natures changed one into another; nor was it (sc. the 'incarnation) for a supplying of the natural functions, in such 'a way that the flesh should not act in its own nature. But 'they attribute the things of both natures to One, while they 'vindicate to each the proper things of its own nature. The '*ousia* of the Godhead is preserved and is impassible while it 'is in the *ousia* of flesh; and the flesh also remains in the *ousia* 'of flesh while it is in the nature and person of the Godhead. 'For the body is one, and both natures are one Son; for God 'the Word in flesh is not said to be another, apart from Him 'who is in our flesh; nor the flesh in like manner: but in the 'Son it is in God the Word; that He may act completely in 'the nature of men, inasmuch as He is man, and remain as 'God, in that He is by nature God; and that, being without 'sin and having kept the likeness [ὁμοίωσις] of His own image, 'He might be delivered up to death for our redemption[2];

[1] This is evidently the beginning of Nestorius's statement of his own position.

[2] The text is confused; literally it runs: 'He who, because (He was) without sin, and when He had kept [............?], should be delivered up to death for our redemption, [and when] He had kept the likeness of His own image'. I conjecture that the words 'the likeness of His own image'

'†that forthwith that saying should come to pass—not however 'as regards the form [μορφή][1]—"He received a name better 'than all names"[2]; that so the nature of man should be exalted. 'But an *ousia* that is no more that of man but that of God 'the Word cannot receive (further) honour or exaltation†[3]. 'It is our nature that has been honoured in another nature, 'and not in our own nature. For the exaltation of our 'nature to that "name better than all names" is shared in 'common by the human nature of Him who is the exaltation 'of that which abides in His *ousia*; which human nature is 'able to be what it is (i.e. keep its identity) whilst in the *ousia* 'of God the Word. For this is an incomparable exaltation; 'but a change of *ousia* into *ousia* puts an end to that *ousia* 'which should have been exalted, and likewise to the exaltation 'itself. Nor is it a condescension on the part of God the 'Word if *He* has changed into another *ousia*, since this latter 'does not belong to that nature which originally condescends. 'But this is the meaning of "condescend":—If, for example, 'a king makes himself as his subjects, he is said to "con-'descend"—though he is truly king—and because of the 'garments of subjection that he has put on he is said indeed 'to have condescended, for that in outward fashion he employs 'that which is proper to himself in that which belongs to

should follow 'when He had kept', and that the second 'He had kept' should be omitted.

[1] The Syriac word ܕܡܘܬܐ, *d'mûthâ*, is the natural equivalent for the two Greek words ὁμοίωσις (Gen. i 26) and μορφή (Phil. ii 6, 7). When therefore there is reference to the passage in Gen. we should understand that it translates the former Greek word, when to Phil. ii the latter. Now all through this work Nestorius appears to use μορφή in a strongly theological sense which is practically equivalent to the sense he gives to φύσις (*k'yânâ*, "nature"), ὑπόστασις (*q'nômâ*), and οὐσία (*ousia*). This is certainly so whenever there is a reference to Phil. ii.

[2] Phil. ii 9.

[3] The words between †...† represent the best sense I can obtain from the Syriac, which is obscure.

‘another, that, just as others are under the institutions of the
‘law, so he too may come under the law of his own good-
‘pleasure, being the while himself king and master of legal
‘institutions. For there is no exaltation if He is exalted to
‘His own nature: but only if He should give it that which it
‘had not before—not that He should take away from it that
‘which it was. For if the exaltation is of that which previously
‘existed, and the humiliation also is the humiliation of that
‘nature which previously existed—of what then was the exalta-
‘tion? First he (the Apostle) says of an *ousia*[1], that it was
‘exalted; then of the name into which it was exalted, that it
‘was "above all names". Now if thou take away the *ousias*
‘from receiving exaltation and humiliation, there is no *ousia* to
‘have been exalted. Therefore, that "He humbled Himself"—
‘he (the Apostle) says this of a union of good-pleasure, and
‘of the incarnation, and of the kind of humiliation which He
‘shewed in taking the form of a servant. And again he says
‘that what took place was a union of good-pleasure, not of
‘nature: "in fashion He was found as a man", not "in *ousia*".
‘For "the form of a servant" is "in the form of God": "the
‘form of God" became "in fashion as a man"—for in His
‘own *ousia* He was God—that both humiliation might be
‘attributed to that which took the form of a servant, and
‘exaltation to the form of the servant, in that it received "a
‘name better than all names". (The union) is not to be
‘conceived of as a change of *ousia*—either into another *ousia*
‘or unto a physical compounding into a single nature—but as
‘one of good-pleasure, through humiliation and exaltation.
‘For a physical (union) implies the passible and changeable,
‘such as a nature which is created and made, not the increate
‘and unchangeable and unalterable.

‘Wherefore in the incarnation this man (Cyril)[2] assigns

[1] Cf. Phil. ii 7, 9. Note the substitution of οὐσία for μορφή.

[2] There is no doubt that ܗܢܐ (οὗτος) here refers to Cyril: as will appear further on. The ‘wherefore’ will denote: ‘in view of what we

'nothing to the control of the man, but only to God the Word '—in such a way that He employs the human nature for His 'own operations. So Arius and Eunomius and Apollinarius 'taught: for in name they say that Christ is God, but in fact 'they deprive Him of being God; for they assign His human 'things by nature to His (i.e. the Word's) own *ousia.* And 'they make void the generations of the descent of the Messiah, 'and the promises to the Fathers that from their seed the 'Messiah should spring according to the flesh. For this reason 'it was that the Evangelists recorded all those things that truly 'shew the human nature, lest perhaps, on account of His 'Divinity, it should not be believed that He is man also; and to 'shew moreover that He it is that was affirmed by the promises. 'And for this cause he (the Evangelist) mentioned the Blessed 'Virgin as being a woman betrothed to a man; and wrote 'even his (Joseph's) name and race and craft and place: that 'there might be nothing to cause doubt and prevent her from 'being believed to be truly a woman. For the same reason he 'wrote also of His being despised, and the announcement of 'His conception, and His birth, and the manger, and the 'making known of Him that was born with her that bare Him, 'that it might be established that He was truly man: the cradle 'in a manger, the wrapping in swaddling clothes, with those 'things that are natural to babes: the gifts offered for His 'sake, His gradual growth in stature and wisdom before God 'and men, His conduct in the world, His watchings, His sub-'jection, the petition He made, and all His fulfilling of the 'Law, His baptism and the voice that was uttered concerning 'Him that He is the Son—even He who is Son from the 'womb by the union—the witness from the marking of His 'conduct, the voice of the Father, the manifestation of the 'Holy Spirit, His earthly life full of care for us, and not

have said it is clear that Cyril' etc. Possibly the underlying Greek was διὰ τί; or διατί; and was read by the translator as διότι.

'in the phantom or the mere fashion of a man, but in human 'nature and body, and a reasonable soul which thought and 'reasoned in the nature of men: that He might be all that He 'was by the nature of man without ceasing from the union 'with God the Word. But the union was not one of natures 'into a single nature, nor a confusion, nor a change, nor 'a changing of *ousia*—whether of God into man, or of man 'into God—nor a mingling of natures, nor a compounding 'into one nature, so that they should be mingled and be 'affected by one another as being physically united as to 'natural functions. Now all these things they make void by 'a union of nature and of *hypostasis* (*q'nômâ*), and they take 'away from Him all those things which He has by His human 'nature and assign them by nature to God the Word: His 'human fear, His betrayal, His trial, His answering, the smiting 'on His cheek, the sentence of the cross, His setting forth, 'the laying of the cross upon His shoulder, the bearing of His 'cross and its being taken away from Him and laid on others, 'the crown of thorns, the crimson garments, the setting up of 'the cross, the crucifixion, the driving of the nails, the gall that 'was offered to Him, the other acts of violence, the delivering 'up of His spirit to His Father, the bowing of His head, the 'taking down of His body from the cross, the embalming, the 'burial, the resurrection on the third day, His manifestation 'in the body, His speaking and teaching:—(all which things 'were done) that men might not suppose that it was the 'phantom of a body that He had, but truly a body of flesh. 'And indeed the body and soul were no phantom and illusion, 'but true and natural. Nothing is concealed: all the human 'things which men now blush to say of Him the Evangelists 'were not ashamed to say: though these persons do not blush 'to attribute these things to the Divine nature by means of a 'union of physical *hypostasis* (*q'nômâ*)—God suffering the 'passions of the body which is physically united, thirsting 'and hungering and being needy and anxious, thinking, and 'making petition that He may conquer these very human 'things that He suffers, and fight against human nature to 'the undoing of our glorying and the undoing of our redemp- 'tion. And these men will make void the proper things of 'God the Word also, and make them human. That He (the 'Word) should act and suffer physically in His own nature 'by physical sensation, receiving sufferings physically by His 'own *ousia*, even as the body suffers by means of the soul and 'the soul by the body—this it would be a frightful and horrible 'thing for us to think literally or to say to men endowed with 'the least intelligence concerning the Son (making Him) a 'slave and a creature, (and asserting) that He was changed from 'impassible to passible, or from immortal to mortal, or from 'unchangeable to changeable. Even if one should make Him 'into the *ousia* of the angels, and impassible, and say that He 'does not act by His own nature and operation and power, 'but by that which He has become—He would flee away from 'being of like passions even with such a nature. But one that 'is physically united cannot flee; for even if He did not 'physically suffer the passions of the body, yet psychically He 'would suffer instead of the soul; for He would be instead of 'a soul that did not think as an intelligence; and in matters of 'the intelligence He would be instead of the intelligence; and 'He would be man in outward fashion only, and would be 'a deluder in the fashion of a man: as though He possessed 'the proper things of soul and body and intelligence, while 'these were deprived of their natural operations.

'Such things are said by those who are the would-be 'orthodox—to wit, that He is of the impassible and inde- 'fectible and unchangeable and unalterable nature of the 'Father—and then, like the Jews who, setting Him at naught 'while they called Him the Messiah, actually crucified Him, 'these persons give to Him the title of an unchangeable and 'impassible and indefectible nature, and then attribute to Him 'all the passions and defects of the body, and assign all the 'things of the soul and of the intelligence to God the Word 'by means of a hypostatic union. And, like those who 'change Him from His nature, they say once and for all that 'He is impassible and immutable and unchangeable, and 'henceforth forbid it to be said that He is immortal and 'impassible and unchangeable; and they are enraged at any 'one who says repeatedly that God the Word is impassible: '"You have heard it once", they say, "that is enough for 'you". And they maintain two perfect natures, of the God-'head and the manhood, and then maintain a change of the 'natures by the union; assigning nothing either to the man-'hood or to the Godhead; making these the natural things of 'the manhood and those the natural things of the Godhead, 'and yet not keeping the Divine things in the (Divine) nature, 'since they make God the Word to be in the nature of both '*ousias*, hiding away the man and all His proper things—He 'for whose sake and in whom the incarnation took place, and 'by whom we are freed from the captivity of death.

'In name, then, they pose as orthodox, but in fact they 'are Arians; and they undo the perfection of God the Word by 'all the naturally human things they say about Him: such as, 'that He should act from the union of a physical *hypostasis* '(*q'nômâ*), and suffer naturally all human things. And, that 'He employed human nature, it was not so that the manhood 'itself should act and suffer for our sakes, but that God the 'Word should so act: not that He should employ a person, 'but a nature—for a union as to person is impassible[1], and 'this is orthodox; but the other implies passibility, and is the 'invention of heretics who fight against the nature of the 'Only-begotten.

'To whichever union a man inclines he is sure to claim the 'credit of orthodoxy and not the reproach of heresy. Now all 'his (Cyril's) contrary arguments concerning the hypostatic

[1] i.e. the Word can remain impassible in such a union.

'union he has written without reserve in his "Chapters", and 'much has been written by many about them. But it will not 'do for us to make our book interminable by treating of things 'that are obvious; we have rather to reveal to all the gradual 'growth of this species of impiety; the which having myself 'foreseen, I have not withdrawn from what is right and 'orthodox, nor will I unto death. And even though through 'ignorance all oppose me—and even some of the orthodox—'and are unwilling to hear and learn of me: well, let them 'have time to learn from the heretics themselves by fighting 'against them, even as they have fought against him who 'fought on their behalf.'

Another passage in which Nestorius freely expresses his own conceptions in relation to those of Cyril must also be quoted at length if justice is to be done it.

'But perhaps some one will say: You have only read 'us a letter. Read also the blasphemies that are in your 'writings. You have perhaps written a letter with reserve 'and caution, according to the views of him to whom it was 'written. But your doctrines, which have been stated 'authoritatively by you, clearly interpret your meaning. And 'so a letter is not enough for us; but we have examined your 'doctrines that we might accurately learn everything about 'you. And not even so did we dare to assume authority, but 'we have set the doctrines of the Fathers also before us, and 'have compared them with these; and so, having made our 'examination with all accuracy, we have also given sentence, 'adducing the Fathers against whom you have fought. Where-'fore, whereas you were called and did not answer, we have 'done all things justly: we have condemned your letter, we 'have examined your teachings, and we seek also to set up 'the teaching of the Fathers as law. What then ought we to 'do that we have not done? This man[1] was present and said 'the things that ought to be said, and taught also; but you 'withdrew at that time, and now you blame and slander us. 'Why do you not accuse yourself instead of us? For we 'did not judge you in secret, but openly. If we omitted 'anything, if we acted on insufficient knowledge, tell us now, 'if this be the case, how it is—though, if we were not 'justly roused against you, you ought to have said so then, 'not now.

'For my part, though I could accuse them of having done 'and omitted many things, I pass on now from this subject, 'lest any should say, "he treats immoderately of these matters". 'But I will convict them of judging me unjustly from these very 'things that they did against me. For they spoke deceitfully 'and led many astray, though they did not keep this examina-'tion secret, but,...[2] as this man wished—for he wished the 'matters not to be duly examined lest he himself should stand 'condemned; for he persuaded them all, as one who should 'know the secrets of the heart, and they who were in collusion 'with him so presented the matter to the many as though he 'were the vindicator of Christ's Divinity, and was preventing 'me from maintaining the opposite. And so he carried them 'all away into opposition to me, insomuch that they would 'not listen to a word until I should utterly make an end of 'Christ's humanity,—as though I were maintaining to him '(Cyril) that Christ was man in *ousia*, but God by an equality 'of honour. And he employed prejudice against me, and was 'saying against me, making God a man, that Christ should not 'be considered to be anything at all save only God the Word. 'And I of necessity aimed my arguments against him, main-'taining that He is also man; and I proved it to him from the 'Divine Scriptures and from the Fathers. And this also he

[1] Clearly Cyril is meant.

[2] Some words seem to have dropped out, for no good sense is obtained by taking the 'but' with what follows.

'used against me, as though I had said that Christ was man 'only. For when I demanded[1] that he should make con-'fession in this matter he was unwilling to confess; whilst 'he tried to keep secret that of which I was speaking and 'making confession. For I was not accusing him of not 'confessing Christ to be God, but of refusing to say that 'Christ is perfect man in nature and operations, and that 'God the Word did not become the nature of man but is '*in* the nature and operations of man—so that God the Word 'should be both by nature[2]. And these things I will demon-'strate from the things that were written when he took passages 'from my teaching and from his own, which latter—whether 'they were so from the first, or whether, out of enmity to me 'and through the machinations of heretics, he changed them 'to the opposite sense—are really like those of Arius, since, 'inconsistently with the *ousia* of God, he attributed all the 'human things to the nature of God the Word through a union 'of *hypostasis* (*q'nômâ*), as though He (the Word) should suffer 'all human passions by physical sensation.

'"From the book of Nestorius", he says, "from the '17th quire, *On the Faith*":—From what book of mine, and 'from what 17th quire did you bring forward what you wanted 'when there was none to gainsay you?—But I do not care 'so much about this if the passages adduced were clear, and if 'they required to be discussed. But concerning those things 'by which he led many astray and drew them from the Faith, 'as though an examination had been made of the Acts (ὑπομνή-'ματα) (of the Council), I wish to persuade you all: those

[1] Reading ܕܬܒܥ ܗܘܝܬ for ܕܬܒܥ ܗܘܐ ('he demanded'). As the text stands it might be translated: 'in the case of that (other) man, when he demanded that he should make confession and he was unwilling to confess'. If this be correct John of Antioch is probably referred to.

[2] i.e. the result of Cyril's refusal to confess Christ as perfect man is that the Word must be both natures at once. It is fairly obvious from the Syriac that this is the meaning.

'things, namely, of which they accused me with prejudice '(*or* prejudged me)[1] without examination; that those who 'have received my (account) and his without investigation[2]... '.................."When the Divine Scripture is about to speak 'of the birth of Christ from the Virgin, or of the death, it is 'nowhere found that it puts 'God,' but either 'Christ', or 'the 'Son', or 'the Lord'; for all three of these titles are indications 'of the two natures: sometimes of this, sometimes of that, and 'sometimes of this and that. For example, when the Scripture 'relates to us the birth from the Virgin, what does it say? ''God sent His Son'. It does not say 'God sent God the 'Word', but it takes the word that declares the two natures. 'Because the Son is God and man, it says 'God sent His Son, 'and He was made from a woman'[3]. And when thou seest 'the name given, which declares both natures, thou wilt call 'the Child of the Blessed Virgin 'Son'; for the Virgin mother 'of Christ bore the Son of God. But because the Son of 'God is twofold in natures, she did not[4] bear the Son of God, 'but the manhood, which is Son on account of the Son who 'is united thereto".

'I ask you now to examine these statements carefully. 'I pass over what they have left out[5]—and clearly they have 'not even preserved the connexion. It is for these statements 'then that he accuses me of dividing up and setting apart the

[1] *Praeiudicio me damnauerunt* is the meaning.

[2] A line is wanting in the MS. Probably the words contained a reference to the work of Nestorius from which what follows is quoted. The passages will be found in *Sermo* x of Loofs's collection pp. 265 ff. and similar ones elsewhere. See *supra* p. 62.

[3] Gal. iv 4.

[4] This negative is not found in the Greek text printed by Loofs (*ib.* p. 274), which runs ἐγέννησε μὲν τὸν υἱὸν τοῦ θεοῦ, ἀλλ' ἐγέννησε τὴν ἀνθρωπότητα, ἥτις ἐστὶν υἱὸς διὰ τὸν συνημμένον υἱόν.

[5] Evidently this passage is one of those that are said above to have been quoted by Cyril in a garbled form. It *is* a little shorter than the Greek; but the omissions are unimportant.

'Godhead on the one hand and the manhood on the other; 'but of employing the words "honour" and "equality" of the 'One, inasmuch as there is a drawing together of things 'separate, by love, not as to *ousias*. Thus he accuses me on 'the score of both the Godhead and the manhood; for "God 'the Word", he says, "is flesh and man, but the manhood 'is Son and Lord (and) God: and this came about (forsooth) 'by love and cohesion!" This is his chief misrepresentation. 'You must be continually on the alert then—for you are the 'judges in this matter—and if you find me to be of this way 'of thinking you must condemn me. And for my part, I will 'condemn myself, and even beg of you to visit my guilt with 'retribution[1], as it is just, even though I should make ten 'thousand supplications to you, and bring forward all manner 'of arguments in justification of my not employing the word '"*ousia*" but merely "love", and maintaining that by this He 'is called Lord and Christ and Son. But if I say the contrary: 'let them shew that the union was of *nature*[2] and that the 'union was *a nature*. But I from a union of *natures*[3] speak 'of one person, one equality, one honour, one authority, one 'lordship. In short, in whatsoever things the person of this 'and that (nature) is by nature, in the same these (natures) 'also are in the union of the one person. For a person is *of* '*natures*: it is not *a nature*; and it is *by nature*, but is not '*a nature*. For the Son of God the Father is by nature con-'substantial with[4] the Father; and whatever is in the nature of 'the Father, this the Son also is. But not everything that the

[1] This seems to be the force of the expression

ܕܬܩܒܠܘܢ ܒܡܫܠܡܢܘܬܐ ܠܚܘܒܝ

lit.: 'that you would receive with handing over (to punishment) my guilt'

[2] i.e., evidently from the context, into one nature.

[3] Text has 'nature'; but it seems necessary to read the plural, as a little below.

[4] Lit. 'Son of the nature of': a common Syriac equivalent for ὁμοούσιος.

'Son is by nature as a person is the Father also; for Son, which 'He is by nature, the Father is not: nor is the Son Father; 'for He is in the nature of the Father, and is by nature Son. 'For they are distinct in person, but not distinct in *ousia* and 'nature, but one, without division, without severance, without 'distinction, in all things that the person has by nature. 'So it is by person that He (the Son) is distinguished.

'But not so as regards the union of the Godhead and 'the manhood—He (i.e. the Word) is not by the union in all 'those things that the person by its nature is, so that in the 'one person [He should become] another *ousia*. For He took 'him (man) into His person—not into the (Divine) *ousia* or 'nature, so that he should be either consubstantial (i.e. ὁμοούσιος) 'with the Father or else another son altogether—and not one 'and the same Son[1]. For the manhood is the person of the 'Godhead, and the Godhead is the person of the manhood, 'but they are distinct in nature, and distinct in the union.

'Examine, now, and see what sort of things that man '(i.e. Cyril) has written: "One (i.e. Nestorius) who attributes 'two natures to the Son, and says that each of these is separate '(*or* independent)[2], removing and distinguishing God apart, 'and the man apart." Now if I had said without qualification '"God" and "man", and not "two natures, one Christ", you 'would have had a pretext for misrepresenting me, as though 'I should call the man "God and man", in that I spoke of '"two natures" and "God". I did not say that the Man is 'two natures—even though He should be called God because 'of the union; nor again did I call God two natures—even 'though He should be called flesh in the union. You have 'not the least excuse for misrepresentation because I said that 'the one "Son" and "Christ" indicate two natures. But

[1] Nestorius argues elsewhere that a union of two natures into one must either result in the loss of one in the other, or else produce a nature that is different from both the original ones.

[2] ܒܗ ܘܠܗ.

'I said that the Son is God and man. First I had said that 'the name "Christ" and "Son" indicates the two natures; 'and then I went on immediately to mention the natures. But 'that the Son is God and man,—this is not said without 'qualification (lit. by itself), but "He is two natures" is 'added. But thou (Cyril) art enraged against me—for I cannot 'think otherwise—for not saying that God the Word is both 'natures by a change of *ousia*. But is it this that I have said— 'that the man was in human nature, and that the man is 'Son by the union, and not by nature—is it this that troubles 'you (plur.)? Or is it that which he also has said: that 'when flesh was born He (the Word) is said to have been 'born? for he clearly reckons the birth of His flesh to be 'His (the Word's) birth. Thus he also has said that flesh 'was born: but he makes it His (the Word's) own. What 'then is new in what I have said: to wit, that when the man 'was born the Son of God is said to have been born from 'Mary the Virgin? since the humanity itself is Son of God 'by the union with the Son, but not by nature. For by the 'union God the Word made the things of the flesh His own: 'not that the Divinity is born in the birth which is of the 'flesh, nor again that the flesh was naturally born in the 'birth of the Divinity: but by the union with the flesh God 'is called flesh; and flesh, by the union with the Son, (i.e.) 'God the Word, is called Son. Or was He not united, and 'are we misrepresenting Him?

'Who has led you astray? Is this agreement one (charac- 'teristic) of those who are in error?[1] For this agreement is in 'regard to the two natures. Now that the words "Son" and '"Christ" and "Lord" indicate two natures even he (Cyril) 'has proclaimed. "The natures", he says, "which are brought

[1] Lit. 'Is this agreement of those who are in error?' The genitive may be objective, and thus equivalent to "with"; if so Nestorius means that he has shewn Cyril to hold the same view as himself about the two natures, and he asks: 'Is Cyril then in agreement with heretics?'

'together into a true union are different; but of the two there 'is one Son, while the natures continue without confusion 'in the union, the difference of the natures not being de- 'stroyed by the union."[1] And again: "The flesh is Son 'by the union, but not by nature, ...[2] for that is not foreign 'to Him with which He sat with the Father". And Ambrose 'has said: "Though in two (characters) the Son of God 'speaks—since in Him there are two natures—it is He that 'speaks. Nor does He always speak in one kind: behold 'Him now in glory, and now in the sufferings of a man. For 'as God He teaches things divine, because He is the Word; 'but as man He teaches human things, because He speaks 'in our *ousia*. 'This is the living bread that came down 'from heaven': this bread is the body, even as He said: ''This bread that I will give you is my body that came down': 'this is He whom the Father sanctified and sent into the 'world'". Does not the Scripture itself teach you that the 'Godhead has no need of sanctification, but the flesh. Why 'have you set aside these utterances and anathematized mine? 'for I have said nothing different....'[3]

These two passages, which follow one another in the *Bazaar of Heraclides*, may be left without remark. Some of the phrases and arguments used in them have already been examined, and further comment would be superfluous. But the space for which Nestorius can be allowed to speak in his own person, pending the publication of the entire book, may be extended to let us hear him on the theme that "distinction of natures does not imply local or any other interval between them". The passage is from the later part of the book and has in view the terms of the *eirenicon* between Cyril and the

[1] See the first of the letters of Cyril read at Ephesus.

[2] Three dots in MS seem to denote words omitted from context.

[3] Here there is a lacuna of 12 fols. in the MS, the leaves being torn out (according to the writer of our copy).

Antiochenes (the "Easterns") who had been on the side of Nestorius, to whom they were linked by every tie of country and friendship and theological tradition, though in the hour of his greatest need—the plain fact must be written down—they deserted him. The supporters of Nestorius, including the Emperor himself, were cowed: they dared not resist the clamour of clergy and monks and people. Cyril's "friends at court" were more influential than the friends of Nestorius, and Cyril himself had been trained in the school of his uncle Theophilus and left no means of securing the victory unused. But though the Antiochenes could abandon Nestorius himself to his fate, and perhaps allow themselves to be persuaded that he had really erred in some points of his exposition and argument; they could not give up the doctrine of the Incarnation which he had championed, however onesidedly or unwisely, and they could not believe that Cyril was really sound in the faith of the Fathers. There was imminent risk that the whole patriarchate of Antioch, the whole of the Church of the East—as the East was counted then, would refuse to fall into line with Alexandria and the West. This was more than even Cyril could face without a qualm. So then took place between the Easterns and Cyril that quieter discussion of the question on its merits which Nestorius had passionately desired. The Easterns acquiesced in the condemnation of their unfortunate champion; but for the rest they held their ground so firmly that Cyril had to content himself with the Easterns' acceptance of the term *Theotokos* interpreted in a sense that would have satisfied Nestorius himself. The terms of the gloss could indeed be collected from his own words. And ever after Cyril, suspected by his own school of thought of having made concessions which were inconsistent with the kind of union of the "substances" that they and he believed in, busied himself to explain that the Easterns did not really mean what they said or what Nestorius had meant. It is to these efforts of Cyril that Nestorius refers in the following passage, but it is particularly for the sake of its positive statement of his own position that it is cited here.

'I say, adhering to the Divine Scriptures and teachings, 'that two natures were united. When I mention "God the 'Word", this is in regard of nature, but when I speak of Him 'as "Son", this is in regard of the person: but He is one 'and the same God the Word. In the same way when I men'tion "God", this is as to nature: but "Father", "Son" and '"Holy Spirit" belong to person. Thus the Godhead is one, 'but the persons are three; for the Father is God and the Son 'is God and the Holy Spirit is God. The persons are not 'without the *ousia*[1]. So in like manner as regards Christ: 'there are two natures, one of God the Word, and one of the 'manhood; but there is one person of the Son, which same 'person the manhood also employs, and one [of the] man, 'which same the Godhead also employs—not in nature, but 'in the natural ("physical") person of the natures. For the 'natures remain without confusion even in the union. And 'the natures are not without person[2], nor was the person[3] 'without *ousia*. Nor, as in the case of an animal nature, 'was the union for the completing of one living thing, which 'in order to be complete has taken of both natures, but of two 'complete natures. From one nature the other can be under'stood by means of appropriation,—not by nature, but by 'the natural ("physical") person of the natures....[4]

'*Cyril.* [Quoting another passage from Nestorius to shew that he means something quite different from the Easterns.]

[1] This argument is aimed at the letter of Cyril to Acacius of Melitene, in which he explains that the Antiochenes accept the distinction of natures in Christ only as a mental one—denoting the natures which were united into one. Nestorius discusses this letter at length.

[2] The text has 'persons': but Nestorius has consistently denied duality of persons. The Greek was probably ἀπρόσωποι, "impersonal"; i.e. the natures were not left without personality, inasmuch as they both had the same person.

[3] Singular here.

[4] *Bazaar of Heraclides* pp. 310, 311.

'He names two natures, and separates them from one 'another, setting God apart by Himself and similarly the man 'by himself, who is conjoined to God only by proximity and 'equality of honour and authority; for he speaks thus: "God 'is not distinguished from Him that is seen. Because of that 'which is not separated I do not separate the honour: I separate 'the natures: I unite the worship".'[1]

[Cyril says this is something different from what the Easterns mean. Nestorius goes on for several pages to point out that when he says he does not separate the honour and the worship he means it—he gives the united honour and worship to the person. He insists that what he means by the passage is a union of two complete and distinct natures in one person.]

'It (the union) is into one person; and in this it consists. 'For God the Word did not employ an inanimate body, nor 'yet a soul devoid of will and understanding, nor was he 'instead of the soul or the intelligence; for this doctrine 'distinguishes the Church of the Arians and Apollinarians, 'which does not accept the union of two complete natures. 'I do not separate the natures that have been united by removal 'or isolation; nor yet do I speak of a conjunction of love and 'proximity, as in the case with those who are apart and are 'united by love and not as to *ousias*; nor again do I say that 'the union is one of equality of honour and authority, but of 'natures, and of complete natures; and by a bringing together 'of the *ousias* I posit a union without confusion. By "one 'honour" and "one authority", then, I mean a union of natures, 'and not a unity of honour and of authority....Where have 'I said in these passages that I "separate the natures from each 'other, and speak of God the Word apart and of the man 'apart"? or that "they are conjoined by a proximity of love 'and by equality of honour or authority"? For by saying "I 'do not separate God from Him that is seen", I do not imply

[1] *Bazaar of Heraclides*, p. 312. The passage is from Cyril's letter to Acacius of Melitene (see Migne *P. G.* vol. lxxvii col. 193).

'"proximity", or "equality of honour", or "agreement"; but 'I say that I do not separate God Himself in His nature 'from the nature that is seen, and "on account of God who 'is not separated (from the man), neither do I separate the 'honour".... Though I said "I separate the natures and I unite 'the worship", I did not speak of a separation of removal, 'that I should put the natures apart one from another, as 'thou with thy misrepresentation hast accused me of saying. 'If there were no other kind of distinction of natures save 'only removal, thou mightest well have accused me of making 'this sort of distinction; but as there are many others, and 'particularly in the case of natures, with which our whole 'controversy had to do, what I said was that the union of 'the natures was without confusion or alteration. Why dost 'thou keep before thee and investigate up and down this 'notion, that I in my mind mean to separate the natures? 'And how dost thou assert that they (the Easterns) "in no 'wise divide those things which have been united", whereas 'thou hast already said formerly that they are distinct? "Our 'brethren of Antioch", sayest thou, "speak of a difference of 'natures as recognizing, only and merely mentally, those things 'of which Christ is known to be constituted: because the God-'head and the manhood are not one thing as to natural quality, 'as I have said, but there is one Son and Christ and Lord who 'is truly one; for we say that He is one person".'[1]

The above extract, it will be noticed, ends with Cyril's assertion that the Easterns only meant to recognize a "mental" distinction of natures or *ousias* in the Person of the Incarnate Word of God, that is to say, a logical distinction, or one which existed in their own minds only, and not a real distinction between the Godhead and the manhood of our Lord. That is a thoroughly Alexandrine conception. It is one that has

[1] *Bazaar of Heraclides*, pp. 314, 315. The passage quoted from Cyril continues that referred to in the last note.

appealed in the past, and appeals today perhaps as much as ever it did, to the reason and the emotions of numbers of Christians. But sympathy with this conception, if we feel sympathy, must not be allowed to blind our eyes to the fact that the Antiochenes did not mean this[1]; and, further, that such a conception is not easily reconciled with the authoritative decisions and formulas of the Church. If they are indeed patient of such a conception, it can only be by a method of interpretation which ignores the plain meaning of words; and such a method of treating careful definitions of the Faith cannot be justified—unless indeed it be held that the union of natures is one of the things that it is as "pious to exaggerate" as it is "impious to minimize", while the same indulgence is denied in regard to the equally Catholic doctrine of the permanence of the distinction between them. This point will come before us again in the conclusion of our enquiry. But before we reach this conclusion we must hear what Nestorius has to say about his adversary's definition of the union as "hypostatic", clearing our minds of any prejudice in favour of a particular form of words and attending only to the sense in which they are used. And we must also let Nestorius tell us what he thought of the doctrine of Flavian and Leo in relation to his own unassailable convictions.

[1] Nestorius returns to the charge a little further on in the book than the passage quoted above. 'They do not', he says, 'conceive of the natures without *hypostases* nor of the expressions as existing in the mind without the *hypostases* of the natures....Cyril says that they accept the expressions as to difference of natures only in idea, and he himself does not accept the idea of the natures as existing in their *ousias*: but without *hypostases* and without subsistence they take their rise and spend themselves in the mind' (*Bazaar of Heraclides*, pp. 321, 322). And he goes on to argue that Cyril ignores the process of cognition, confusing the objective *ousia*, the idea of the *ousia* in the mind, and the expression which makes known the idea. In saying that the Easterns accept only the idea of the difference of natures, he ignores the fact that the natures have their *ousias*, and so he allows of difference only in the *idea* of the natures and not in the *ousia* (*ib.*).

CHAPTER XI

THE PHRASE "HYPOSTATIC UNION"

IN one of his sermons[1] reported by Marius Mercator as preached on the 12th of December, 430, on the receipt of the letters of excommunication from Celestine and Cyril, Nestorius appeals to Cyril to be a man and come out into the open, and let their dispute be decided on a fair field, instead of hiding in the dark and shooting at him with arrows of gold[2]. He does not believe in his *bona fides*. He cannot think what it is that he really wants or means.

In the *Bazaar of Heraclides* he argues the matter at length[3], asking what in the world Cyril means by a "hypostatic union" if not what he himself understands by a union of two distinct *hypostases* and natures in one Person.

It is by the arguments of Nestorius himself that we must judge of his meaning; and I am loth to interpose between him and that hearing which has been so long denied him. But a few words, by way of preface, may supplement what has been already said as to the different meanings which the terms involved in the discussion bore[4], and call attention to the ambiguity of the phrase, which long usage has rendered familiar in a particular sense, and for theologians hallowed. Nestorius, as we have seen, is always consistent in his use of

[1] *Sermo* xviii in Loofs *Nestoriana* pp. 297 ff.

[2] An allusion to Cyril's presents to the officers and ladies of the Court.

[3] pp. 186—196.

[4] See *supra* ch. iii.

the term *hypostasis* in connexion with the doctrine of our Lord's person. It always has, for him, in this connexion, the sense of "substance", and he maintains that the two substances, Godhead and manhood, though united in the one Person, continued to retain their respective and different characteristics, which are summed up under the term "natures". Cyril, on the contrary, is not so definite in his usage of either of the terms *hypostasis* and "nature", that we can say at once exactly what he meant by any composite phrase in which either of them occurs. To describe the union he uses the adjectival form of both these terms: he speaks of it as "hypostatic" and as "natural". We too must ask, like Nestorius, what he means. It will be enough to examine the former phrase.

"Hypostatic union" (ἕνωσις ὑποστατική) may mean a union, or unification, of two *hypostases*, the result of which is the formation of a new *hypostasis* which is something other than either of the two out of which it is compounded. If this is what Cyril intended, using *hypostasis* in the sense of "substance" (and Nestorius evidently thinks this is the obvious meaning of the phrase), then Nestorius could not, of course, regard the phrase as anything but a summary statement of the doctrine of the Person of our Lord which he dreaded. For it would express the blending or compounding or confusion of the Godhead and manhood (the two *hypostases*) which he himself believed to still remain, each in its own nature, although united in our Lord's person. Nor was the case better if, with this use of the adjective, *hypostasis* was given the sense of "person". For then the phrase would signify that two persons had been made one, and Nestorius insists that though it is a person in whom the union is realized, the union itself is not of persons:—the component parts of it, so to speak, are not persons, but the distinct substances of Godhead and manhood with their distinctive characteristics. It is in this sense that he repudiates the term "*prosôpic* union", which he suggests is possibly what Cyril means; a "personal union", in the sense of a unification of persons, is as unsound a doctrine as the unification of "substances".

But, on the other hand, in the phrase "hypostatic union" the adjective may have its full adjectival force as a description of the union when realized, rather than as a statement of the mode in which it is brought about or of the elements which produce it. In this sense the phrase would still seem to Nestorius (who would naturally take "hypostatic" to mean "substantial") to be an unsatisfactory expression, as implying a doctrine which did not safeguard the distinction between the substances in the Incarnate Word, Emmanuel. It would not give adequate recognition to the reality of the human nature and experiences of the Lord Jesus Christ; it would tend to "dehumanize the manhood"; or else it would suggest a "mixture" which resulted in the degradation of the Godhead. If, however, Cyril really meant by it only that the "substances", while retaining their distinctive properties, found their union in one Person—so that it was the Person who was "one", while the substances were "two"—, and that therefore genuinely Divine and genuinely human experiences alike were His; then Nestorius was in complete agreement with him. To the phrase "personal union" in this sense Nestorius could have no doctrinal objection, even though he might think it a somewhat equivocal phrase, capable of being misunderstood.

As after all these years we read the words of Cyril, a canonized Doctor of the Church, whose terminology has become our own, we are scarcely conscious of the ambiguity. We assign to his terms a conventional meaning, and familiarity with them makes us suspicious of any other form of words:—if Nestorius objected to them, it was because he was a heretic. But again it must be said, it was a period when terms were "in the making". We read Cyril more easily than we read Nestorius, but anyone who carefully examines his expressions will find himself often arrested. And if he compares the accounts of Cyril's teaching which he finds in the works of Catholic theologians and historians of doctrine with his very words, he will find many a gloss inserted[1]. If it is clear that he used expressions which could only be interpreted as "orthodox" (in accordance, that is, with the definitions of Chalcedon), it is none the less clear, I believe, that he also used expressions which, if interpreted in accordance with the common contemporary usage of the terms, were *prima facie* and so far as they went unorthodox. And it is not clear that he consciously attached to such expressions a meaning which would free them from suspicion. His use, for example, of the expression "natural union" (ἕνωσις φυσική) gives strong support to the view that he really used the parallel expression "hypostatic union" in the sense of "substantial" rather than in the sense of "personal" oneness. We give Saint Cyril the benefit of the doubt, and we use his phrases in an orthodox sense; though we know that many devout Christians have passionately clung to them as true interpretations of the doctrine of the Incarnation in a sense which the Catholic Church has disallowed. We cannot wonder that Nestorius, in his zeal for Catholic truth, as he understood it, insisted on putting them to the test of a careful dialectic. Technical terms must always be ready to run the gauntlet. Happily for them, though perhaps unfortunately for those on whom they are imposed, there is not always a Nestorius in the line.

He cannot find any peace of mind in the fog, or golden haze, whichever we prefer to call it, of the ambiguous phrase which half conceals and half reveals the truth he sees so clearly. He is, no doubt, a little impatient; but I do not think there is anything unfair in the process to which, himself a trained theologian attacked on technical grounds, he subjects the technical language of his chief opponent. A recent historian of the Council of Ephesus writes that, before the

[1] This is true, for example, of Dr W. Bright's account of Cyril's teaching.

Council opened, Cyril "endeavoured to drive Nestorius into a corner by acute arguments"[1]. I do not know what evidence there is of such a personal encounter, or whether Nestorius ever had an opportunity of plying Cyril face to face with questions in his turn. Here, at any rate, in his book, we can read the questions that he would have asked, we can see how far he was ready to meet acuteness with its own weapon, and we can judge whether he or Cyril was the more likely to be driven into the corner. He addresses himself, in this part of his book, directly to his antagonist, as though he was indeed face to face with him, but they are written words of Cyril that he cites.

'Thou shewest surprise when thou hearest expressions of 'mine which are thine also; for there is no union which does 'not demonstrate a difference: as also (a difference is implied) 'by a worship of consession[2]....Therefore, either give up 'speaking of two natures united without confusion, or confess 'and say this. And does it not appear to thee absurd to speak 'of a union of the two different natures in the sense of a union 'of *ousia*, and not in the sense of a union of person?

'"But", thou hast said, "if we reject the *hypostatic* union 'as incomprehensible or unbecoming we fall into the error of 'speaking of two Sons, for it will be necessary to distinguish 'and speak of the man separately who is honoured with the 'name of Son, and separately of the Word of God who possesses 'the appellation and the reality of Sonship by nature. It is not right therefore to distinguish the one Lord Jesus Christ 'into two Sons." ....
'What wouldst thou have a *hypostatic* union to mean?—'which does not allow us to understand that the *ousia* of man 'exists, nor to understand a man by nature, but only God the

[1] Hefele *History of the Councils* Eng. tr. vol. iii p. 44.

[2] Nestorius is arguing that Cyril's phrase "*with* which He sat" implies a difference of natures quite as much as any phrase used by Nestorius himself to express the distinction.

'Word by nature: i.e. that even He who is God is not (now) 'what He is by His nature, on account of a *hypostatic* union 'which does not admit the distinctions and definitions of things 'that are different[1]. Therefore this union is one of those which 'are defined by the term "*ousia*[2]". But if it (the union) be 'rendered inactive it is no longer a union, but *from* a union '(i.e. the result of a union)—not (actually) a union[3]. And if 'all definition of the natures is destroyed, how has the union 'not destroyed the distinctions of the natures? And if they '(the natures) are not thought of (as existing) in nature[4] nor 'yet in union, how is it that thou hast said that He made His 'own the proper things of the flesh, saying that He has this by 'nature and that by the union, and that His suffering and 'dying in (human) nature are His (the Word's) because he 'made them His own?

'In what sense, then, art thou considered to uphold a '*hypostatic* union? What is this *hypostatic* union which cannot 'be understood? Or how can we accept it without under-'standing? Or how hast thou understood it? How is it 'lofty and "incomprehensible", and again "not becoming"[5]? 'Teach us............

[1] i.e. a hypostatic union abolishes the distinctions and definitions belonging to the things united in it.

[2] i.e. the union thus effected results in a single *ousia*.

[3] The context shews that this means that if the union results in one *ousia*, then the component parts are obliterated, or fused so as to be indistinguishable; hence it can no longer be called a union, but only the *result* of a union, for a true union implies the continuance of the natures united.

[4] φυσικῶς probably.

[5] Cyril's words were "if we reject the hypostatic union as incomprehensible and unbecoming, we fall into the error", etc. (in the first of the letters read at Ephesus). They were aimed undoubtedly at Nestorius and others like him who wished to understand with their minds the doctrine they professed with their lips. Nestorius replies that no one would say at the same time that a doctrine was both "incomprehensible" and "unbecoming", inasmuch as the first epithet precludes him from the use of the

'For neither thou nor the whole Synod can suffice to 'give a name to the union. But I also speak of a union; 'but thou dost not receive what I say because I distinguish '(in) the union. If I say concerning those things which have 'been united: He (Christ) is body in *ousia* and not body in '*ousia*, and they (the natures) are distinct from one another, 'this as created and that as increate, this mortal and that 'immortal, this eternal with the Father and that created at 'the end of the times, and this consubstantial with the 'Father and that consubstantial with us—for the union does 'not abolish the *ousias* that were united so that they cannot 'be known—(if I say this) thou sayest to me: "Thou art 'dividing": yet thou thyself hast gone so far as to use these 'words—having been led into them in order to accuse me— 'for thou hast said: "The natures which came unto a true 'union are different; but of the two there is one Lord Jesus 'Christ: not as though the difference of the natures were 'taken away by the union". Dost thou then allow us to think 'thus concerning a *hypostatic* union also? Or is it that, having 'made a distinction by saying that the natures that were 'united were different through their diversities, thou dost wrest 'this admission into accordance with thine own teaching "lest 'thou shouldst admit the suspicion of severance"[1]? And 'what shall I say of the words "admit the suspicion of sever-'ance"? Or what of the word "suspicion"? Dost thou 'understand "severance of natures" according to the mean-'ing of "natures", and as "without confusion", yet without 'there being any "suspicion" of a limitation of the natures

second: if he declares it "incomprehensible" he disqualifies himself from passing any further judgement on it, as to whether it is "becoming" or not. The answer is of course "eristic", but Nestorius scores his point in the debate; and it is a good instance of the manner in which he retaliated, when attacked, and of the way in which he annoyed his opponents. J. F. B-B.

[1] The same letter of Cyril is referred to. The Greek is *ἵνα μὴ τομῆς φαντασία παρεισκρίνηται διὰ τοῦ λέγειν τὸ "σύν"*.

'in thy mind, as when the fire was united with the bush and 'the bush with the fire, and they were not confused[1]? Thus 'thou shewest them (the natures) to be without limitation and 'without difference. But I hold them to be limited and dis-'tinct. If then thou speak of a *hypostatic* union, say clearly 'what thou meanest—for I confess that I did not then under-'stand[2], and even now I have no need that thou shouldst 'teach me[3],—that I may agree with thee. Or, if I do not 'accept thy meaning, say that I do not accept it; and, if 'the judges agree with thee, let them either convince me or 'condemn me as one who cannot be removed from his error. 'Say, then, what thou meanest by a *hypostatic* union. Wouldst 'thou have us to understand *hypostasis* as *prosopon*, as we 'speak of one *ousia* of the Godhead and three *hypostases*, 'understanding the *hypostases* as *prosopa*? If so, by *hypostatic* 'thou meanest *prosopic* union. But the union was not one *of* '*persons*, but of natures: "The natures which came unto a 'true union", thou sayest, "are different; but there is one 'Christ of the two". Dost thou mean the one person of 'Christ, or (again) a *hypostasis* of the *ousia* and of the nature—'as it were an express image of His *hypostasis*[4]—and dost thou 'speak of (*or* mean) a union of natures by "hypostatic union"?

[1] This illustration probably applies to the first part of the sentence only, and not to the immediately preceding clause, for Nestorius presently employs it himself with reference to the union of the natures in Christ.

[2] When he first received Cyril's letter—or at the Council.

[3] The meaning of this is not obvious. I suggest reading ܐܠܐ, 'but', for ܘܠܐ, 'and not': the sense then will be, 'and even now I have need that thou shouldst teach me, that I may agree with thee'. This is obviously the sense required. I have noticed other cases in the MS of the interchanging of ܐܠܐ and ܘܠܐ.

[4] ܐܝܟܢܐ ܕܪܘܫܡܐ ܕܩܢܘܡܗ, 'as it were an impress of His *hypostasis*', is of course a reference to Heb. i 3, καὶ χαρακτὴρ τῆς ὑποστάσεως αὐτοῦ. In the Peshitta this is rendered ܘܨܠܡܐ ܕܐܝܬܘܬܗ "and the image of His being" (*îthûtheh*). The translator of Nestorius has either not seen the allusion to Heb., or (more probably) preferred to

'But I also say this; and in this I applaud thee, that thou 'hast so spoken and made a distinction of the natures—of 'God the Word and of the manhood—and a conjunction of 'these into one person. Or hast thou not said "differences 'without confusion", and (again) "it (the union[1]) continued 'without any difference by which it should be severed"? And, 'even though thou do not grant a difference, i.e. a difference 'of natures, yet thou unwittingly grantest a natural severance.

'But is there no distinction in the union when those which 'have been united therein remain without confusion, like the 'bush in the fire and the fire in the bush?

'But it does not appear that thou meanest this[2]; and thou 'blamest me as though I did not accept the *hypostatic* union. 'But any other *hypostatic* union of different natures I am not 'acquainted with[3]; nor do I know of anything else that is proper 'to a union of different natures save only a single person, 'through which and in which both natures are recognized, 'and which makes the things that belong to these (the natures) 'to belong to the person. For, that the body is the temple of 'the Godhead of God the Word, and that the temple is united 'to God by the highest kind of (*or* by a perfect) conjunction[4], 'so that He (God) should bring for Himself the things of 'this temple into an intimate association[5] with the Divine

give a more exact rendering, using *q'nômâ* for ὑπόστασις (as he regularly does), and giving a different rendering of χαρακτήρ, and one which better expresses the idea of *depicting*, or *expression*, than the simple word "image".

[1] The fem. shews that 'it' refers to 'union'.

[2] i.e. apparently the view that Nestorius approves.

[3] Or, perhaps, 'I do not recognize': referring to the sort of *hypostatic* union which he has just said he would approve of.

[4] ܒܢܩܝܦܘܬܐ ܪܡܬܐ, *supremâ coniunctione*.

[5] The word ܒܝܬܝܘܬܐ corresponds in formation to (and doubtless stands for) οἰκειότης, which with other derivatives of οἰκεῖος is constantly used in the controversy in this sense. Cf. Leo *Ad Flav.* "et aedificante

'nature,—this it is right to confess, and it agrees with the 'tradition of the Gospels: but not that He made them[1] (the 'things of the body) into His own *ousia*. What other *hypostatic* 'union, therefore, thou wishest to teach me by speaking of a 'supreme and divine and ineffable union, I do not know: 'unless it be that of a single person, whereby this is that and 'that this. Wherefore I everywhere persistently proclaim that 'it is not right for those things which are said, either of the 'Godhead or of the manhood, to be attributed to a single 'nature, but rather to a person, lest, when the two (sets of 'properties[2]) are united into an *ousia*, there should be a mere 'phantasm (φαντασία) of the human things. For that which 'He (the Word) is by *ousia* He is not said to be as to *ousia* in 'all the things (i.e. the properties of the natures); but (He is so 'in) all things that proclaim the person; and God the Word, 'who is said to have become flesh, and the Son of man, is 'recognized through the form (ܕܡܘܬܐ = μορφή) and person 'of the flesh and of the man, which (form and person) He 'employed that He might make Himself known to the world. 'For God the Word is not said to be those things which the 'flesh is said to be *by nature*, so that it should be said that '"there was when He was not", or, "from things that were not 'He was made",—or whatever may be said of the flesh before 'it was made, or whatever happened to it after it was made 'through the changes of growth and waste—(that it should 'be said) in short that He (the Word) is consubstantial with 'us....

'So also the flesh is not said to be everything that God 'the Word is by nature; for it is not without beginning, or 'unmade, or incorporeal, or invisible, or consubstantial with 'the Father and the Holy Spirit. Even though that which He

sibi sapientia domum, verbum caro factum est, et habitavit in nobis, hoc est in ea carne quam assumpsit ex homine".

[1] Feminine, representing the Greek neuter.

[2] The fem. shews that this is meant, and not directly the natures.

'who is Son and Lord and God is said to be, the flesh also 'is similarly said to be in the union: because a union has taken 'place into the person of the Son of God: not *into an ousia* 'nor *into a nature*, but *of natures*: not into a *nature*, but into 'a *person*: for all the things of the person belong to it (the 'flesh) except the *ousia*[1].

'What other *hypostatic* union, then, is it that thou speakest 'of which, as thou sayest, I reject as being "either incompre-'hensible or unbecoming", and thus "fall into the error of 'saying two Christs—one, a man who is honoured with the 'title of Son, and, apart from Him, the Word of God, who 'possesses by nature both the name and the reality of Son-'ship"?

'How can it be that he who speaks of one Son, one Christ, 'one Lord in the union means that the Son, the Son of God, 'is one separately and apart, and that it (i.e. the flesh) is another, 'and thus speak of two Sons? For this could no longer be 'called a union. But each one of the natures is in its own '*ousia*; nor is God the Word said to have become flesh in His 'own *ousia*, but by a union with flesh; nor again is the flesh 'called Son apart from the union with the Son of God. Hence 'in (the union of) the two there is one flesh and one Son. 'Now that which (either nature) receives through the union to 'be and to be called, this it is not and is not called when (the 'natures) are marked off and distinguished one from another. So 'God the Word is in His own nature God, and incorporeal: but 'in the union of the flesh He is called flesh; and the flesh, 'which is by its nature and in its *ousia* corporeal is, neverthe-'less, by the union with God the Word the Son of God, both 'God and Son. Yet those things which *by nature* are different 'and are united in a union *of natures* are not said to be two 'fleshes, nor again two Sons..
'Now it is as it were by grace (*or* favour) that it (the flesh) is in

[1] i.e. the divine *ousia*.

'His (the Word's) *hypostasis*, and that in His own form (μορφή)[1] 'He made for it a form—not through a commandment[2], nor 'yet by honour, nor yet by a mere making worthy by grace, 'but in His own natural form He made it His form[3], so that 'it should not be other than, but the very same as, He who 'received it into His own person, that this should be that, and 'that this[4]..

'I know not then in what sense thou speakest of the *hypo-'static* union, that I should receive it, or not receive it, as 'something "incomprehensible or unbecoming, so that the 'man should be isolated and spoken of apart as having the 'title and honour of Son, and the Word, who is of God, also 'apart, even He who has the Sonship and the appellation and 'the title by nature".

'That word "apart"[5]—how dost thou understand it.......

[1] There is a reference to Phil. ii 6, 7. Nestorius in the earlier part of this treatise frequently uses "form" (*d'mûthâ* = μορφή), with a reference to the passage in Phil. ii, not in the sense of mere figure or outward manifestation, but almost as equivalent to *hypostasis* (in the sense in which it leans towards πρόσωπον), or even οὐσία, and φύσις: i.e. in a strongly theological sense. Compare Leo's use of "forma": "agit enim utraque forma cum alterius communione quod proprium est".

[2] i.e. not by an advancement which is the reward of keeping the commandments. Nestorius rejects this error in the earlier part of his work, and (if I remember rightly) has before referred to it simply as "through a commandment".

[3] The sentence up to this point is rather obscure, but I think the above gives substantially the sense of the text. Nestorius is probably concerned here with shewing that expressions used elsewhere to describe the union, such as "union of love", "of grace", were employed by him only to guard against the idea of physical union (or union into *one* nature), and not with any intent to express a loose or local union. Elsewhere when he has spoken of a union of love or good-pleasure it is always God's love that is meant—not a mutual love between the man and the Word as two persons, but God's condescension in causing the union.

[4] i.e. clearly, that both "forms" should be one in the one Person of the incarnate Word of God.

[5] Gr. ἰδικῶς.

'How sayest thou that we should not understand the nature of 'man "apart"—aside from the *ousia* of God the Word—as 'being Son not [by nature][1] but through the union? Yet 'thou also sayest that there is a difference between the natures 'which have been brought together into the union of the one 'Son, and that the difference of the natures is not taken away 'by the union of the natures: "not" (thou sayest), "as 'though the difference of the natures is taken away by the 'union". If then the differences of the natures are not re-'moved, the nature of the flesh is "apart" the nature of man-'hood; but that which is Son and *homoousios* with the Father 'and the Holy Spirit is separately and "apart" the (nature) 'of the Godhead; but in the union the flesh is Son, and God 'the Word is flesh. Wherefore, he who speaks thus does not 'speak of two Sons, nor of two fleshes; nor does he speak of two 'fleshes by nature,—the flesh on the one side and (its) Sonship 'on the other; but in the person the natures use their properties 'mutually, like the fire in the bush. The bush became fire, 'and fire the bush; yet severally they were bush and fire, not 'two bushes nor yet two fires, for both were in the fire, and 'both in the bush. For there is no division; but by the union 'of two natures the two natures become a person. Either, 'then, cease to speak of distinct natures which remain with the 'distinctions of their natures and are not destroyed, or else say 'that they remained in different natures..........................

'But dost thou perhaps speak of a *hypostatic* union which 'is into one nature,—so that after the union the natures do 'not retain their own properties,—thus correcting the things 'thou hadst before said? Rather it is that thou aimest at 'making them (the things Cyril had said) incapable of receiving 'approval from me; for thou dost wish to say what is different 'from that which I say—since it is not for the truth but

[1] The word ܒܟܝܢܐ, 'by nature', or ܒܐܘܣܝܐ, 'in *ousia*', has dropped out of the text.

'through perversity, as an enemy, that thou happenest to be 'displeased with me—that thou mayest seek an occasion of 'differing from me. And this union (that thou meanest) is 'one that destroys the natures, and so I do not accept it.

'In thine enmity against me thou hast thought out[1] difficult 'words and definitions, as thieves do, that thou mayest conceal 'thy meaning and not be understood; and thou sayest this 'and that and everything. Thou dost not, however, make '(the expression) "*hypostatic* union" to mean an abolition of 'the natures, but rather a physical union which comes from a 'compounding into one nature.

'As the soul and body make up the one nature of a man, 'so (as thou wouldst have it) was God the Word united to 'manhood[2]: and this thou callest a *hypostatic* union. But 'here, even though the natures continue, yet the union is 'into one passible and made and created nature. For a 'physical union is a second act of creation; for what each 'has not by its nature, this it receives by nature in the 'physical union. Now things that are united into a physical 'union are united so as to have the passions, each of the 'other, physically, and do not freely receive each other's 'passions: like the body and soul, which by their natures 'are not susceptible of the proper things of one another, yet 'by a physical union become partakers one of another, and 'receive and cause sufferings to each other by physical necessity, and by a sort of physical mixing, so that each of them 'will suffer (physically) what neither could suffer apart. For 'in the union the soul does not of itself suffer hunger and 'thirst, nor is it (by itself) pained by cutting or burning or

[1] The Syriac verb is pointed as 1st pers. sing. If this be correct the text must, I think, be defective in other respects, thus: 'Thine enmity against me, with thy definitions by means of difficult words, I have thought over...like thieves; that thou mayest conceal', etc.

[2] St Cyril uses this illustration in the second of his letters read at Ephesus.

'smiting ; and the body, again, without the soul has no per-'ception of these things; but by a physical union of the 'different natures they are mutually capable of experiencing 'these things, and share them by a necessity which comes 'of the union.

'If, in this way, thou meanest "*physical*" by "*hypostatic*" 'union, thou speakest like the Arians; for it is a physical and 'not a free union if He (the Word) suffered with physical 'passibility. He suffered, they say, through a physical union '(with the flesh); for the passions of the soul are the passions 'of the body by a physical compounding. But the Unmade 'who by His nature is increate was not compounded so as to 'suffer like that which is created and made.

'Now it is not merely because the soul is in the body and 'the body in the soul that they exhibit a union of one nature; 'for not in every body that has a soul within it does it (the 'soul) cause a union, nor can the soul in this case always make 'the body its own; but there must be a compounding like that 'by which it was fashioned into one nature (with the body) 'by the Creator, and by which it is physically limited and 'confined so that it cannot go abroad, being held and retained 'without any choice. (Natures) then in a physical union are 'set loose or bound together by a creative act. If then God 'the Word was united with the humanity by a union into one 'nature, and even if the natures themselves remain without 'confusion,—yet the Maker and the made will have been 'fashioned into a physical union by change, willy-nilly. And 'He who is able to create all, that is God, will be the nature 'of the union, and not the *hypostasis* of manhood, which (only) 'in the nature (of the union) is known to be living[1]. For 'neither is the body without the soul living by its own *hypo-'stasis*, but it becomes living by the creative act implied in a

[1] The Syriac noun probably stands for ζῷον, or ζωϊκή, in the widest sense of "living being".

'physical union. If this be so, then the man receives through 'God (the Word) to become living, and has not this by[1] his 'own *hypostasis* and nature, but gets it from the *hypostatic* 'union which subsists in one nature[2].

'Therefore he (Cyril) refuses to say[3] that the man is man, 'and is living by his own *hypostasis* and nature, and that God 'the Word is God the Word by His own *hypostasis* in such a 'way that He retains His own nature in the union, and did not 'receive from the union to be living. Now that he (the man) 'should be man he received through an act of creation on 'the part of the Father, Son, and Holy Spirit: that he should 'become the Only-begotten Son he received from the union 'with God the Word, not from his own nature, nor yet through 'a *physical* and *hypostatic* union. But that which he comes to 'be by a physical union, this he does not receive to be from 'aught else than from physical creation: I mean, that he should 'become one living thing, which he was not by the body alone, 'nor yet by the soul alone, nor yet by both[4], but by an act of 'physical creation.

'But this (kind of union) is corruptible and passible; but 'a union *of natures* into a person is impassible and incorrup-'tible; for it comes by free appropriation—for the union is '*not in*voluntary—by condescension and exaltation, by au-'thority and obedience[5]. And it (this latter kind of union)

[1] Reading ܒܩܢܘܡܗ for ܩܢܘܡܗ.

[2] Nestorius's argument seems to be that, as the body is not really animal unless it is united with the spiritual soul, and thus by the union becomes something that it is not apart from the union, so neither can the manhood of Christ (if the *hypostatic* union be considered to be the same as that of soul and body in man) remain hypostatically human when united with the Word; for a creative act has been performed upon it, making it into a new nature which is shared by the Word also.

[3] i.e. if he understands *hypostatic* union in this sense.

[4] Nestorius has already said that mere position—the fact that a body has a soul in it—does not constitute a living organism.

[5] These two words are not the ordinary ones in Syriac for "authority"

'is to be so understood, not by the lapsing or nullification or 'extirpation of one of the natures or of the proper things of 'both natures, but in the sense that the natural properties 'remain distinct both as to mind and as to will, with a dis- 'tinction which is that of natures (united) in one agreement. 'For there was one and the same will and mind in the union 'of the natures[1], so that both should will or not will exactly 'the same things. They (the natures) have moreover a mutual 'will[2], since the person of this is (the person) of that, and (the 'person) of that (the person) of this.

'He who is (the resultant) of a union of natures speaks 'in one person of this (nature) from (the standpoint of) that, 'and of that from this, as from one person.

'He (Christ) is not a single *hypostasis* or nature; for the 'Godhead is not confined in the body, as is the case with 'all natures which are united into a *hypostasis*; for these are 'bounded by the nature which confines them in their existence '(*yâthâ*), and they have no existence apart from each other[3].

'If then this is what thou meanest by saying that God 'the Word was united *hypostatically* with flesh, and if thou 'callest this an "incomprehensible and unbecoming" union, 'I do not hesitate to say clearly that they who so speak[4] are 'impious, and that this opinion is unorthodox....................

and "obedience", they rather express the ready alacrity of the human will answering to the call of the divine.

[1] Nestorius is not here denying the existence of a human will in our Lord—he has just before asserted it. He means unity of will with regard to the objects of will, in other words, complete agreement of wills,—a moral, not a psychical union. The same applies to "mind", which in Syriac, as in English, can mean "attitude of mind". Nestorius is never tired of proclaiming the existence in Christ of a complete human intellect. That doctrine lies at the root of his whole position.

[2] Using St Leo's word "invicem", we might translate this "sed et *invicem* sunt voluntates, (Deitatis et hominis)". Cf. *supra* p. 183.

[3] Lit. 'and outside themselves they are not'.

[4] i.e. who hold this Arian view of the union.

'Wherefore thou meanest (by "hypostatic union") a volun-
'tary union whereby we think of a union without confusion
'and without physical sufferings (on the part of the Word)—a
'union into one person, not a physical union.

'Now we can speak of the person which comes from a
'physical union as being of two natures: just as man is neither
'body nor soul (taken separately), but is a nature which has
'resulted from a union of these things, and a physical person.
'But God (the Word) "took the form of a servant" into His
'own person and Sonship. It did not come from some other—
'as in the case of those things which are united into one
'nature—that He took the form of a servant; nor was "the
'form of a servant" the *ousia* of man: but He that took it
'established it as [His own][1] form and person and became
'in the form of men, (but did) not (become) the nature of men'
(*Bazaar of Heraclides* pp. 186—196).

[1] I think we must supply this in the text—the context seems to understand it, and its omission is not grammatically justifiable if it is to be understood. There are perhaps other clerical errors in the context: the words 'nor was "the form of a servant" the *ousia* of man' do not yield a very satisfactory sense.

CHAPTER XII

THE TEACHING OF NESTORIUS IN RELATION TO THE TEACHING OF FLAVIAN AND LEO

THE conclusion to which a fresh study of the remains of Nestorius's teaching collected in Dr Loofs's *Nestoriana* had brought me was that there was nothing in the teaching of Leo and the Chalcedonian definition which he would not have endorsed, that his conceptions were indeed essentially in harmony with the "orthodox" doctrine as to the Person of our Lord. The date of his death was uncertain. The tale that he lived till the eve of the Council of Chalcedon was very meagrely supported by external evidence and seemed to lack intrinsic probability; it was generally discredited. There were no means of knowing for certain what his attitude would have been towards the definition of Chalcedon, though it was of course certain that he would have regarded Eutyches and Dioscorus as worthy successors of Cyril and, while fervently abhorring their doctrine, would have been able to respect them more as men who "came out into the open" and frankly and unashamed said what they meant.

The recovery of the *Bazaar of Heraclides* removes the atmosphere of uncertainty which would otherwise have continued to veil the question. It is no longer a hypothesis that Nestorius would have welcomed Leo as an ally. It is a fact that he lived to read Leo's letter to Flavian; that he regarded the treatment of Flavian at Ephesus as a repetition of the history of his own case—the same doctrines were condemned, and had he himself attended the former Council of Cyril he would have suffered on the spot as Flavian suffered; and it is a fact that he welcomed the proceedings of the Council of Chalcedon as a final triumph for the Faith for which he had contended. We have his own words. In this victory all personal questions were swallowed up. The Faith, indeed, was all he had ever cared for. It had been, he says, in order to remove all personal *animus* that after the Council he had wished to return to Euprepius and to inform the Emperor that—

'Notions of self-advancement in connexion with the episcopal 'office had no influence with me, but that I was only longing 'for my own country....Having witnessed the intrigues and 'attacks formerly prepared against me...and how through their 'bitterness against me they became embittered against the 'faith, it seemed to me wiser and better to sacrifice myself for 'that which was more important; for when enmity is removed 'men often return to their better selves' (*Bazaar of Heraclides* p. 286).

And again:

'The goal of my earnest wish, then, is that God may be 'blessed on earth as in heaven. But as for Nestorius, let him 'be anathema....And would to God that all men by anathe- 'matizing me might attain to a reconciliation with God; for 'to me there is nothing greater or more precious than this. 'Nor would I refuse to retract what I have said[1] were I but 'assured that it was required of me to do so, and that men 'would hereby be brought to God, and that I should be in 'honour with God for the sake of the things of God, which 'I have conceived of in a manner according to God and not 'according to man' (*ib.* p. 363).

[1] Nestorius doubtless means that he would readily make concessions as to the language to be employed.

It was the same feeling that had prevented him from writing to Leo, as he had been urged to do, especially since he had read the *Letter to Flavian* and found in it the faith plainly set forth without fear of the Emperor's favour to Eutyches.

'My reason for not writing is this: not that I am a proud 'and unreasonable man, but that I might not be a hindrance 'to him, by reason of the prejudice that exists against my 'person, in the course that he was running so well. And I have 'elected to bear the accusations made against me, to the end 'that, while these accusations rest upon me alone, others may 'accept the doctrine of the Fathers without hindrance; for 'what things were done against me are of no account to me' (*Bazaar of Heraclides* p. 370).

He describes the pleasure with which he learnt that the Church of Rome, which in the person of Celestine had condemned him, was now in the person of Leo ranged on the side of a true confession.

'When the bishop of Rome had read what had been done 'against Eutyches, he condemned Eutyches of impiety. Now 'when I came upon that exposition (sc. Leo's *Tome*) and read 'it, I gave thanks to God that the Church of Rome was 'rightly and blamelessly making confession, even though they 'happened to be against me personally' (*Bazaar of Heraclides* p. 337).

He declares repeatedly at the end of his book that Leo and Flavian and he held the very same opinions, and that the scandalous treatment of Flavian ('who filled my place') at the "Robber Synod" was only a repetition of what had happened to himself: the same parties and the same doctrines had been at issue, and only the persons were different. It was one and the same struggle for the truth of the Incarnation, and in this epilogue to the drama of which he himself had been the central figure, and the subsequent overthrow of the Eutychian party, he recognized the Hand of God. Here is one of the chief passages in which he expresses his conviction :—

'Who was it that constrained them to utter these doctrines 'of mine which by interdicts were forbidden to be read, and to 'fight for these very things and contend with all persistency 'that they should be said, while I was silenced and deprived of 'the right to say them and was not believed? It was God, who 'had raised up those who, when they uttered my doctrines, 'should be believed that these (doctrines) are true,—those 'upon whom there rested no suspicion that they uttered them 'for any friendship or love of me. It was God who did this: 'not on my account—for who is Nestorius, or what his life or 'his death in the world?—but for the sake of the truth which 'He had given to the world and which was being made void 'by error He rebuked them that were leading men astray. 'And because men were suspicious of me, and would not 'believe what was said by me—for I was held as one who hides 'the truth and withholds his exact meaning—God gave to this 'teaching a preacher who was clear of this suspicion, even Leo, 'who without fear proclaimed the truth. And whereas many 'were prejudiced and overawed by the idea of the Synod and 'also by the person of the Romans[1], and would not believe 'what I said[2], and my case remained without examination, God 'allowed these things to fall out contrariwise. For He would 'remove the bishop of Rome who had ratified[3] the machina-'tions of the Synod of Ephesus against me, and make him[4] 'to approve and affirm the doctrine of the bishop of Con-'stantinople. And he who had been all-powerful was now 'esteemed of no account, I mean Dioscorus the bishop of 'Alexandria. "Of no account", I say, for he took to flight 'as a means of avoiding deposition and being driven into exile.

[1] The Roman legates appear to be meant.

[2] To 'say things' is continually used in this work in the sense of "to hold or teach doctrines".

[3] ܕܡܫܪܪܘܬܐ... ܥܒܕ ܗܘܐ appears to be a periphrasis for ἐκύρωσεν.

[4] i.e. put another bishop there who should etc.

'And all this happened that they (those of Flavian's party)[1], 'by suffering the same things themselves, might believe those 'things that were done by an Egyptian against me also in the 'former Synod, and know that it was through the treachery of 'the Emperor and the court nobles that I was regarded as 'one who resisted the Synod, since it could not terrify me into 'relinquishing the truth or force me to submit to the Emperor 'in those matters which were done against me; for it was 'because they (Flavian's party) had never investigated the 'truth that they held me for a blasphemer. But God, in order 'to shew that the Emperor's friendship for me was a mere 'pretence, and not genuine but for the purpose of acquiring 'money, shewed in the case of Eutyches and Flavian what 'the worth of his assistance was to those whom he did not 'even allow to take part in the assembly, and to those who, 'taking part in it, were not permitted to speak a word beyond 'what was commanded them, so that through fear and con'fusion they were even incriminating themselves. And because, 'again, they (Flavian etc.) supposed that my assertion that the 'summons I received (to attend the Synod of Ephesus) was 'not to a fair judgement, and that they were summoning me 'to be condemned and not to be tried, and were attempting 'to lure me into a plot for my destruction and death—because 'they supposed that this was mere idle talk, God allowed 'Flavian to come to the Synod and to suffer what he suffered, 'in order that He might convince them that those also (of the 'first Council of Ephesus) were murderers. For it is evident 'that this (that was done to Flavian) is what would have been

[1] The Greek construction has no doubt been altered in the Syriac. It is evident that these words refer back to those who, prejudiced by the decision of the Synod, would not examine Nestorius's cause. This was probably quite clear in the original construction. Nestorius is drawing a parallel between the two synods of Ephesus—he and Flavian, who held the same doctrines, were each condemned at Ephesus by a bishop of Alexandria.

'done to me formerly by those others. And again, because it 'was supposed that they (of the first Synod), being bishops, 'would not allow themselves to do anything that was improper 'or unjust, whether out of attachment to the Emperor or 'through fear or violence; once more God has exposed them 'and convicted them before all men of acting otherwise. And 'He has left nothing without a witness, but by every means He 'has exposed the causes which led to error, and has caused 'them to be proclaimed upon the housetops, so that there may 'be no excuse for those who affect ignorance; for as by every 'means Pharaoh was convicted by God, and remained without 'excuse—since neither by the logic of words, nor by deeds, 'nor by the reproof of men or of God would he be persuaded, 'but died in his blasphemy—so these also remain without 'excuse.

'When I have seen these things, then, that God has done, 'would you have me keep silence and hide so great a dispensa-'tion of God? The prophets of God would not have been 'approved—those who by lying prophets were anathematized 'as lying prophets, as it were by (true) prophets—unless they 'had suffered to be anathematized for God's sake by lying 'prophets. Their sons would not have been worthy of the 'honour and the doctrine of prophets if they had kept to the 'communion of lying prophets. Those of the Jews who be-'came Christians would never have been singled out to be 'saved if they had adhered to the judgement and the injustice 'of their fathers against Christ as that of holy and righteous 'men. They would never have become apostles of Christ if 'they had clung to the whole synagogue of the Jews and the 'priests and the lawyers and the heads of the people as to 'teachers of the Law and as prophets. They would not have 'believed in Christ or have died for Christ unless they had 'reckoned death and contempt as an honour instead of a dis-'grace; nor at this present time would they be held in honour 'by peoples and leaders and lords unless they had suffered 'death and shame at the hands of princes and peoples. They 'would not have been worthy to be thus revered by kings and 'princes and powers if they had observed the commands and 'laws of kings and judges and princes. Our fathers would not 'at this time be accounted orthodox teachers had they striven 'to avoid the condemnation of the Synods of heretics and con-'sented to confess their doctrines and play the hypocrite. We 'should not have been accounted worthy of the teaching (which 'is the fruit) of their labours had we accepted without exami-'nation the united opinon of those opposed to them as coming 'from Synods. In short Meletius and Eustathius would not 'have been bishops of Antioch had they acquiesced in the 'election and the judgement of a Synod of heretics opposed 'to them; nor would Athanasius have been bishop of Alexandria 'if without doubting he had accepted his sentence of deposition 'as coming from orthodox men. John (Chrysostom) would 'not have been bishop of Constantinople if he had accepted 'the judgement of deposition pronounced against him without 'examination as coming from a (true) Synod; nor again would 'Flavian have been bishop of Constantinople had he agreed to 'the decision of the ecumenical Synod which deposed him as 'coming from a Synod; nor would all those of whatever city 'who have suffered all these things on my account (now) be 'shining as the sun if I had given heed to my accusers rather 'than to God; nor to those doctrines to which each and all 'of these have belonged in God should I have been worthy 'to belong. But not mine is the work, but Christ's who has 'strengthened me; for every man shall give an answer to God 'for those things he has said and done, whether it be that he 'has caused offence or has laboured with all zeal to remove 'offences. But if, when a man has done all that in him lies, 'he that has stumbled will not be persuaded, then let his 'stumbling be laid to his own account, and not to his who has 'spoken to him and cried out without being heard' (*Bazaar of Heraclides* pp. 366—370).

Nestorius certainly did his best to get a hearing for the "sound doctrine" on the side of which he took his stand and for the sake of which he bore so much unflinchingly. The "heresies" against which he foresaw his opponents would have to contend, because they would not listen to him and be forearmed[1], came only too surely and wrought havoc in the Church of Christ. He had only "cried out without being heard", and even the "great dispensation of God" which exposed the errors against which he protested, and led him at the end of his life to break silence once more, brought no reparation to him. His *apologia*, the final vindication of his teaching, remained unheeded, if not unknown. The Church's condemnation had been passed upon him, and he and his teaching have been ever since *anathema*.

In the same "dispensation of God" his work has come to knowledge again in an age in which the doctrine of the Incarnation is exposed to dangers, from opponents and defenders alike, which are at least as dissolvent as those against which he cried unheard.

[1] See *supra* p. 158.

CHAPTER XIII

CONCLUSION

Nestorius says that if he held the views attributed to him he would condemn himself, and even beg that his guilt might be visited with retribution, as would be just, even though he made ten thousand supplications for mercy and brought forward all manner of arguments in justification of his words. He had had all through the weary years of the struggle "one only end in view—that no one should call the Word of God a creature, or the manhood which was assumed incomplete". With this end in view he had been forced to oppose the "would-be orthodox", as he calls them, who were, he thought, either Arians or Apollinarians in disguise.

'It is my earnest desire that even by anathematizing me 'they may escape from blaspheming God, and that those who 'so escape may confess "God, holy, and almighty and im-'mortal", and not "change the image of the incorruptible God 'for the image of corruptible man"[1] and mingle heathenism 'with Christianity, but that they may confess God as He is 'in His image, and man as he is in his image, so that the 'passible and the immortal be confessed in their own natures; 'that Christianity may not confess, after the manner of heathen 'ungodliness, either any change of God or any change of 'man. And let there be with the truth, yea, yea, and nay, 'nay,—the Redeemer and the redeemed—so that Christ may

[1] Cf. Rom. i 23.

'be confessed to be in truth and in nature God and man, 'being by nature immortal and impassible as God, and mortal 'and passible by nature as man—not God in both natures, nor 'again man in both natures. The goal of my earnest wish, 'then, is that God may be blessed on earth as in heaven: but 'as for Nestorius, let him be anathema; only let men so speak 'of God as I pray for them that they may speak. For I am 'with those who are for God, and not with those who are 'against God, who with an outward show of religion reproach 'God and cause Him to cease from being God' (*Bazaar of Heraclides* pp. 362, 363).

Reading his own words, carefully and consecutively, as we can read them now, it is impossible to believe that Nestorius was "Nestorian".

But there is other evidence. Theodoret was as obnoxious to the opponents of Nestorius as Nestorius himself. His doctrine has lately been subjected to a fresh examination by a French scholar[1], who, by a careful comparison of the anathemas of Cyril with the replies to them composed by Andrew of Samosata, on behalf of the Eastern bishops, and Theodoret of Cyrrhus, is led to the conclusion that the two Christologies, of Antioch and of Alexandria, in spite of notable differences, were alike perfectly orthodox. Underneath all their differences of terminology and expression the doctrine is essentially the same. It is true he excludes from his investigation the counter-anathemas of Nestorius himself. But, as we have seen, it is certain that Nestorius intended to express the ordinary doctrine of the school of Antioch—and who should know it, if not he?—and that in his counter-anathemas at all events there is nothing that is explicitly unorthodox. The evidence shews that he was personally

[1] Père J. Mahé in the *Revue d'histoire ecclésiastique* vol. vii, no. 3 (July, 1906).

sacrificed to the agreement which was made between Alexandria and Antioch, and suggests that personal rather than doctrinal reasons determined his fate and the destiny of the band of enthusiastic Christians who would not be parties to such a transaction.

And we may look still further afield. For the large body of bishops and others, who could not accept the ecclesiastical condemnation of Nestorius, found a home in Persia, where the imperial decrees, without the aid of which the condemnation could not be effective, did not run. And there, on the foundation of the old Eastern Church which had seldom had much to do with the Church of "the West", they built up the great Syriac Church which, in numbers and learning and missionary zeal combined, surpassed all others and was till the fourteenth century the Church of the East *par excellence*, reaching far into India and China[1]. A few years ago the collection of the canons of the Councils and Synods of this Church, known as the *Synodicon Orientale*, was published with a French translation[2], and writings of some of its early representatives have been made available for use in the same way. After the revival of monophysitism at Constantinople, and the controversy of "the Three Chapters" (the condemnation of Theodore, Theodoret in part, and Ibas[3]), and when a new

[1] A convenient sketch of the history of the Church will be found in the *Annual Report* of "the Archbishop's Mission to the Assyrian Christians" published by the S. P. C. K. See also M. Labourt's history cited p. 200, n. 1.

[2] By M. Chabot—vol. xxxvii of the *Notices et extraits des manuscrits de la bibliothèque nationale*.

[3] It must be remembered that again, in this painful episode, political considerations, rather than theological, were dominant. The Emperor Justinian wished to conciliate the Monophysites, who would not accept the Council of Chalcedon; and the formal condemnation of their chief opponents in the past offered an easy means to secure the end in view. Motives of state policy dictated this early instance of anathemas on the famous dead, who while they lived had been held in high honour and had died in "the peace of the Church". (The effect this condemnation might

terminology had been introduced or popularized by Leontius of Byzantium in the first half of the sixth century, some of the terms employed by the Nestorians might seem to express a definitely unorthodox doctrine. But it does not appear that the Nestorian Church ever changed its traditional terminology; nor indeed could it be expected to change it, in view of all the facts of the case; and if they speak of the union as "prosôpic", and not as "hypostatic", it is not fair to assign to the phrase the new Byzantine meaning of it. Indeed, it would be a mere blunder to do so. (They mean to assert that the one-ness is to be found in the Person, and that the distinction between the *hypostases* Godhead and manhood is preserved.) In any case, during the whole period when the teaching and terminology of Theodoret and Nestorius were well remembered as well as standard ("standard" they have always remained), the Creeds of the Councils of the Nestorian Church are perfectly orthodox. No trace of heresy has crept into them. I can find no trace of "Nestorianism" in the Nestorian Church of that time. And a writer, like M. Labourt, in his recent and valuable history of Christianity in Persia[1], who notes at an early date how "singularly attenuated" "Nestorianism" had become[2], is really unconsciously misinterpreting the facts. I cannot find evidence that "Nestorianism" ever existed in any but this "singularly attenuated" form. In other words, it was never more than a tendency.

But it was a tendency. At the back of it all there is something that goes deeper than mere differences of terminology. And if we are to get down to it, we must not shrink from

have on the Christians in Persia could of course be disregarded, as they were outside the Empire; and the opposition to it in Africa and the West, where the theological issues were understood, seems to have come as a surprise to the Emperor.)

[1] *Le Christianisme dans l'empire perse* (pp. 224—632), Paris, 1904.

[2] *ib.* p. 268.

asking ourselves one of those large questions which we are usually content to "let lie". What is the ultimate significance of all our doctrinal controversies? What real difference does it make to us, what theory we hold of the Person of Jesus Christ? Why, for example, does Gibbon seem to any theologian so extraordinarily absurd when he makes merry over the long controversy which was waged between two competing definitions, which differed from each other by a mere *iota*—the smallest letter in the alphabet?

The answer is not hard to find. It is just because, be it articulate or inarticulate, our whole philosophy of life is based on Jesus. We see in Him the Saviour of the World; One who has shewn Himself in word and in act able to bind men to Him by the closest of ties, to give them power to overcome temptation to evil, and to assure them of forgiveness and bring them the peace of God. That is the practical Gospel. But when we say that, and just because we believe it, as a practical truth, for us as we are, in the world as it is, we say a great deal more and we believe a great deal more. He can only be that if He does really in His own Person, as well as in His whole attitude to life, embody the meaning of human life, the solution of the enigma of existence—

> what we are, and whence we came;
> whence we came and whither wending.

He can only be Saviour of men constituted as they are, and placed as they are, if in His own actual experience—thought, feeling, will—indeed, in His whole being—He represents and expresses a perfect human life. This is the philosophy of the Gospel.

So it is that the Catholic doctrine of the Incarnation expresses a philosophy of life; and variations in the definitions of the Person of Jesus, if words have any significance at all, carry with them variations in the theory of the meaning of human life, the place of man in the universe.

The whole ecclesiastical system is based on the antithesis —the Divine: the human;—God and man. And Christianity, as at once a historical religion and a philosophy of life, an interpretation of actual facts of human experience, is based on the theory of the Incarnation:—the belief, that is, that once in human experience this fundamental antithesis found its synthesis. Once a Person lived a human life who united in Himself the human and the Divine, who was conscious of the antithesis, who could feel the war of wills, who could be tempted as we are tempted, who had to learn obedience by the things which He suffered, who shared the limitations of human existence:—One who was fully conscious of all these things, and yet at the same time was conscious of Divine origin, of insight into the Divine will and Divine power to fulfil it, of oneness with the Divine by which He transcended the limitations of the human.

So acting on, and following up, this belief, that the true relations between God and Man, the true interpretation of the meaning of the universe and of human life, were visibly realized in Him, the Church has always taught that what was actual in Him was potential in all men; and that just because of Him and in and through Him, so far as they could become one with Him, they too in their individual experience might hope to realize the synthesis.

This is however an entirely different thing from the denial of the antithesis, as practically true, a present reality of experience.

We are, of course, face to face here with a profound problem—though it can perhaps be stated simply, sufficiently for the purpose.

The doctrine of the Incarnation seems to proclaim as ultimate reality the oneness of God and man, the Divine and the human, Godhead and manhood: but as practically true the antithesis of both. If then we have a real unity in our philosophy of life—our theory of being—we seem to proclaim the Divine and the human as correlates or counterparts of each other—the spiritual and the material (to use somewhat antiquated terms) as different modes of one existence[1]: or it might be said that neither was complete without the other.

So, in the representative instance of our Lord Himself, this is the obvious doctrine of the Church, which has always resisted any theory which failed to recognize in Him both alike:—He, the one being, is complete in Godhead and complete in manhood. To His full being manhood is as essential as Godhead. It is this in another form that is the thought of the writer of the Epistle to the Ephesians in the passage "and He gave him to be head over all things to the church, which is his body, the fulfilment of him who all in all is being fulfilled" (Eph. i 22, 23)—the true meaning of which words has only lately been given back to us[2]. The Christ Himself is not complete without His Body, and the Body itself will not be complete till the Church is complete—that is to say till all mankind is actually one with Him. Then and not till then will He be "all in all fulfilled". Till then the antithesis holds.

This great thought, it is true, perhaps does not find very explicit recognition in the ordinary theological teaching of the Church. But consciously or unconsciously it is the spring and life of its practical work and of the institutions by which it seeks to train its members. It is the life of Christian ethics, both of its principles and of its *praxis*. And so alike in the doctrine of the Incarnation on the one hand, and in the whole

[1] It is, I believe, generally recognized by theologians that the theoretic dualism of spirit and matter is not Christian. The world, including all that we call matter, has its origin in the will and love of God alone, and the idea of the world at least has always been conceived by Christian theology as eternally existent in God. It is only the practical dualism, the "logic of facts", that has impressed itself on Christian thought.

[2] "There is no justification for the rendering 'that filleth all in all' (A.V.)." Such idiomatic uses of the middle of the verb as are cited afford no justification for taking it here in what is really the active sense. See the Dean of Westminster's note *ad loc.*

sacramental system on the other hand, the Christian philosophy of life is embodied, with full recognition of Divine and human; maintaining fearlessly the apparent contradiction of the transcendence and yet the immanence of God; and proclaiming as the ultimate goal of life the complete realization of manhood in union with God.

The mystic temperament has tended, in every age, to concentrate attention on the synthesis, and has seemed to others, in doing so, in the effort to attain the synthesis, to ignore or annihilate the human. Yet the Church—with St Paul and the Fourth Gospel as her guides, and the practical salvation of men as they are as her mission, and the facts of everyday life as the sphere of her activities:—while she has given shelter to the mystic, and has ever held before men's eyes the vision of the synthesis as the ultimate reality—the Church in all her definitions and doctrinal statements has maintained the antithesis. She has never spoken of the "humanity" of God or the "Divinity" of man. Any theology that did—were it old or new—would be obviously false to the facts of everyday experience. Any theory which denies the distinction between the Divine and the human is essentially monophysite, and, if it seems to tend to the glory of God and the ennoblement of man today, it may issue tomorrow in the supersession of God by man—a world without God. In the days of Nestorius the danger was that the doctrine of the Church should be robbed of its moral appeal to men as they are, and it was his ethical insight and practical instinct that made him oppose a form of thought which seemed to him in his own words to "dehumanize the manhood" of the Lord. 'The manhood', he says in the striking passage already quoted[1], 'has been brought 'into a state of complete cohesion with Him, but it has not been 'deified, as the wiseacres among our younger *doctrinaires* would 'have it'.

[1] *Supra* p. 64 *ἀπηκρίβωται γὰρ εἰς ἄκραν συνάφειαν, οὐκ εἰς ἀποθέωσιν κατὰ τοὺς σοφοὺς τῶν δογματιστῶν τῶν νεωτέρων.*

He was resisting the covert monophysitism of his times: a tendency of thought which may be traced all down the history of the Church, assuming various forms at different epochs:—the tendency, that is, in some form or other to deny the distinction between the Divine and the human:—primarily, of course, in the Person of our Lord, but, so far as the doctrine of His Person expresses the Christian theory of existence, in effect and by consequence to deny it altogether.

As spectators of the controversy we are really watching the struggle between mystical unity and practical duality. Neither side really denied the chief contention of the other; but each suspected his opponent of failing to recognize what was to himself the main premiss.

One of the earliest champions of the Nestorian side after the Council of Chalcedon, Narsai, a student and teacher in the school of Edessa, and afterwards the first head of the school of Nisibis (from 457 to 507), whose homily in defence of the three great Doctors, Diodore, Theodore, and Nestorius, can now be read in French, declares that though these three "just" men were unjustly persecuted by emissaries of Satan, yet in spite of all the victory remained with them[1]. And we have seen good reason to think that he was right. As a matter of fact, though Nestorius as an individual was condemned, all that he contended for was amply conceded in Leo's letter to Flavian and at the Council of Chalcedon—which was silent about Theodore, the teacher to whom Nestorius was most indebted; which pronounced Ibas and Theodoret orthodox, the chief champions of the same school of thought; and declared unmistakeably the duality not only of natures but of substances[2], as distinct as

[1] See the Homily with a French translation by Abbé F. Martin in the *Journal asiatique*, Nov.–Dec. 1899 and May–June 1900.

[2] "Consubstantial with the Father as regards His Godhead", "consubstantial with us as regards His manhood", and the term "Mother of God" only with the qualification "as regards His manhood" which was just the limitation which Nestorius desired.

they were ineffably united: and in spite of the later chaotic disputes in connexion with the controversy over the "three chapters", and the Council (the "fifth general council") which declared that the distinction was to be understood to be "logical" only, and in spite of all the turmoil between East and West of the sixth and the seventh centuries, duality finally triumphed in the doctrine of two wills. The human is not the Divine even in the Person of our Lord. And therefore it is not in us.

Many a phrase no doubt can be cited from orthodox Greek fathers, whether in regard to the doctrine of the Incarnation or in connexion with the doctrine of the Eucharist, shewing the thought that in virtue of the Incarnation, or through the Eucharist, men may become Divine:—the *ipse per se hominem adunans Deo* of Irenaeus, or phrases such as that of Athanasius ἐνηνθρώπησεν ἵνα ἡμεῖς θεοποιηθῶμεν (He became man in order that we might be made Divine) and some of those of Gregory and others about the Eucharist. But "deification" is a process: the process for which the Church and its whole system of sacraments exists:—but still a process, not an achieved result. Men may *become* Divine in Christ: they are very far from *being* Divine. This is the thought of one of St Paul's most pregnant sayings, in which he expresses both the antithesis and the synthesis, in words that no familiarity can dull—"Him that knew not sin He made sin on behalf of us, in order that we may become God's righteousness in Him" (2 Cor. v 21). The saying remains, in its ethical assertions as well as in the metaphysical implications that underlie them, as startling today as it must have been when it was first read out to the Corinthians of old; and nearly every word in it has emphasis.

Apart from the theory of the synthesis—the traditional doctrine, that is to say, of the Incarnation—Christian philosophy and Christian piety cease to be. Apart from belief in the practical truth of the antithesis the whole fabric of Christian religion and Christian ethics crumbles to the ground. The assertion of so obvious a truism would call for apology were there not signs today that the Nestorian controversy may have to be fought out again in a new form in the twentieth century. Piety has always resented the appeal to history, and has always claimed to know Christ no longer "according to the flesh". But even if we admit that individual experience is the finally convincing test of spiritual things, we need to remember that Christianity owed its triumph over many other ennobling philosophies and "mysteries", its early rivals, to the fact that it was based upon belief in a Person, born of a woman, who had lived the life and died the death of men, before He proved Himself to be victorious over death. A historical religion, while it may strictly limit the scope of the reference, can never ignore the facts of its early history, nor can it tolerate doctrines which are inconsistent with any of those facts.

We have seen that the ideas, for which Nestorius in common with the whole school of Antioch contended, really won the day, as regards the doctrinal definitions of the Church; though Nestorius himself was sacrificed to "save the face" of the Alexandrines. The manhood of Christ was safeguarded, as distinct from the Godhead: the union was left an ineffable mystery.

The views against which Nestorius protested would have robbed us altogether of the historical Christ of the Gospels. Though inspired by the inevitable philosophical craving for unity, and the supreme desire of genuine piety to see in the manhood of Christ the real deification of human nature as an entity, they would have made of the Saviour of men a Person not really human, and of Redemption a magical, instantaneous, rather than an ethical, gradual, process. The possibility of an ethical valuation of His human life and experiences was in large measure saved by the stand the Nestorians made: for the Church of the West, though all its doctrinal traditions linked it to them, was, as we have seen, by a strange political accident, arrayed for the moment against them. That the Son of God should continue to be the Lord of human life we owe to Nestorius first—for it was in his day that the tendencies to an unhistorical interpretation of the Person of the Lord (always present in the Church from the times of the Gnostics) first became a serious menace to the traditional doctrine of the Incarnation within the Church itself—and after him to the "Nestorians" of later times and other lands.

But more and more, all down the centuries since, the manhood receded farther and farther behind the Godhead. The Person, who has been the stay of the religious hopes and aspirations of the great majority of Christians all down the ages, has been the Divine Person, whose manhood has been the mystery: till now again, in our own times, the human Christ has come back to us in the fulness of His manhood. The Alexandrine—the mystic religious—conception has prevailed so long, that now that we are again permitted, indeed constrained, to examine freely and trace afresh the human history of our Lord's life on earth, the life which he lived as man among men, to "recover the primitive portrait", there is the new danger that the reaction may mislead as much as it helps. For the new distinction between "the Christ of History" and "the Christ of Faith" is as false as it is in some ways specious. The real Christ of History is the Christ of all the ages since the Advent, and of all the ages still to come. Cyril and Nestorius both spoke Greek, but they were to each other *βάρβαροι*. The same kind of difference separates men today. The Nestorian controversy has its warnings for us in this respect. For though the doctrine of one Person in two natures, living always in two spheres of consciousness, comes probably as near as we can come towards satisfying the double demand of piety and of practice, of philosophy and of redemption, the problem is, if not insoluble, still unsolved. The Gospels represent Him to us as one who knew Himself as man and as God. Metaphysicians and psychologists have their special lines of investigation and their own proper terms: but is there yet any better definition of the union of the natures than is contained in the words "He knew Himself as man and as God"?

If the teaching of Nestorius is to be put to a practical test; and, I imagine, he would have asked nothing better himself; the test is ready to hand. We know what those Christians, whose boast it was that they believed as Nestorius believed, could do and dare and endure to spread the Faith in the Incarnate Word, their Lord and his Lord, to the ends of the earth. They are his "letters testimonial", to be "known and read of all men".

It is of course possible to see a Divine judgement on doctrinal error in the disasters which befell that Church of the East Syrians after nearly a thousand years of undaunted missionary enthusiasm—disasters which make it necessary for us, after an interval of half as many years again, to try once more slowly to win to Christ great tracts which were once the sees of Nestorian bishops. It may even be possible—who knows?—to see in Tamerlane, that scourge of humanity, the minister of the Wrath of God. The problem presented by the extinction of once flourishing Christian Churches is one on which we need not enter here. Only we may note that the judgement, if it were judgement, fell with almost equal weight on Nestorians and on anti-Nestorians, on monophysites and on orthodox, alike; and it will scarcely be supposed that it was more accurate definitions, or a sounder faith, that enabled Europe to repel the Turk. And in view of its history it is difficult to believe that there was anything fundamentally wrong with the faith of the Nestorian Church. Whatever the explanation of its overthrow may be, for one who believes in the providential government of the world, it is clear that for centuries its devotion to the Person of our Lord carried it triumphantly through extraordinary difficulties and was signally "blessed" in results. And now that it is well known to us in its humiliation, we find that there is, so far as we can learn, nothing essentially unorthodox in the faith of its members or in the writings of the Fathers to which it appeals.

The question which has been under consideration is clearly not one of merely antiquarian or historical interest. No question affecting the doctrine of the Person of our Lord can ever be thus described with truth. But it is also closely connected with one of the great problems by which the Church of England is faced today:—its relation to the separated Churches of all kinds. On the one hand are those Societies of Christians who would dispense with all doctrinal definitions, as needless accretions to the simple primitive faith, or even dangerous impediments to the free growth of knowledge, petrifying what should be the flowing stream of interpretation of Christian experience. These are outside the range of thoughts which the Nestorian controversy suggests. But on the other hand are historic Churches, Christian Societies with all the notes of genuine national churches—the Sacraments, the Creed, the historic ministry—such as the Church which has maintained unbroken its continuity from the fifth to the twentieth century. With this great ancient Church, which "was a centre of light and power when we (in Cambridge) were a reed-fen"[1]—not of her own seeking, but in tardy and still very meagre response to repeated appeals for help—the Church of England has already been brought into peculiarly close relations, through the action of successive Archbishops of Canterbury. We are on intimate terms of friendship. Only between us, between the two

[1] I quote the words from a letter written by Archbishop Benson, the founder of the Anglican Mission, on its "distant and yet touching and lofty object", after a great meeting at which he was present in the Guildhall in Cambridge in 1895 in support of the Mission.

Christian Churches, there is as yet no ecclesiastical intercommunion. The terms are sympathetic, as between two alien bodies, external to each other; between whom there can only be a *συνάφεια σχετική* such as Nestorius was said to maintain—a "conjunction of relations".

If what was said of Nestorius was true, and if it be true that the so-called Nestorian Christians of today "divide" the Person of Christ; then between us and them there must still, it seems, be division: we must still be sundered in the supreme bond of Christian fellowship, the supreme act of Christian worship, the Sacrament of Union. But if it is, and was, mainly a question of tendencies and terms: if the Nestorians of today are not unsound in regard to the doctrine of the Incarnation[1], and if Nestorius himself did not really "separate" the natures in the one Person of the Lord, then the way would be smoothed to a real "union" between his Church and ours. If we both believe that in our Lord Jesus Christ, God and man, Godhead and manhood, while really distinct, were yet brought together, reconciled, united, really, truly, ineffably, indissolubly—has not the time arrived for genuine Christian fellowship, ecclesiastical intercommunion? The age of anathemas is gone. To have realized this will be perhaps the chief merit of the twentieth century of the era of our Lord. If they are willing to cease to pronounce their ancient anathema on Cyril, we shall not surely ask them to disown their early hero Nestorius.

[1] The Letter of Leo to Flavian and the Council of Chalcedon are, I am informed, formally recognized in their official collection of conciliar documents.

APPENDIX

ON THE HISTORY OF THE SYRIAC TERMS *ÎTHÛTHÂ*, *ÎTHYÂ*, *K'YÂNÂ*, *PARṢÔPÂ*, AND *Q'NÔMÂ*

(by the English translator of the *Bazaar of Heraclides*)

THE words *îthûthâ*, *îthyâ*, *k'yânâ*[1], *parṣôpâ*, and *q'nômâ* have played a part in Syriac theological and Christological discussions parallel to that played in Greek by οὐσία, φύσις, πρόσωπον, and ὑπόστασις. The object of this note is to determine, as far as may be, the theological value of these Syriac terms. It is hoped that what is here offered, however incomplete, may throw some fresh light upon their meanings, and perhaps help to clear away some misconceptions.

I. *Îthûthâ* and *îthyâ*.

These words, which may be discussed together, are derived from the root *îth*, which corresponds to the Heb. *yesh*, "being", "existence". Properly *îth* is a substantive in the construct state (i.e. that form which precedes a genitive). In use it corresponds to the verb substantive "is", but it is conjugated by means of the nominal, not the verbal suffixes. Syriac has a separate word for what in Greek and Latin is expressed by γίγνομαι and "fio".

In derivation, then, the terms *îthûthâ* and *îthyâ* answer to the Greek οὐσία. According to its formation *îthyâ* should

[1] Whenever the word "*nature*" occurs in the following pages in translations from Syriac works it is to be understood that it renders *k'yânâ*.

express the idea of "being", "existence", according to a more concrete concept than that conveyed by *îthûthâ*. This grammatical distinction holds good (generally speaking) in practice.

(1) In the Peshitta version of the N.T.

Îthyâ does not occur at all in Pesh., and *îthûthâ* only once, viz. in Heb. i 3, where it translates ὑπόστασις, which there practically means οὐσία. Thus ὃς ὢν ἀπαύγασμα τῆς δόξης καὶ χαρακτὴρ τῆς ὑποστάσεως αὐτοῦ is rendered, "who is the ray (*or* effulgence) of His glory and the image of His *îthûthâ*".

(2) Other Syriac writings.

(*a*) Bardaisan.

A characteristic use of *îthyâ* in the earlier Syriac writers is to express the notion of an independent or elemental Being; while *îthûthâ* strictly denotes the being or existence which such a Being has: though it also is sometimes found in the more concrete sense of "a Being". Hence St Ephraim and writers of all ages after him constantly use these words absolutely to denote "the Deity", or "the Divinity".

Bardaisan, according to the notices of him found in the works of St Ephraim[1], used *îthyâ* and *îthûthâ* to denote certain elemental substances which God first created and from which He then fashioned the world; thus air, fire, and water were *îthyê*[2], or elements. In the *De Fato* itself Bardaisan is

[1] Most of Ephraim's references to Bardaisan are collected by Nau in his recent edition of the *De Fato*, otherwise called *The Book of the Laws of Countries* (*Patrol. Syr.* pars I t. ii). This work was first edited with an English translation by Cureton in his *Spicilegium Syriacum*. It was composed by Bardaisan's disciple, Philip, and takes the form of a Socratic dialogue between Bardaisan, two or three of his disciples, and an unbeliever.

[2] Cf. Nau *op. cit.* p. 502. It is this teaching that Ephraim has in view when, in his commentary on Genesis (Ed. Rom. i 6 D), he writes: "Since water and wind were not yet created, nor fire and light and darkness established, they, being younger than heaven and earth, are (part of) the creation...and are not *îthyê*".

made to speak in one place of *îthyê* as synonymous with the borrowed Greek word *estûksê* (στοιχεῖα): "He said to me, Not in so far as they are fixed, O Philip, will the Elements (*estûksê*) be judged, but in so far as they have power; for Beings (*îthyê*) when they are fashioned together are not deprived of their *nature*, but they lose somewhat of their own proper force by being mingled one with another, and they are subdued by the power of their Maker; and in so far as they are subjected they will not be judged, but only in that which is their own"[1]. *Ithûthâ* does not occur in the *De Fato*.

(β) St Ephraim.

We may take St Ephraim next, since he affords more information than Aphraates, who is a decade or so earlier chronologically. Of his extant works perhaps the most instructive for our purpose is the second of two tracts *Against False Doctrines* published by Overbeck. In this work Ephraim examines some of the speculations of Mani as to the origin of the world. Here again we find *îthyâ* and *îthûthâ* employed to denote the two Manichaean Beings, or first principles, the Good and the Bad, Light and Darkness. Ephraim himself, however, does not appear to recognize these as real *îthyê*. He writes[2]: "But if everything is one *nature* and from one good *îthyâ*, how can it be divided; and how can that impassible *nature* be cut up?...And if the earth has no feeling, and the stones are incapable of suffering, how is it, since there is but one *îthyâ*, that both rational souls and dumb stones come from it? So then it is not one homogeneous *îthûthâ*".

Again: "Now if it (Light) is a *nature* that is stable and continuous, the sons of Darkness when they ate it—if they did eat it—could not have dissolved its *nature*. For even as they could not destroy its being (*îthûthâ*), so that it should cease to be—for, lo, it is—so they were not able to dissolve the stability

[1] Nau *op. cit.* col. 548; Cureton *op. cit.* p. 4 (text).
[2] Overbeck *S. Ephraemi Syri aliorumque Opera Selecta* p. 61.

of its being (*îthûthâ*)". Ephraim speaks in this tract of God as the Self-existent Being, the "*îthyâ*-in-His-*îthûthâ*"; and indeed the Divine Being was the only *îthyâ* he really recognized. He says that the "hateful idea of the filthy *hûlâ* (ὕλη)" which the heretics regarded as an *îthûthâ* was got from the Greeks, but that "all the sons of the truth have preached but one *îthyâ*" (i.e. God)[1].

(γ) Aphraates.

There are only two passages in Aphraates' *Homilies* in which the words occur: (1) "We praise in Thee the hidden Mercy that sent Thee—even Him who had pleasure in us that we should live by the death of His Only-begotten; we glorify in Thee the Self-existent Being (lit. the *îthyâ* of Himself) who separated Thee from His being (*îthûthâ*)"[2]; and (2) "We adore Thee, the Self-existent Being (the *îthyâ* of Himself) who made us out of nothing"[3].

The first of these passages well illustrates the difference between *îthyâ* and *îthûthâ*.

(δ) Later writers.

In the above passages *îthyâ* is simply "a Being", and especially "the Being" *par excellence*, the Deity[4]; while *îthûthâ* is similarly "being", and often the Divine being. As yet there is no suggestion of the ideas which we connect with the word "essence". Although *îthûthâ* seemed the natural word to take over all the theological functions of οὐσία, it did not in fact do so. *Îthûthâ* in theological (as distinct from philosophical) language can only represent οὐσία when applied

[1] Nau *op. cit.* p. 502.

[2] Ed. Parisot, in *Patrol. Syr.* I ii col. 100. Dom Parisot, who completes his edition of Aphraates' *Homilies* in this volume, has added a concordance of all the Syriac words in the *Homilies* and an admirable Index Analyticus.

[3] *ib.* col. 117.

[4] Cf. the Syriac *Acts of Judas Thomas* (Wright *Apocryphal Acts* vol. i p. 279), "To be glorified art Thou, ineffable Being (*îthyâ*)".

to the Divinity. A Syrian might translate οὐσία, meaning the Divine οὐσία, by *îthûthâ*, but—I speak under correction—he would not dream of using such an expression as "the *îthûthâ* of the humanity" in Christ, although οὐσία is frequently so used (e.g. by Nestorius). Thus we read in one of Narsai's *Homilies*: "Three *hypostases* (*q'nômê*) the Church learned from our Lord—the Father, the Son, and the Holy Spirit—one *îthûthâ*"[1]; and again: "This is what the crying of Holy three times means; but that of "Lord" teaches concerning the *nature* of the Deity (*îthyâ*) that it is one"[2]. The orthodox (?) Isaac of Antioch also writes: "Thy *nature* is not mixed with our *nature*, nor is our *nature* fused with Thy *nature*. Our completeness, Lord, is preserved in Thee, and Thy *îthûthâ* dwelleth in our body"[3]; and again: "From the Father is His *îthûthâ*, and from the mother is His humanity. He had no father on earth; He had a Father on high. Virgin is the Child in His *îthûthâ*; virgin is the Child in His humanity"[4]. And the Monophysite Philoxenus writes: "And, being Himself God, the Son of God is man, and the man Son of God; the Son of the *îthûthâ* is Son of the Virgin, the Son of the Virgin is Son of the *îthûthâ*"[5].

When a Syrian wishes to speak of any other οὐσία than the Divine he prefers to use the word *k'yânâ*, "nature", or to take over the Greek word in the form *ûsiyâ*. The latter is the regular practice of the translator of Nestorius's *Heraclides*, even when the Divine οὐσία is meant; and even in original Syriac writings *ûsiyâ* is often employed in the same way.

1 *Narsai Homiliae et Carmina* ed. Mingana (Dominican press Mosul) 1905, vol. i p. 381. Narsai was the founder of the second School of Nisibis, after the expulsion of the Nestorians from Edessa *circa* 457 A.D. (cf. Mingana's Preface p. 8).

2 *ib.* p. 382.

3 *Homiliae S. Isaaci Syri Antiocheni* ed. Bedjan, vol. i p. 790.

4 *ib.* p. 811.

5 *The Discourses of Philoxenus* ed. Budge vol. ii p. 97 (Introduction). Dr Budge has missed the construction in his transl. of this passage (p. 32).

Finally the expression "Son of the *îthûthâ* of the Father" came to be a recognized rendering of the Nicene phrase ὁμοούσιον τῷ πατρί. In a fragment of the Nicene Creed preserved in the mutilated MS of the *Heraclides* the Greek phrase is so translated. The more common rendering is "Son of the nature (*k'yânâ*) of the Father"; and in many allusions made by Nestorius to the creed clause it is so turned. We find both expressions in the *Acts of Sharbil*, a document which was written probably at the end of the fourth or beginning of the fifth century and shews many traces of Greek influence, thus: "For He who put on a body is God, Son of God (i.e. θεὸς ἐκ θεοῦ), Son of the *îthûthâ* of His Father, and Son of the *k'yânâ* of Him that begat Him"[1]. The latter phrase is that employed in the Nestorian Creed of today, which probably goes back at least to the time of Narsai.

II. *K'yânâ*.

This word means "nature", and is capable of all the shades of meaning in which we use "nature". In translations from the Greek it invariably renders φύσις, as may be seen by comparing the Peshitta version with any passage in which φύσις occurs in the Greek. It occurs in the Syr. N.T. in a couple of places in which φύσις is not found in the Greek.; thus, in 1 Cor. xv 38 ἴδιον σῶμα is translated "the body of its *k'yânâ*"; and in Ja. i 21 for τὸν ἔμφυτον λόγον we have "the word which is planted in our *k'yânâ*". Bardaisan's disciple, Philip, uses it in the *De Fato* to express that which belongs in common to the members of any particular order of beings: mankind has one *nature*, the animals have another. He contrasts it with Fortune and Free-will: "And we men are found to be governed by *Nature* equally, by Fortune differently, and by Free-will each as he wishes"[2]. He also employs it of *Nature* in the widest sense: "*Nature* has no law, for a

[1] Cureton *Ancient Syriac Documents* p. 43 (Syr. text).

[2] Cureton *Spic.* p. 10 (text).

man is not blamed because he is tall in his stature or little, or white or black, or because his eyes be large or small... for, lo!...as to those things which are not done by our hands, but which we have by our *Nature*, we are not indeed condemned by these; neither are we justified"[1]. Again: "From *Nature* there is a sufficiency in moderation for all bodies; and from Fortune comes the want of food".

But *k'yânâ* had probably a wider application than the Greek φύσις. Bardaisan, in the work referred to, speaks of God "who ordained how should be the life and perfection of all creatures and the state of *îthyê* and *k'yânâ*". And Ephraim in the tract *Against False Doctrines* writes: "And who can fix a *nature* that cannot be fixed? For who can fix the *nature* of fire so that it be not divided by the wick of a lamp? Although fire is a *nature* it is capable of being divided, because of its *nature* not being fixed. But a ray of the sun no man can divide, because it is fixed, all in all, in a *nature* which is indissoluble"[2]. Here we have *k'yânâ* used—in one instance at least—in exactly the sense in which Bardaisan or Mani would (according to Ephraim) have used *îthyâ*, "Being": fire is a *k'yânâ* with a *k'yânâ*. We have seen that Ephraim objected to using *îthyâ* except of God; he prefers to call all dependent beings *natures*. Another good example of this use is found in a late (saec. xiii) Nestorian writer, Solomon of el Baṣra: "Darkness is a *k'yânâ* which subsists of itself; and if it were not a *k'yânâ* it would not have been numbered with the seven *k'yânê* which were created in the beginning in silence. Others say that darkness is not a *k'yânâ* that subsists of itself, but the shadow of bodies"[3].

Where we should speak of material things as "substances" a Syrian would call them "*natures*"; thus, "oil is a liquid substance" would be "oil is a liquid *nature*".

[1] Cureton *Spic.* p. 8. [2] Overbeck *op. cit.* p. 63.

[3] *The Book of the Bee* ed. Budge, p. 16. Ephraim (Ed. Rom. i 6 F) speaks of darkness as a *k'yânâ* in this sense.

III. *Parṣôpâ*.

This is πρόσωπον in a Syriac dress. It frequently translates the latter word in the N.T.: always in the sense of "face", "appearance", with the possible exception of Jude 16 where θαυμάζοντες πρόσωπα is rendered "glorifying *parṣôpê*". Syriac has also a word of its own for "face", and this sometimes takes the place of *parṣôpâ* in rendering πρόσωπον—especially in the expression πρόσωπον λαμβάνειν, where the idiom is borrowed from the Semitic.

In Payne Smith's *Thesaurus* (s.v.) several examples are quoted in which *parṣôpâ* is used absolutely to denote men, individuals: e.g. "illustrious *parṣôpê*" = "illustrious persons". There can be no doubt that the later Syrians (say, after the middle of the fifth century) sometimes used the word in practically the same sense as we use "person", "personage". But I do not remember to have met with a similar usage in the earlier writers (Aphraates, Ephraim, etc.). Aphraates certainly never uses the word in any sense but "face" or "appearance".

But there was a tendency to make *parṣôpâ* denote not so much the actual human visage as a mask or presentation (true or false) of some real or supposed person or thing. Hence we have the very common idiom to do something "in the *parṣôpâ* of another", i.e. as, truly or falsely, representing another: as acting for or pretending to be another. One or two examples may illustrate this. Rabbûla in his *Canons for Monks*[1] writes: "Let not the brethren in the *parṣôpâ* of sicknesses (i.e. feigning sickness, *or* on the plea of sickness) leave their monasteries"; again: "Let not the monks leave their own locality and, in the *parṣôpâ* of others (i.e. under an assumed personality), obtain judgments by bribery". Examples of this usage are constantly occurring. We meet also with such cases as "in his (own) *parṣôpâ*" = "propria persona".

[1] Overbeck *op. cit.* p. 213.

Parṣôpâ is, of course, the word by which the Nestorians, following Nestorius's own use of πρόσωπον, have always expressed their conception of the unity of person in Christ. Nestorius rejected the expression μία ὑπόστασις because, as will have been observed from the passages quoted in this volume from his *Heraclides*, he continued to understand ὑπόστασις in its older sense as almost equivalent to οὐσία (cf. the anathema to the Nicene Creed, ἢ ἐξ ἑτέρας ὑποστάσεως ἢ οὐσίας). The Nestorian Syrians similarly rejected the phrase "one *q'nômâ*" because, as we shall see, *q'nômâ* in this connection meant to them something very like what ὑπόστασις meant to Nestorius. Hence they have always expressed the union of the natures in Christ by the formula "two *k'yânê* and two *q'nômê*, one *parṣôpâ*". We shall quote presently, when discussing *q'nômâ*, two Nestorian definitions of the words *q'nômâ* and *parṣôpâ* which were given in the seventh century.

IV. *Q'nômâ*.

This is the most difficult of the terms which we have to deal with, and at the same time by far the most important theologically. Its derivation is uncertain. It is sometimes (probably erroneously) connected with the root *qûm*, "to stand up". The Syrians themselves apparently so derived it[1]: at least they explain it by derivatives of *qûm*.

Before we can hope to understand what *q'nômâ* meant to those who employed it in the controversies of the fifth century we must try to find out what sort of background it had in earlier usage.

(1) In the N.T.

By far the most common use of *q'nômâ* in writings of all ages is that in which it is coupled with the personal suffixes and means "self"; "my *q'nômâ*" is "myself", "egomet ipse", "his *q'nômâ*" is "himself", "ipse" or "se ipsum", and so on.

[1] Cf. Payne Smith s.v.

Thus employed it is rather more emphatic than *naphshâ* (lit. "soul"), which is used, much in the same way, as a simple reflexive, "me", "se", etc. It is in this idiom that *q'nômâ* is employed in the Peshitta N.T. with one exception—if indeed it be a real exception: in Heb. x 1 the words οὐκ αὐτὴν τὴν εἰκόνα τῶν πραγμάτων are translated, "not the things' own *q'nômâ*". We must leave the discussion of this passage until we have seen more of the use of *q'nômâ*.

According to the usage just noticed *q'nômâ* sometimes has the force of the Greek ὅλως; thus at Mt. v 34 in both the Old Syriac MSS of the Gospels for μὴ ὀμόσαι ὅλως we have "do not swear yourselves (lit. your *q'nômâ*)". Similarly at Jn. ix 34 ἐν ἁμαρτίαις σὺ ἐγεννήθης ὅλος is rendered in Syr. Sin. "thou thy *q'nômâ* wast born in sins", where Prof. Burkitt conjectures that ὅλως was read for ὅλος. Two similar instances occur in Bardaisan's *De Fato*[1], in both of which we must translate *q'nômâ* with the possessive suffix by "at all". Similarly St Ephraim says of the moon that it is sometimes invisible "for two actual (*or* whole) days (lit. for two days their *q'nômâ*)"[2].

(2) Aphraates.

Aphraates several times employs *q'nômâ* in the ordinary idiom in which it = "self"; but two passages in which he uses it call for special notice. In *Hom.* vi § 11 he says that "God and His Christ, though They are one, yet dwell in many men; and They in their *q'nômâ* (sing.) are in heaven"[3]. In *Hom.* xxiii § 7[4] he says, "at another time when he (Moses) prayed his prayer did not suffice for the *q'nômâ* of himself". Nöldeke recognizes in this latter instance only an extension of the

[1] Ed. Nau *op. cit.* col. 560 l. 22, and col. 567 l. 9. Cureton *Spic.* pp. 8 l. 1 and 9 l. 9.

[2] Overbeck *op. cit.* p. 72 l. 20.

[3] Parisot *op. cit.* i col. 285 l. 10.

[4] *ib.* ii col. 21 l. 12.

pronominal use of *q'nômâ*[1]; and I think the same pronominal force is felt in the former case also, and that Parisot is right in translating "dum *ipsi* in caelo remanent". I believe also that the same is to be said of the use of *q'nômâ* in Heb. x 1, and that we should translate the Syriac, "not the *actual* things *themselves*"[2].

But the real question is, What idea underlies this pronominal use? Is it that of reality, actuality, subsistency, or that of personality? Nöldeke says (*Gram.* § 223) that "*q'noma* 'person'" is "often employed with the personal suffixes to express the reflexive with accuracy". But according to this usage it is employed indifferently of persons and of *things*; and, like our word "self", it may merely emphasize the reference to a particular entity, whether it be a person or a thing. "Self" does not necessarily imply personality.

For further enlightenment we must examine passages in which *q'nômâ* is used as a simple substantive. Let us try to understand what St Ephraim's notion of *q'nômâ* was.

(3) St Ephraim.

In the tract already quoted, *Against False Doctrines*, he writes: "But the spiritual *q'nômâ* of the angels bears witness that their *nature* is incapable of increase. And not only these holy ones are lifted above this, but not even does the *nature* of the unclean demons receive increase or suffer diminution in any part of its being (*îthûthâ*); nor is the *nature* of the sun ever greater or less than what it is; for these things and those like them are complete *q'nômê*, and keep always the quantity of their *nature*. But anything that diminishes or increases, or waxes or wanes, or loses, or grows weak, is by its creation a perishable *nature*—though even over *natures* which are not perishable the imperishable Will that made them has

1 *Syriac Grammar* § 223.

2 The expression *q'nômâ dîlhên* is only a strengthened form of *q'nômhên*.

authority"[1]. Here Ephraim uses *q'nômâ* to express that which is indivisibly one in its existence and nature. It differs from his conception of *îthyâ*, in that this to him denotes the ultimate Being, whereas a *q'nômâ* may be created. It differs from *k'yânâ* (as used to denote what Bardaisan and Mani would call *îthyâ*—see above under the discussion on *k'yânâ*) in that a *k'yânâ* may be divided—as fire—while a *q'nômâ* is naturally incapable of division or any essential modification. There is here no suspicion of the idea of personality—St Ephraim did not regard the sun as a person.

In another treatise published by Overbeck (also against Mani) Ephraim refutes Mani's doctrine that Good and Evil are two co-eternal principles mutually antagonistic. He argues that good and evil are not Beings at all, but conditions resulting from the right or wrong use of free-will: "Now if Evil exists *q'nômically* (*q'nômâ'îth*, an adv. of *q'nômâ*), as they say, it is possible for it to be repelled (only) by the Good—which also exists *q'nômically*—for power must resist power, and *q'nômâ* be repulsed by *q'nômâ*, and force by force be conquered; for our word without the hand is not able to move a stone, nor can our will without the arm move objects about. And if inanimate and weak objects cannot be moved by our will, how shall it be a match for mighty Evil?"[2]

Here Evil is certainly personified; but this is quite independently of the use of the word *q'nômâ*: a morally bad Being *must* be a person. What the writer means by "and *q'nômâ* be repulsed by *q'nômâ*" is shewn by the illustration: a mere word cannot move a stone: there must be something with a corresponding *q'nômic* existence, some reality. Just so, if Evil is a *q'nômâ*, the will, not being a *q'nômâ*, cannot resist it. We are not concerned with St Ephraim's logic.

Some fifty years ago the Rev. J. Brande Morris made an ex-

[1] Overbeck *op. cit.* pp. 63 f.
[2] *Op. cit.* p. 57.

cellent translation of a selection of St Ephraim's works, to which he added many useful and scholarly notes. Having made a special study of Ephraim's writings he came to the conclusion that this Father had no fixed theological terminology to express the distinct personality of the Father, Son, and Holy Spirit in the Trinity. He consequently refused to translate *q'nômâ* by "person" and used either "subsistency" or "reality". On pp. 398 f. (in the second Hymn *On the Faith*[1]) there is an important passage, which may be given in Morris's translation: "Thou hast heard of God that He is Father; by His Fatherhood know His Begotten. For if the Father begetteth, the Son that is from Him did He beget from Himself. That One Offspring which is the Only-begotten Son, let not thy questionings sunder! thou hast heard of the Brightness of the Son; do not thou insult Him by thy questioning! Thou hast heard of the Spirit; surname Him by the Name that they have called Him. Thou hast heard His Name; praise [Him] by His Name: to pry into His Name is not allowed. Thou hast heard of the Father and the Son and the Spirit; by the Names hold the Realities (*q'nômê*). These Names are not blended together: the Three are in truth blended together. If thou confessest their Names, and confessest not their Subsistencies (*q'nômê*), thou art in name a worshipper, in deed an unbeliever. Where there is nothing in subsistency (*q'nômâ*), the name which intervenes is an empty one; whatsoever hath no subsistency (*q'nômâ*), of that the appellation also is void: the word subsistency (*q'nômâ*) teacheth us that it is some reality". This is a most instructive passage: on the first occurrence herein of *q'nômê* Morris remarks that it is used "in a sense approximating to Person"; but he observes that from the subsequent language it appears that the writer "regards *q'nômâ*

[1] This Hymn is one of three published in the Roman Edition of St Ephraim's works vol. iii p. 164. Though only found in one MS of the 12th century these hymns bear every internal mark of genuineness. Their interest is Trinitarian and not Christological.

...as the reality which every name implies, and not as that reality viewed in a definite sense, as modified by those properties which constitute its personality".

There is a somewhat similar passage in the preceding Hymn (Morris p. 380). The writer is speaking of the mysterious relation of Father and Son in the Godhead: "Confess that there is a Father and a Son in reality as in Names. The root of the name is the subsistency (*q'nômâ*); by it the names are bound together. For who ever set a name on aught when the subsistency (*q'nômâ*) belonging to it had no existence?" Further on (p. 382): "The name of the fruit belongeth to the fruit alone, the name of the tree to the root alone. Two powers and two subsistencies (*q'nômê*) in one power and love are mingled. For if there be the name of the fruit, and there is not the subsistency (*q'nômâ*) of the fruit, then hast thou named the tree a stock by the name of the fruit that it bare not[1]; as then the tree exists in name, and likewise in subsistency (*q'nômâ*), the fruit is also like it, in that it also is so in name and in reality. If the fruit be in name, but the stock in its subsistency (*q'nômâ*), a falsity and a reality is there in thy naming them, since one exists and the other does not....The Father thou learnest by His Name, and the Son by His Surname; thou hast heard 'Father', the Name is enough for thee; and the Son's Name sufficeth for thee. There is no face (*parṣôpâ*) there that thou shouldst be informed by the face (*parṣôpâ*); their names are to us as faces (*parṣôpê*). By their names even men when far off are distinguished; by their names are they learnt. In place of faces (*parṣôpê*) are appellations, and in place of forms (*or* features) are names. The voice riseth instead of light, and instead of the eye is the hearing".

Morris remarks on this passage: "St E. again and again

[1] That is, if the Son is not a reality you must not speak of a "Father". Observe that the word *sh'rârâ*, "truth", "reality", is several times employed in these passages as a synonym of *q'nômâ*.

speaks of the *Names*, but does not use the word *q'nômâ* alone (though even the metre would not interfere with his doing so) for Persons. To express this he contends that the Names have a reality to answer to them". That is, I venture to think, a correct statement of the case. To Ephraim *q'nômâ* did not mean "person": it meant "substantia" or "substratum". We see also from this passage that *parṣôpâ*, though tending towards the meaning "person", was as yet too materialistic a word to stand for the Persons of the Trinity.

Commenting on Gen. i 1 Ephraim writes (Ed. Rom. i 6 A): "In the beginning, it says, God created the being[1] of the heaven and the being[1] of the earth: i.e. the *q'nômâ* of the heaven and the *q'nômâ* of the earth". He argues from this that the passage does not admit of being interpreted away, and the words "heaven" and "earth" of being taken figuratively: we must understand that "they are truly heaven and earth".

From all this it would appear that the idea which underlies the various pronominal uses considered above is not that of personality, but that by the use of *q'nômâ* the notion of actuality or reality is coupled with a noun or pronominal suffix in order to give it emphasis.

We now come to the question, What did *q'nômâ* mean to the Syrians of the fifth and following centuries who used it in the great Christological controversies?

The first point to be noticed is that at this period it is the regular word to translate ὑπόστασις. In the *Heraclides* of

[1] The word *yâth* is here employed in the Peshitta in the attempt to render literally the Hebrew objective particle *eth*. Like *îthûthâ yâth* is said to mean "being" or "essence"; but as I have scarcely ever met it in the earlier writers except when coupled (like *q'nômâ*) with pronominal suffixes in the sense of "self", and as it seems never to have acquired any specifically theological colouring, I have not attempted to discuss its use.

Nestorius it stands for the latter Greek word in quotations made from the Nicene anathema; also in extracts from and references to some of St Cyril's letters of which we possess the originals, and in other places where the *hypostatic* as opposed to the *prosopic* union is clearly meant. It again represents ὑποστάσεως of the Nicene anathema in the Syriac version published by Martin[1]. It is true that in Heb. i 3 ὑπόστασις is rendered by *îthûthâ*; but that version dates back before the rise of the Christological controversies; and in any case ὑπό-στασις there means, according to its older sense, οὐσία, the Divine being considered in its unity; and we have seen that *îthûthâ* is the one Syriac term that exactly expresses this. Yet even here we find *q'nômâ* for ὑπόστασις in an extant Syriac version of a letter of Andrew of Samosata to Rabbûla of Edessa in which Heb. i 3 is quoted in connexion with the Nestorian controversy[2]. Finally the Nestorian Catholicus Isho'yabh III (647—658) writes in a letter to Sahdona, or Sahda: "Learn then from those who know the language that the Greeks call *q'nômâ îpôstâsîs*" (i.e. ὑπόστασις)[3].

The next point is that Syrians of all communions spoke of three *q'nômê* in the Trinity. This, of course, corresponds to a well-known use of ὑπόστασις in Greek theology—one, however, which did not always pass unchallenged.

A third fact is equally well ascertained, though it has not always been recognized, viz. that Nestorians and Monophysites alike regarded the doctrine of one *q'nômâ* in Christ as tantamount to the assertion of one nature (*k'yânâ*): exactly as Nestorius himself (and some of those who, accepting the

[1] *Loc. cit.*

[2] Overbeck *op. cit.* p. 223 l. 21. Cf. also in the present vol. p. 178, note 4.

[3] Printed by Budge in his edition of Thomas of Marga's *Book of Governors* vol. ii p. 136; re-edited by R. Duval in his edition of Isho'yabh's letters, *Corpus Scriptorum Orientalium* 3rd series t. lxiv p. 131.

Council of Ephesus, afterwards declared for Monophysitism) maintained that unity of ὑπόστασις implied unity of φύσις.

Before proceeding to quote one or two formal explanations of *parṣôpâ* and *q'nômâ* which were given by Nestorian writers of the seventh century we may notice a couple of passages in which Narsai, a fifth century writer, employs *q'nômâ* in a non-theological sense. He says in one place[1]: "Something, be it never so contemptible, is better than nothing, by how much the *q'nômâ* that exists (lit. stands) is more real than the shadow". Notice here (besides the familiar contrast of substance with shadow) the use of the verb *qûm* ("to stand") to explain *q'nômâ*. In describing the horrors of Gehenna Narsai says there will be there "immaterial fire (lit. fire without *k'yânâ*), worms without body, and unsubstantial darkness (lit. darkness without *q'nômâ*)".

Early in the seventh century Babai, a distinguished Nestorian theologian, and abbot of the great convent on Mount Izlâ[2], wrote a work on the union of the two natures in our Lord. This work is unpublished; but there is a MS of it in the Vatican Library[3]. M. Labourt when writing his excellent little book *Le Christianisme dans l'empire perse* had access to a copy, and he has given several extracts from the treatise *De Unione*, and amongst them the following:

"We apply the term *hypostasis* to the particular substance (οὐσία), which subsists in its own single being, numerically one and separate from the rest; not in so far as it is individualized, but in so far as, if it belong to the class of things created, rational, and free, it receives various properties—such as virtue or blame, knowledge or ignorance, and if it be among things that do not possess reason, in like manner various properties in consequence of contrary temperaments, or in an altogether different way....*Hypostasis* is invariable in respect of its own

[1] Mingana, *op. cit.* vol. i p. 37.

[2] See Wright *Syriac Literature* p. 167.

[3] Wright *ib.* p. 168 refers to *Catal. Vat.* iii. 372.

nature and in its kind (εἶδος), for the *nature* of the *hypostasis* is common to it and to all like *hypostases*. But it is distinguished from the *hypostases* that are like it by the individual attributes which the *person* possesses: Gabriel is not Michael, Paul is not Peter. But in each of these *hypostases*, the nature which is common to them all shews itself, and reflexion leads to the recognition of the single nature which embraces the *hypostases* in common, whether it be the nature of men or the nature of other things. But the *hypostasis* does not embrace the universal.

As to *person*, it is that characteristic of the *hypostasis* which distinguishes it from other *hypostases*. The *hypostasis* of Paul is not the *hypostasis* of Peter. On the count of nature and of *hypostasis*, there is no difference between them; for both of them have a body and a soul, are alive, rational and corporeal. But by *person* they are distinguished each from the other, in virtue of the individual particularity which each possesses, whether it be on account of wisdom, or of strength, or of figure, or of appearance or temperament, or of paternity or sonship, or by masculine or feminine sex, or in any way, whatever it may be, that distinguishes and reveals the particular characteristics and shews that *this* man is not *that* woman, and that *that* woman is not *this* man, although on the count of nature there is no difference between them. And because the particular characteristic which the *hypostasis* possesses is not the *hypostasis* itself, the term *person* is used of that which makes the distinction."[1]

The Syriac word rendered *hypostasis* is no doubt *q'nômâ*, though M. Labourt does not say so. But even if it be only the Greek word transliterated it matters little, since *q'nômâ* was at this period its recognized Syriac equivalent. No doubt the words "in so far as...it (the *hypostasis*) receives various properties" mean, "in so far as it is receptive of", etc.: it is *person* that adds these distinguishing attributes.

[1] Babai *De unione* ch. xx *apud* J. Labourt *Le Christianisme dans l'empire perse* pp. 283—285.

We have already spoken of the Catholicus Isho'yabh III who wrote later in the same century (eighth) as Babai. Several of his letters deal with the case of Sahdona, bishop of Mâḥôzê dhĕ Arîwân, who seems to have attempted to bring about an understanding between the Nestorians and the Catholics on the ground that the latter used ὑπόστασις in the same sense as πρόσωπον, and that the word *q'nômâ* might be capable of a similar interpretation. Isho'yabh writes to the clergy and people of Sahdona's diocese as follows[1]: "You have purified your believing Church from all the wicked and multiform error of those who by unity of *q'nômâ*, that is to say of *nature*, destroy the confession of our faith". Again, in the same letter: "For you all know, as men taught of God, that one *q'nômâ* necessarily indicates one *nature*...and, that we should understand this *q'nômâ* as *parṣôpâ*, i.e. *parṣôpâ* by *q'nômâ*,... this the ancient meanings which attach to the words utterly forbid....And that there cannot arise from the Divinity and the humanity a single subsistency (*m'qîmûthâ*) or a single *q'nômâ* the impossibility of the things cries out as with a loud voice". In the letter to Sahdona already quoted he explains the difference between *parṣôpâ* and *q'nômâ*: "For *parṣôpâ*, O brother, is that which distinguishes the *q'nômâ*, and it has a great variety of ideas connected with it, and has a ready aptitude for being bartered and exchanged[2], and, as I have said, it contains a complex idea. But *q'nômâ* merely contains the idea of essence[3] as isolated; and by the simple declaration

[1] Budge *op. cit.* ii 133; Duval *op. cit.* p. 223.

[2] i.e. personality is something that is capable of being transferred or delegated. The writer is probably thinking of the union of natures in Christ, where (according to Nestorius) the person of the Word takes the place of a separate human πρόσωπον, without, however, impairing the perfection of the human ὑπόστασις.

[3] The word *k'yânâyûthâ* is explained as "quiditas naturalis, quae de omni re definitione statuitur". Thus it is nearer to "essence" or "substance" than to "nature" (*k'yânâ*).

of its existence it remains apart[1], embracing the whole idea of essence[2] as it is exhibited (i.e. in a concrete specimen); and it does not admit of being bartered and exchanged". Further on in the same letter: "Nor should you, O brother, have recourse to another error, to the effect that some say that among the Greeks *parṣôpâ* and *q'nômâ* are the same. Learn then from...those who know the language that the Greeks call *q'nômâ îpôstâsîs*, i.e. *q'nômâ*, and 'that which subsists' (*qayyâmâ*), and 'subsistency' (*m'qîmûthâ*), and 'substance' (*qûyyâmâ*); but *parṣôpâ* they call *prosopon*, i.e. *parṣôpâ*, and 'face', and 'individuality' (*p'rîshûthâ*), and '(that which is capable of) perception', and 'that which declares a free and independent self (*yâthâ*)'".

Let us ask finally what the Monophysite Syrians thought about *q'nômâ*.

In the Introduction to his edition of the *Discourses* of Philoxenus, the Monophysite champion, who died early in the sixth century, Dr Budge prints a tract by the same author in which he is arguing against the Chalcedonian doctrine of one ὑπόστασις and two natures in Christ. His point is that it is folly to allow two *natures* when you speak of one *q'nômâ*: "There is no *k'yânâ* without a *q'nômâ*, neither is there a *q'nômâ* without a *k'yânâ*. But if there are two *k'yânê*, then there must be two *q'nômê* and two Sons"[3]. Similar arguments are employed for several pages. When Philoxenus says that there is no nature that has not a *q'nômâ* he surely means by this word a "subsistency" and not a "person".

Again, in Wright's *Catalogue of the Syriac MSS in the British Museum*, p. 937[b], there is a quotation from a MS

[1] I take this to mean that *q'nômâ* is an essence with existence predicated of it, which circumscribes and isolates it and constitutes it a single entity.

[2] See p. 230, note 3.

[3] p. cxxiii (text), p. xxxix (transl.). The reader is warned that where "Person" occurs in Dr Budge's translation the Syriac word is regularly *q'nômâ*.

of the eighth century which contains a catena of passages from the Fathers in favour of the Monophysite doctrine. It is to this effect: "Wherefore, the Synod of Chalcedon did nothing different from the former heretics, in that it confessed one Son and one Christ but [separated] the two inseparable *natures*, and understood *q'nômâ* as *parṣôpâ* after the view of Nestorius, as Theodoret testifies".

This statement is somewhat confused: but when we take it to pieces it implies that *q'nômâ* cannot mean the same as *parṣôpâ*, but is equivalent to *nature*. Then, the strange misstatement about Nestorius I take to mean this: that the writer, being convinced that Nestorius taught two persons, concluded that he spoke of two ὑποστάσεις (i.e. *q'nômê*) in the sense of two πρόσωπα. Though Nestorius maintained two ὑποστάσεις in Christ, he denied that this implied two πρόσωπα or two Sons.

Chronological Table of Syriac Writers referred to in the foregoing Appendix

BARDAISAN, died c. A.D. 222, called "the last of the Gnostics".

PHILIP, disciple of Bardaisan, wrote the *De Fato*, probably after his master's death.

APHRAATES, the "Persian Sage", wrote the last of his *Homilies* A.D. 345.

EPHRAIM, died A.D. 373 (for a list of certainly genuine works see Burkitt, *S. Ephraim's Quotations from the Gospel*, in *Texts and Studies*, vol. vii no. 2).

RABBÛLA, bishop of Edessa, died A.D. 435.

SHARBIL, Acts of, composed about the beginning of the fifth century.

ISAAC OF ANTIOCH, fl. (probably) towards the end of the fifth or the beginning of the sixth century.

NARSAI, died c. 502.

PHILOXENUS, bishop of Mabbog, died c. A.D. 523.

BABAI, died about the middle of the seventh century.

ISHO'YABH III, Nestorian Catholicus, died c. 658.

SAHDONA, or SAHDA, contemporary of Isho'yabh.

CAMBRIDGE: PRINTED BY JOHN CLAY, M.A. AT THE UNIVERSITY PRESS.